D1231795

The 50·50 Marriage

Books by Gayle Kimball

The 50•50 Marriage

Harriet Beecher Stowe's Gospel of Womanhood

Women's Culture: The Women's Renaissance of the Seventies

THE
50·50
marriage

gayle kimball

BEACON PRESS

BOSTON

Portions of this book appeared in slightly different
form in *Family Journal*.

Copyright © 1983 by Gayle Kimball

Beacon Press books are published under the auspices
of the Unitarian Universalist Association,
25 Beacon Street, Boston, Massachusetts 02108
Published simultaneously in Canada by
Fitzhenry & Whiteside Limited, Toronto

Printed in the United States of America

(hardcover) 9 8 7 6 5 4 3 2 1
(paperback) 9 8 7 6 5 4 3 2 1

Library of Congress Cataloging in Publication Data

Kimball, Gayle.
  The 50 • 50 marriage.

  Bibliography: p.
  1. Marriage—United States.   2. Parenting—United
States.   3. Married people—Employment—United States.
I. Title.   II. Title: Fifty-fifty marriage.
HQ1426.K55   1983   646.7'8   82-70571
ISBN 0-8070-2726-X

To Jed

I hope he'll grow up

to be like the men in this book

Acknowledgments

My deepest gratitude goes to the 150 couples who gave their precious time, already filled with family and work, to participate in this study. They are pioneers, aware of the fact that examples of equal marriages are needed. Their encouragement of my research sustained me.

I began interviewing when I was pregnant; as a parent who also teaches and writes I rely on an extensive support system. My thanks to child-care providers Mike and Lavina Smith, who are so competent and caring I can work free of guilt. My son's father, Les Hait, takes care of him faithfully on Saturdays and Tuesday and Thursday evenings. Thanks to my son Jed for teaching me about being a parent.

Paula Hamman transcribed taped interviews. Andrea Bowman typed drafts with numerous insertions and deletions, as did Bev Taylor and Judy Paine. Mike King did the computer analysis of surveys comparing egalitarian and traditional couples; Jeanette Alosi helped with the computer work. The Faculty Development Program headed by John Morgan at California State University at Chico provided some funds for interviewing. The Chancellor's Office of the California State University System provided extensive funding for my production of seven videotapes on women's issues; video travel funds enabled me to interview scholars whose ideas I quote in this book.

The following graciously made editorial comments on various chapters: Stuart Bramhall, Ain Haas, Murray Markland, Barbara Kimball, Carol Burr, Susan Suntree, Harriet Jardine, Dolores Blalock, and the students in my Femininity/Masculinity class, Spring 1982.

Couples whom I interviewed and who gave permission to acknowledge them by name are Nancy Allured & Ray Gleason, Barbara Becker & Slack Ulrich, Sandra & Daryl Bem, Judy & Doug Blanchard, Susan & Michael Cabat, Pat & Ron Cameron, Nona & Carroll Cannon, Nancy & Seth Chase, Mary & Dave Cook, Juanita & Clinton Dixon, Joan & Michael Easley, Sue & Matt Epstein, Shirley Anne & David Evenson, Carol Fitzgerald & Doug Becknell, Kot Flora & Larry McGranahan, Janice Gagerman & David Frankel, Esther & Fred Geil, Emily & Ted

Graser, Kathleen & Steve Guinn, Linda & Ain Haas, Corky & Rod Hensch, Lyn & Ed Hill, Joan & Robert Hillman, Norma Hymes & Vincent Esposito, Linda Kallman & Stephen Bromberg, Renee & Hank Kogel, Carol & Glenn Laque, Judy Leavell & Ted Sokal, Ellen & Stuart Little, Laurel Leone & Steve Wagner, Claire & Andy Lien, Moon Jee Yu-Madrigal & Orlando Madrigal, Laurie & Jim Mann, Mary & Tony Mahowald, Diane & Leroy McDermott, Elise Moss & Philippe Stassart, Dianne & Martin Neumann, Jenny & Barry Oremland, Christine Overall & Ted Worth, Ruth & Al Paige, Joann & Patrick Perry, Jo Ellen & Duanne Polzien, Wendy Roberts-Benard & Jim Benard, Caroline Rider & Paul Weiner, Mary & Ron Sagerson, Kathie Sheldon & Steve Tarzynski, Darlene & Dave Sloneker, Kathleen Sodja & Charles Marshall, Rusty & Daniel Siegfried, Gail & Edwin Steiner, Susan & Philip Suntree, Ann Tabor & Steve Sheridan, Karline & Martin Tierney, Laura Waterman & Dan Friedman, Syril & Gary Whitlock, Evie & Ed Whitsett, and Ann Wright & Richard Wallat.

Introduction

In discussions with my friends and students several years ago, I asked if anyone knew of a long-term marriage in which both partners were growing, were genuinely interested in each other, and shared tasks and power equally. Since most of us could not think of anyone, or of any books describing how equal marriages work, I set out to find couples whose relationships were worthy of emulation. Thinking that feminist groups would be a likely source of referrals to equal marriages, I wrote to all the National Organization for Women chapters, except those in California. I did not want this study to be loaded with Californians as we are not viewed as typical. N.O.W. chapters all over the United States were my major source of interviewees. I also advertised in *Ms.* and other feminist magazines, with some success, and sent queries to men's groups' newsletters and magazines for the black community. The couples themselves were the second-largest source of referrals. Some knew of other egalitarian couples, although it was amazing how frequently they did not know of any. In all, I interviewed 150 couples.

I defined egalitarian couples as those in which husband and wife share moneymaking, housework, child care, and decision making. In all but two of the couples I interviewed both husband and wife do paid work: One Nebraska woman is a full-time homemaker and so is one Missouri man. Only parents were included (including one couple with foster children) because the arrival of a baby often leads couples to a traditional division of labor.

Both partners were interviewed together for at least an hour, usually on a two-extension telephone. I found the phone interviews to be very conducive to frank discussions, easier perhaps than when an interviewer is watching as well as listening.[1] My student Karen Eberwein did eighteen of the interviews and shared my fascination with the process. Since egalitarian couples are accustomed to discussing their feelings about their relationships with each other, they were articulate and open. I looked forward to my once- or twice-a-week interview sessions because they allowed me to share in real-life dramas. The interviews continued from 1979, before I gave birth to a son, until 1982 when he was two. I found I was able to ask better questions about parenting as a result of first-hand experience. During that time my own real-life script included separation from Jed's father partly because of our differing expectations about role-sharing. That experience intensified my desire to learn how other couples succeed at role-sharing.

The couples interviewed are located throughout the United States and Canada: 30 percent in the Midwest, 28 percent in the West, 21 percent in the Northeast, and 17 percent in the South, and 3 percent in Canada. Their ages range from early twenties to late sixties: more than half are in their thirties. Most are white, one couple was Asian-American, one black, and one racially mixed. They are not representative American families; they are in the vanguard rather than the mainstream. They are mainly upper-middle-class, highly educated professionals, the women having almost as many graduate and professional degrees as the men.[2] Almost all have at least some college education. Most have intact marriages, although 15 percent are both in second marriages. The majority have been married six to fifteen years, one third for less than five years; 4.5 percent are living together but not married. Most have one or two children. (See Appendix 1 for a more detailed description of the couples.)

I asked the couples the following questions:

How do you share child care and housework?

What influences led you to role-sharing?

How do you deal with conflict?

What do you do for fun?

How did you cope with Hollywood film-type myths leading to unrealistic expectations about marriage and parenting?

What advice would you give to a young couple who wished to have an egalitarian relationship?

Have we left anything out?

I also interviewed three traditional couples for purposes of comparison. I interviewed published specialists in family issues: sociologists Jessie Bernard, Lillian Rubin, and Nancy Chodorow;

men's liberation activists Warren Farrell and Herb Goldberg; feminist author Robin Morgan, and pediatrician Benjamin Spock. I interviewed marriage counselors Thea and Tom Lowry, and, in 1980 in Stockholm, numerous Swedish experts on equality programs. All their insights were useful for placing the 150 couples in a broader perspective.

A personality survey designed by Sandra Bem that tests for psychological androgyny, or a person's ability to combine masculine and feminine traits, was completed by eighty-nine egalitarian couples and seventy-five traditional couples. (The latter were identified by the former.) My aim was to see if role-sharing couples had different personality types from those of traditional couples. They did: traditional couples fell in sex-typed feminine and masculine categories while egalitarian couples did not.

In the following chapters themes that emerged from my interviews with egalitarian couples are developed. The men and women have a secure sense of self that permits them to withstand social pressure against role-sharing. For example, some men are accused by their acquaintances of being "wimpy" or henpecked if they change diapers and cook dinner, and women are seen as poor mothers if they are not with their children twenty-four hours a day. Many nontraditional couples are strengthened by their liberal political ideology that values equality and social justice (some were influenced by the 1960s political rebellion against conventional authority), as well as by feminism. Success in their careers adds to their ego strength and flexibility, as do university degrees. Some feel they escaped traditional role training by being a first-born daughter, who was expected to achieve, or a late-born son, who received less attention from his parents.

Their marriages are intensified by giving priority to family over career. The most frequently repeated statements are that husband and wife consider each other best friends and spend much time talking to each other. Communication skills are valued and sought by going to a marriage counselor, by reading, or by talking with friends The couples learn how to cope with conflict by negotiating, compromising, and "fighting fair." Conflicts over housework and child care, for example, might be resolved by making contracts that are spelled out concretely in charts: John cooks every other night, puts the children to bed on the nights he does not cook, and pays the mortgage and utility bills.

Egalitarian marriages tend to fall into three categories: (1) those that began traditionally and changed to role-sharing after the woman returned to paid work (these were the most troubled relationships), (2) second marriages that successfully react against a traditional first marriage, and (3) intact marriages that began equally (usually younger couples influenced by feminism). (Appendix 5 contains examples of interviews with representative couples of each type of marriage.) Two different styles of marriage emerge: one that is easygoing, casual, and low key, in which for example, whoever feels like doing a task does it with no specific assignment, and the other more structured, with specific division of tasks and financial responsibilities and specific times set aside for talk and leisure. The structured style is sometimes accompanied by more interpersonal intensity, more visible ego, more willful personalities, more ups and downs, and more conflicts than is the low-key style.

Readers are invited to describe their own experiences combining equal parenting and two careers, for a future book on raising children in a role-sharing family (see Appendix 6). Please write to Dr. Gayle Kimball, E.W.S.-420, California State University, Chico, CA 95929. Any comments from readers are welcomed.

Contents

1
The setting

"We are the head geese breaking the path: there are more behind us."
—A Delaware husband

"We're at the cutting edge of change."
—A California husband

A Wisconsin man who is part of an equal marriage reports that "men with feminist wives who have left them have come to me and said, 'What do you do?' I try to talk to them and tell them books to read, but there is nothing about how to make an egalitarian marriage work." The experience of 150 couples who live in thirty-three states and three Canadian provinces provide examples of equal marriages. Their knowledge is gained from daily efforts to share decision making, housework, child care, and moneymaking, as they described in interviews.

The introductory quotations to this chapter indicate that these couples are not typical. They are in the vanguard of a movement for equality between the sexes, spurred on by women's entry into the paid work force and by the women's and men's liberation movements. *Perhaps for the first time in human history the worlds of men and of women are beginning to merge.* Couples who share equally the burdens and joys of being bread-winners, bread bakers, and nurturers of children are pioneers. The couples interviewed are unusual because most families, including dual-career couples, maintain a traditional division of labor, with the man's career primary and the woman responsible for family work. Despite being highly educated and well paid, the interviewees find role-sharing difficult. They are going against the mainstream of a society that is still geared toward the male worker with a wife who takes care of domestic tasks. One couple, co-owners of their own business, think that "our situation is probably the easiest you can get, but even then we find it difficult. We can't find adequate child care, for example."

Learning about the struggles and rewards these role-sharing couples face can be of use to other couples who wish to be equal, including young adults who are unaware of the enormous difficulties involved in balancing careers, marriages, and children. Many men and women want to participate equally in careers and family life but have no examples of how to do so. Because we have so few models and because society neglects the needs of working parents, the experiences of couples who successfully share working and parenting are valuable.

The egalitarian couples' accounts of how their marriages work are also significant because, in an era of high divorce rates, most consider themselves happily married. The fact that the number of divorces in the 1970s was twice the number in the 1960s, so that at current rates half of recent marriages will end in divorce, indicates the stress put on marriage by changing expectations. Role-sharers' experiences in selecting and living with a spouse are the foundation of this book, since the best authorities on modernizing sex roles are those who are doing it.

One role-sharing couple, both of whom are psychologists, define an equal marriage as one in which neither partner has priority over the other or more authority or power—even if one makes more or all the money, has a higher-status job, or is bigger or older. Equal marriage requires that "there should be no monopolies for either sex in any sphere." [1] An egalitarian relationship is one in which tasks, responsibilities, and privileges are shared. Assignment of tasks is flexible, based on practical considerations of proper male and female behavior. If a man likes to cook and his wife does not, he cooks. Since they both use the toilet, she is not the only one to clean it. Power is fluid, not based on a rigid hierarchy of dominance and deference.

Egalitarian marriage contrasts with traditional, patriarchal marriage in which the husband is head of the household and his paid job is most important, while the wife is responsible for nurturing the family. An example of a traditional relationship is the marriage of President Ronald and Nancy Reagan. She states, "In marriage it's the woman who has to do an awful lot of the adjusting. Men think they're making adjustments, too, but they're really not. That's what makes them both happy." Her view is that a wife finds fulfillment in pleasing her husband. A *Ladies' Home Journal* survey of 30,000 readers, however, found that traditionally feminine women who sought their identity in husband and children were the most unhappy respondents and suffered most from symptoms of stress. The more independent respondents, "the changing women," were happier and felt closer to their husbands.[2] Traditional roles are stressful for men as well: A physician reports that 90 percent of the leading causes of death in males are specifically associated with the masculine role.[3]

The underlying assumption in egalitarian relationships is that women's and men's time is of equal value, that a man is not demeaned by washing dishes or caring for children, and that a woman deserves as much leisure time as her husband. Most fair people would agree that men and women are of equal worth, but few act on that assumption, as evidenced by the fact that women earn only 59 percent of what men earn and men generally have higher status in society. Most wives do more housework and child care to compensate for their lower earnings and lower self-esteem or to carve out an area in which they feel in charge, even if they work outside the home for the same number of hours as their husbands (see Appendix 4). Many middle-class couples say they believe in equality between spouses, but their belief is rarely translated into practice. A study conducted by the Catalyst Career and Family Center of 815 dual-career couples found that couples considered their careers of equal importance but acted traditionally, as in moving for his career rather than for hers and in the wife's assuming more household responsibilities.[4] The same pattern was found in a study of 200 married couples, all psychologists.[5] A 1980 Harris poll of 1,503 U.S. adult family members found that 90 percent thought child-care responsibility should be shared by both parents, but only 36 percent reported sharing it equally in practice.[6]

The benefits for couples who share marriage roles are especially recognized by spouses who began their marriage with the burden of economic support solely on the husband and the burden of domestic tasks solely on the wife. Annie and Jack own a small record business; when their sons were three and six, they decided to share its management, switching from traditional roles. As a result, Jack explains,

> We communicate better. I think we have stronger feelings for each other, because we share so much now that we didn't share when we were playing the male-female roles. Plus our sex life went to hell when I was working the long hours. Since we have shared the business, the problems are not so large, because there are two of us working at it and we both know what is going on. We both come up with ideas. There is nothing that has to be kept inside anymore, that one person is brewing on, not wanting to tell the other person.

Many husbands appreciate the freedom they gain with two wage earners in the family: freedom to escape the pressure to earn more money, to quit an unpleasant job, or to study. Another benefit for husbands is having a partner who feels she is living up to her capabilities and therefore does not look to him to shape her identity. As a Colorado husband, Charlie, puts it:

> To me, being egalitarian is the ultimate meaningful relationship, the coming together of equals to nurture each other and form a partnership. To be totally caught up in the male career means no sharing can go on. The other rewards are even greater than the prestige of affluence—a balanced life in which you participate with your children and have a lot of time with your loved ones.

Studies concur that equitable relationships are more satisfying than traditional relationships, because each spouse has access to two worlds rather than one and the children have access to two parents. A study that followed married couples from the late 1930s to the early 1950s found that marriages with the greatest role differentiation were unsatisfying "empty shells." [7] Couples who perceive equal benefits from their relationship are the happiest,[8] and the more housework and child care a husband performs the less likely his wife is to divorce him.[9]

One woman, Lisa, a personnel director in Illinois, reports:

> I work with over 100 women; what some of them put up with is unbelievable, and it makes me appreciate what I've got. If I had to walk in every day and my husband sat there and watched the news while I fixed dinner and tried to get my son fed and bathed, if I had to do everything that 98 percent of the wives do—we would have a lot more problems.

Despite the backlash by reactionary religious and political groups, the reality is that a minority of American families fit the nineteenth-century definition of the family: husband as sole breadwinner, wife as full-time mother. In the majority of marriages today, both spouses are wage earners and 54 percent of the children under eighteen (including almost half of the children under six) have working mothers. The number of working mothers has increased tenfold since World War II. Women's ability to earn income influences their roles as wives, because their financial resources often result in more decision-making power. Economic necessity generated by inflation is an impetus for women to assume more equality.

Equality is also made possible because women are earning more university degrees than in the past—for the first time there are as many female college students as males. Women are marrying at a later age (22 is the average) and having fewer babies (1.8 per mother). Also, the number of women giving birth after age thirty almost doubled between 1973 and 1981. The movement of women into the work force is described as the most significant social change in the twentieth century, leading to the major change in men's role—their increasing involvement in the family.[10]

Societal attitudes and organizations have not caught up with these major changes in men's and women's lives; flexible working hours or adequate day care have not yet been produced in any routine way, for example. One attempt to marshal official pressure against equitable sex roles is the Family Protection Act, a bill proposed in Congress in 1981. The bill attempted to prohibit federal funding for any educational program that "denigrates role differences between the sexes as they have been understood historically in the United States." The Senate version added opposition to educational materials that "do not reflect different ways in which women and men live . . ." Another example of the fear of changing sex roles is the virulent right-wing rhetoric that defeated the Equal Rights Amendment on the grounds that it would turn our sons into pansies and our daughters into tigers and create a unisex society. In fact, equal rights do not extinguish gender or sexual attraction.

An overview of women's and men's relationships in America shows a return to the partnership experienced by the first settlers. In the colonial and frontier eras, women were a valued part of the family's economic team. Women were the manufacturers of raw materials; the husband sheared the sheep and the wife spun and knit the wool into clothes. The man butchered the pig and the woman made its fat into candles and preserved the meat. Women were also valued as baby makers, for agrarian people depended on their children to work the farm and to provide security for them in their old age.

Pilgrim and Puritan colonizers of New England considered themselves the new Zion, God's chosen people of the seventeenth century. Women as well as men were recognized as among the elect, especially since more women had the mystical experience of saving grace that was required for church membership. A woman had a real choice in her marriage partner, perhaps for the first time in history. The Puritans were also aware that women, as well as men, have sexual needs, so impotence was considered grounds for divorce. The first published American poet, Anne Bradstreet, wrote about her children as the fruit of her and her husband's "heat." Many babies arrived sooner than nine months after their parents' marriage, among all social classes, without a great deal of censure of the parents. (Adultery, however, was a serious offense, legally punishable by death.)

Although colonial women's labor was so necessary that they ran taverns and printing presses, they were not considered man's equal. Preachers reminded women that they were made from man's rib to be his helpmate. Paul's biblical passages were quoted out of context to ensure that wives looked to their husbands as their head and did not presume to teach men or speak in public. Women were considered more frail in body and mind; the wife of Connecticut Governor Edward Hopkins was believed to have gone insane because she overtaxed her mind in intellectual pursuits. Women had no voice in secular or church government, and they could not own property. A wife's purpose was to do the mundane labor to free her husband from "all secular vocations" so he could concentrate on spirituality. When Abigail Adams asked her husband, the second president, for representation for women in the new democratic government, he laughed. Economic need propelled women into an active role in colonial society, but they were still considered inferior to men.

The nineteenth century radically altered husbands' and wives' economic partnership. The Industrial Revolution provided machinery that took over women's jobs as manufacturers of raw materials. Immigrants provided an abundant and cheap source of labor, and middle-class women were no longer needed as workers. The new ideal of the lady replaced the reality of the hard-working, competent frontier woman who raised a dozen children, made all their clothes and food, could butcher a pig, and defended her family with a gun. The popular image of the lady was that she did no work except supervise servants. Her job was to teach Christian piety, bourgeois manners, and literary tastes to her children. For perhaps the first time in history mothers became exclusively responsible for their children's care and upbringing, with little help from husbands or extended family. The woman's realm was the home, for she was considered too pious, pure, refined, and delicate to enter the competitive world of business and politics—a definition that put her safely on a pedestal out of men's way. In nineteenth-century novels and sermons woman is frequently described as angelic and child-like.

Her husband's realm, values, and traits were considered opposite to hers. Men gained status by supporting nonworkers who consumed conspicuously. Men were described as brutes who needed their wives to provide a civilizing influence and a peaceful haven as a refuge from males' fierce competition. "A beautiful woman is a practical poet, taming her savage mate," wrote Ralph Waldo Emerson. Even many suffragists opposed legalization of birth control devices on the grounds that birth control would allow men unrestrained exercises of their primitive sexual appetites, to their pious wives' dismay. Virtuous women were so removed from physicality that they insisted that ruffles be painted on a sign displaying a piano's legs, for fear viewers would think of female limbs; they were horrified when their daughters were taught human anatomy, refused to permit gynecologists to observe pelvic examinations, and kept their pregnancies secret. Only women of ill repute were considered sexual beings: Charles Francis Adams, grandson of President John Quincy Adams, was proud that his fiancée excited no sexual feelings in him; such feelings were reserved for a man's mistress.[11]

Because men and women were defined so differently, women turned to each other for companionship, often addressing friends as "beloved" and "dearest darling." We still bear the legacy of separating the concerns and characteristics of women and men, giving prestige to men who can support nonworkers and dividing women into good and bad (adolescents, for instance, use terms such as "cheap," "easy," and "slut" to describe sexually active girls, but no terms are used for boys). The nineteenth century may seem remote, but its social attitudes are still very much present.

In the 1920s a superficial change in mores led to the flapper image and a fantasy of the emancipated woman. Cutting their hair, shortening their skirts, and smoking cigarettes can be seen in retrospect as insignificant changes when women today still represent only 10 percent of all elected officials and have access to the White House mainly as wife or secretary. Lip service is given to the ideal marriage based on companionship and sharing. But in a recent survey of more than 1,000 contemporary couples, 80 percent claimed they shared leadership, but only 12 percent did so in practice.[12]

As economic necessity pushes women into the work world, they are again becoming important providers for their families. The change has occurred recently: In 1940 not quite 15 percent of married women did paid work; the percentage almost doubled by 1960. Yet "women's work is still shaped around the family, while the family is still shaped around the world of men," reports the historian Carl Degler. He titled his history of American women and the family At Odds. The sociologist Jessie Bernard, herself the mother of three children, observes, "to be happy in a relationship which imposes so many impediments on her, as traditional marriage does, a woman must be slightly ill mentally." [13] Even in contemporary society, marriage has continued to put women in a subordinate position.

Married women's entry into the paid work force has occurred so recently that economic partnership has not yet resulted in domestic partnership for most couples. Major changes are bound to occur in domestic relationships as a result of women's earnings, higher education, and fewer and later pregnancies. In the chapters that follow, couples analyze the influences that led them to create equal marriages, the cement that holds their marriages together, their arrangements for sharing housework and child care, and the methods they use to solve conflicts. The last chapter outlines some of the changes needed in the social structure to promote egalitarian families.

2
Egalitarian wives

"I sometimes think the people who are more traditional don't have much of a self-identity and are afraid to be different."
—A Massachusetts wife

She is a thirty-four year-old teacher; her husband is twenty-seven and self-employed. They lived together for five years before getting married. Her first marriage was a major impetus to role-sharing: She put her first husband through graduate school, did all the housework, shoveled the snow, and cooked for his gatherings of fellow students, which included a woman with whom he was having an affair. She vowed never again to do two jobs while her husband did one.

"I don't see myself as needing to be a successful homemaker to have an identity."
—A Wisconsin wife

Married for fifteen years, she and her husband have two sons. She is an accountant and he is a psychologist. So they both can have a career, she commutes thirty-two miles and he fifty-two miles on the train. During four years as a full-time homemaker she discovered that he was better at housework but resented doing it when she was home all day. Also, she could not empathize with his work experiences. The fact that each has a profession has brought them closer.

If a man is looking for a woman to share an egalitarian relationship, the statements introducing this chapter indicate that he must look for a woman who has a sense of self-worth and independence. The studies of dual-career couples overwhelmingly agree that stress is greater for wives than for husbands, especially when they have children.[1] A woman needs strength to combine a career and motherhood. Egalitarian wives feel their education and money-making skills provide them with independence and a sense of co-providing for the family that allow them to speak their minds. Establishing a career as a single person before marrying helps them mature into adults who know what they want and who expect to get it. Their common pattern is to delay marriage and parenting, giving them time to establish identities as individuals and then, with their husbands, as a couple. Some wives resented their first husband's lack of involvement in family life and looked for a second husband who would be more active at home. Their feminist beliefs support their desire to have a family and a career without feeling guilty about not always being available to their children in routine domestic ways, such as baking cookies.

Family Influences

A woman's parents are important contributors to her adult makeup. Optimally a woman's mother is autonomous, she has a career, and she encourages her daughter to have one too, although many women develop egalitarian attitudes in reaction to their mothers' lack of development. Women often characterize their fathers either as strongly encouraging and participating in family life or as offensively patronizing to women. A middle-of-the-road parent seems to have less influence than a very positive or a very negative one. Some young women rebelled against the treatment of their mothers and themselves as second-class citizens, thus stimulating their later achievements. Some first-borns receive attention usually given to boys. Females with numerous siblings sometimes escape the pressure to grow up traditionally feminine because their parents are too busy to direct them into traditional roles.

Many egalitarian women had mothers who provided an example of self-reliance. Widows raised their children alone, and divorce or military service removed the men from other families. Mirroring her mother's independence, a woman reports, "I never expected a man to take care of me and I was always a strong woman."

Some mothers followed traditional roles but exercised power subtly. Megan Lou, reared in the South, remembers, "Despite all of her 'Yes, Billy' and 'No, Billy,' I was aware that my father couldn't function without her, but she could function without him." Another Southern wife, Roberta, remembers her mother as a very strong woman. Roberta was the oldest daughter of the oldest daughter of an oldest daughter, and she felt that she was therefore expected to achieve. Several other Southern women see themselves as descendants of a line of strong women. A sense of tradition and heritage worked favorably for such women. On the other hand, some Southern women report pressure from their neighbors to "act incompetent and men will do the work for you" and to "manipulate your way through life."

Many women had working mothers who did not expend much time or energy on domesticity; studies concur that career-oriented women often had working mothers.[2] Thomasin explained that her mother did not consider homemaking very important: her mother cooked, but it was far from the focus of her life. Another woman remembers that when she was growing up her family existed on TV dinners. A psychologist's mother let her know that housework was neither fun nor glamorous.

Some mothers directly encouraged their daughters to pursue a career: One mother wanted her child to be a great writer or reporter, and another told her daughter to "go for whatever you want." A teacher taught her daughter, Alison, that women as well as men should do something with their brains. Being able to pattern herself on a successful mother was important to a high-level businesswoman; as a result, it never occurred to her that women could not do anything they really wanted to. In contrast, the men in her family seemed weak to her. She resented that her father had not shared in the responsibility of running the household and she felt her mother spoiled him. One woman's mother held high-level banking positions and did not do much housework, while her father was not a presence in her life because he was too preoccupied trying to make a living. Capable mothers gave their daughters a role model and expectations to achieve.

Several women who lacked a positive example in their mothers found one in other older women, such as grandmothers, aunts, or supervisors. One Minnesota woman, Virginia, who grew up viewing women as doormats was astonished when she met a woman with high self-esteem: She had not known it was possible. Clearly, a model of an achieving woman is an important influence.

At the other end of the spectrum, some women wanted to be the opposite of their dependent mothers. A corporation vice-president from New Jersey recalls:

> I was probably influenced in reaction to my mother rather than seeing her as a pattern to follow. My mother has never worked. I think she balanced a checkbook maybe once or twice. When she was finishing high school she told her father that she would like to become an interior decorator and he said, "No daughter of mine is doing that. We're teaching you how to cook and keep the house and you're staying home"—which to this day she resents. When I left home it was a major crisis in my mother's life. I think that had the greatest effect on me, to the point that I should be a little more domestic. But I find something in me that says, "Don't you dare get into this. If you begin to stay home, you might never leave the house." There are times when I feel sort of strange because I don't see the same sort of lifestyle in many of our friends.

The mother of a manager in Ohio, Carol, never had a paying job or drove a car. As a result Carol had a burning desire not to be locked into such a role. The fear of being like her mother motivated a Washington real estate saleswoman not to repeat her mother's life:

> My mom is a real classic case of a woman so out of touch with the world that she took all her anger and turned inside and became sick. My mother and dad were divorced

when I was seven and she never recovered from this rejection, becoming almost a complete invalid. She is a very
bright woman who could have been capable of anything
in the world. I see her as a wasted human being. I tell
Rob that one of the reasons I am a feminist and see how
my life got to be the way it is, is my mother and his
mother. These are two examples to me of women who
could be so much more than they were allowed to be. This
is what I do not want to have happen to me. And I have
three daughters so that makes it even more important.

Suzanne, a professor, reacted against her parents' unequal
marriage. Her mother's opinions were so discounted that she
stopped discussing books and playing bridge with her husband.
Suzanne's father told her how smart she was but said he re-
gretted her brains being wasted on a girl. She lowered her aspirations because of his prejudice:

> I remember as a young girl in high school sitting in my
> classes thinking how unfair and illogical it was for me to
> be sitting there and learning just so I could then be locked
> up at home and hope I could have a son. I could teach
> him and then maybe he would be able to go out and apply
> it. I thought that was highly unfair and it didn't make
> sense.

The dissolution of her unhappy first marriage, the women's
movement, and therapy gave Suzanne the impetus to reject her
father's prejudices about female achievement.

Watching her father hold up his water glass for her mother
to fill turned an Indiana woman into a feminist. When she told
her parents she wanted to be a doctor, they patted her on the
head and suggested she become a nurse. She did go to nursing
school but then decided she would rather have more authority
on the job and went on to complete medical school. A Cincinnati therapist reacted against the roles assumed by women in
her and her husband's families. She described her father as a
king waited on by women. A man standing near the refrigerator
in her husband's family would ask a woman to get him a glass
of juice, and at gatherings the women did all the work while

the men sat and enjoyed themselves. She rebelled against the expectation that women wait on men and do all the "shit work."

Confronting a stressful situation can lead to achievement. One researcher's explanation is that growing up in trying circumstances acclimates a woman to the high stress involved in a dual-career marriage.[3] If a woman's mother is unhappy in her marriage, a conventional marriage seems undesirable to the daughter. The daughter of an influential politician describes him as violent, regularly expelling one child or another from the home. Interestingly, this patriarch was not sexist; he did not distinguish between what boys and girls were expected to do. His daughter believes that his difficult behavior led to her self-reliance. An anthropologist realizes that because her father was always telling her what not to do, she achieved simply to show him she could do it. Overcoming difficulty can make a woman strong, as long as she has enough encouragement not to be crushed by opposition.

A father who respects his daughter and encourages her self-esteem can also inspire high achievement. Gale, a California Ph.D. student, was first-born; her father treated her like the son he expected. He assumed she could do whatever she wanted to do and taught her "masculine" skills such as how to work on their car. She married a physician who as a boy had helped his mother at home and who is willing to relocate when she finds a teaching position. A Michigan woman identified with her father, did not like her mother very much, and did not want to grow up to be "Mrs. Anybody."

Some women grew up in families in which their fathers were actively involved: "You never saw Daddy sitting down with his feet propped up; it was all of us helping so that both of them could sit down when the work was done. I see a lot of that in my husband." A New Hampshire administrator's father took the children on an excursion every Saturday—referred to as children's day—and also did many chores around the house. Women with active fathers brought their expectations for male participation in family life to their relationships with their husbands.

Relations with brothers and sisters have an impact on women's traditional or nontraditional leanings. Inequality in the way tasks were distributed—boys could go outside to play while girls had to stay inside to do housework—produced rebellion in some. The oldest girl in a family of four children felt secondary to her brothers:

> I can remember many times ironing my father's handkerchiefs and folding my brother's wash while my brother was out playing. I told myself that I was absolutely not going to do that when I got to be an adult. When we go to the laundromat Steve folds his own clothes and I fold mine.

A woman who loved sports had to settle for hand-me-downs of her younger brother's used baseball equipment, and her parents went to his ball games rather than hers. Her family's preferential treatment of her brother provided fuel for her later feminism.

Having siblings all of the same sex can lead to nonstereotyped division of labor, and having all sisters (about 20 percent of the women I interviewed had all sisters) can encourage achievement. Yet having brothers can dispel a sense of mystery about men, who come to be regarded as friends rather than a different species.

Being the oldest of three children meant that as a girl one woman was "an authority figure" in the household; she later became a chiropractor. Studies of birth order often indicate that first-borns are apt to be high achievers, living up to their parents' expectations.[4] About 51.8 percent of the women interviewees were first-borns, compared with 40 percent of the men.

Another way to escape pressure to fit a passive, feminine mold is to receive less parental attention than older siblings. An accountant with two older sisters and a younger brother gives an example:

> I think I was kind of a forgotten child in terms of my proper upbringing. There was very little family interaction. My folks were strangers to each other even though they

were living together. I was never taught that I was supposed to be a second-class citizen because I was a female.
My father believed that, but he somehow forgot to teach
me. When my sister, who is ten years older than me,
wanted to go to college he told her that it wasn't necessary for girls because girls just get married and don't need
an education. And yet, I always knew I was going to college. I don't know how I managed to think that.

An oldest daughter, one of eight children, had the same experience of benign neglect. She is now a corporate attorney.

My parents—mostly just because they were busy with a
large family, not because they were enlightened—let me
do whatever. I never had any interference as far as what
was appropriate. It makes you much freer. I was treated
like an adult a long time.

Being an unpopular adolescent was reported by several women
who were bright and assertive as ultimately conducive to their
adult achievement. A physician described herself as an outcast
and a professor remembers being an extraordinarily unpopular
teenager. They feel that in the long run they benefited from not
being cheerleaders and spending hours daily on their appearance and pleasing boys. Although not fitting in meant unhappy
high school years, it proved a stimulus to their success. Popular
girls learn not to win or to excel, particularly in male fields such
as sciences, because doing so threatens some male egos.

Being acceptable was equated with restrictions for many girls,
one of whom grew up to be a physician despite her parents'
limitations. Her mother told her not to climb trees, because
they are for boys, and to sit with her legs crossed. She remembers crying at age ten because she did not want to be a girl. Her
association of ladylike behavior with loss of freedom was the
spur she needed to succeed in the intense competition of medical school.

In general, girls with educated parents are more likely to be
encouraged by their families to have careers.[5] Lower-income
families tend to keep near their relatives and to retain a strong

emotional tie to them that can conserve traditional male and female roles.[6] Black couples are more likely to role-share,[7] perhaps because black women have always had to work and were not put on a pedestal.

A Traditional First Marriage

A woman who does not rebel against a domineering father may react against a first husband who expects her to do a double job and be a subordinate wife. A lawyer describes her first husband as hostile to women who were active or wanted to participate equally, out of his fear of being preempted. This woman became a full-time mother of two who felt as if she had three children to care for. Feeling a void at the center of her life, she developed migraine headaches and resented her husband. She divorced him but remarried him for her sons' sake, then divorced him again when she was in law school.

Rose is a forty-one-year-old writer whose husband expected that he must be taken care of and catered to.

> If he wanted a glass of water he expected me to get up and get the water and I did it. He would go out and play bridge and I was supposed to be home. If I went out, I was somehow neglecting him. We had very little money. Money can help these things and they can not be such burning issues: When there is a certain amount of work to do and you can't buy services it's difficult. When I had a child and he wasn't getting taken care of, he blew up and left the marriage.
>
> I was in high school in the fifties and you went to college and met someone and got married. There was Freudian talk of career women being castrating: I didn't have any rhetoric [in response] and felt that was the right way. I knew there was something wrong about it but just couldn't figure it out.

Rose determined to find a man who cared about her and her work, and her second marriage is a success.

Having an unpleasant first marriage gave some women the incentive to demand more from their second husbands, as in the case of a Colorado actress, Judith:

Too many times women get into a thing of, "If I say this is the way things are going to go, he's going to walk out." So you don't, you hang on to him and make it work. I just happened to have been through enough in my first marriage that I said, "I'm not going to put up with a shitty relationship; if we're going to have a relationship, it's going to be one that we've both got something to play on."

Some spouses in second marriages feel that the poor results of their first experiences are a major impetus to work harder the second time, to bend more: "So we are highly motivated to make it work and part of that is being more flexible about how you do things. That's what egalitarian couples are like—they are people who are willing to be more flexible." Since few of us are raised with the attitudes necessary to transcend sex-typed behavior, the unhappiness of a first, unequal marriage may be required to jolt us into change.

Being Educated and Having a Career

The incidence of role-sharing in marriage increases with wives' education and income: College can have a subversive effect on women, points out Jessie Bernard. Some women took women's studies courses in college and learned to aspire to use their talents. Those who went to a women's high school or college felt their ambitions were especially encouraged, and they learned appreciation for female achievements. Women who work in jobs they like are consistently found to be happier than homemakers.[8] Women with professional careers tend to be less traditional than nonprofessionals and more open to feminism.[9] Wives who have careers that are important to them make more decisions in their marriages and do fewer traditionally feminine household tasks than do less career-oriented women.[10] It is possible to have an equal marriage between a homemaker and a sole provider, but the effects of having one's own income and a sense of importance outside the home make it easier to role-share.

Meeting as colleagues in professional training generates an atmosphere of equality between men and women: "When you meet in law school," reports a woman from Maine, "there is a good key to somebody that they're not marrying Susie housewife." Starting out married life as students or recent graduates, with both spouses working, reinforces the college roommate mode of equal responsibility. An optometrist explains that when he finished school, his wife kept working and continued when they had their two children, so a traditional pattern was never established. They maintained their sharing from the beginning. Other young couples often did not feel the sex-role crunch until the birth of their first child. A wife's dropping out of work for years to bear and rear babies can impede role-sharing and career advancement.

A source of income gives a woman an important independence, self-confidence, and bargaining power. Personal worth and power are often coupled with income in our culture; even if one does not agree, the impact of American values is strong. As a wife's income rises relative to her husband's, so does the amount of housework done by her husband.[11] Studies confirm that the more income a husband earns the less work he does around the house, unless his wife's salary is comparable to his.[12] Income provides a resource for use in bargaining or negotiation.[13]

A power vacuum is set up if one mate has a vocation that gives a sense of accomplishment and the other does not. This is the conclusion of a husband whose first marriage suffered from a disparity in the strength of personality and career experience between him and his wife. He deliberately looked for a second wife who was "doing something she stood up for" to avoid inequality.

Women with little training or education have fewer options in mate selection, as this remarried attorney, Tavia, explains:

If you are independent and can support yourself in an acceptable standard, some of the needs to remarry quickly are gone. Some women frankly cannot support themselves and their family and have to get remarried. They look for someone and will accept less than a man who fully meets all their needs for that very real economic need. I've talked to some and I don't know what other alternative there is. They are left with two or three children and they're working at clerical or assembly-line wages. They can't support themselves. Whereas for me, actually, I was almost better off financially before I remarried. So I had a choice. Also, I was very outspoken at the beginning as far as what I was willing to give and what I need to get.

Women who contribute a substantial income to the family expect help with family work. A pharmacist thinks that women who put up with less are crazy; if her husband had not agreed to share the family chores, they would not still be married. Earning power is necessary for independence, according to Sarah, a South Carolina teacher:

Personally, for me money is important. Any time one person totally supports another person, you cannot have an egalitarian relationship, in my opinion. Somebody is feeling like they're contributing more. I need to feel financially independent.

The pressure to prepare for the "most important day of their life" (so says a current hosiery advertisement, portraying a bride in her white gown), rather than for a career, was strong for many young women. Those who were able to avoid the pressure developed self-esteem. Some women without a strong identity may be reluctant to share family work with their spouses if the home and family are the only areas they control.[14] This is an important distinction among traditional wives: Many of them do not want equal participation by their husbands in family life because that would leave the women unable to exercise power.

Some role-sharing wives' self-confidence led them to have high standards in their selection of a spouse rather than passively

accepting whoever came along. One physician, married to another doctor, explains:

> If you don't have high standards and don't insist on fair
> behavior in your mate then you are sunk. The key to my
> success as an egalitarian couple is my husband. It's not that
> he is responsible. I am responsible because I picked him. I
> owed it to myself and I gave myself the best.

A Montana nurse, Chris, had specific criteria in mind for mate
selection:

> One of the qualities I looked for in a man was someone
> who would not expect that I would wait on him hand and
> foot. There would be no way that I could live with a per-
> son like that; there is just not enough time in the day to
> be everything. You can't be superwoman: I couldn't work
> forty hours a week, take care of my son, keep a clean house,
> cook, and still be an individual myself, which would make
> me happy, make me a better person. I couldn't do all that
> and survive.

Delaying Marriage and Parenthood

Two important factors in preparing for egalitarian marriage are
living alone for some years to establish an autonomous career
and identity and knowing one's mate well before marriage. One
Colorado couple, a teacher and an attorney, lived alone for five
years after college graduation and were married eight years before they had children. Their pattern is typical of egalitarian
couples in their thirties. As one such woman stated, "If you
have some living under your belt you know that nothing is un-
complicated and just because you believe in equality doesn't
make it easy to be equal."

Many egalitarian couples believe that maturity leads to fewer
illusions and false expectations about marriage and that they
have an advantage over inexperienced, younger people who expect their partner to change. A Michigan women feels that wait-

ing until she was twenty-nine to marry was critical; if she had married at twenty-one, which is what she originally wanted, she would have been very traditional. The women's movement and living on her own entirely changed her perceptions. Other women agreed that if they had married in their early twenties, they would have fallen into the usual roles, stayed home to mother their babies, and probably gotten divorced. They needed time to mature, to establish a career, and to practice independence and self-sufficiency. As a Connecticut woman, Joanna explains:

> My growing feminist awareness meant that I didn't feel any rush to get into a relationship. When I did I was twenty-five years old and able to make real decisions about what I wanted. I didn't feel pulled by a domineering man, or feel entrapped, unlike many women who have so many years wasted and then are angry when they realize their error in judgment.

Women who did not wait and entered into an early first marriage as a result of college-senior panic found that they were children playing house. They knew neither themselves nor their spouses very well. The early marriages that survived most harmoniously are those in which the partners knew each other many years before the wedding and both continued their education and career. Generally, however, a New Jersey man, William, notes,

> There is a pattern [of marriage] we are aware of that leads to a nonegalitarian type. If a woman goes from her father's house to her husband's house without any period of independence, that's almost guaranteed to reproduce a hierarchical relationship. The husband in some ways becomes the new father.

Waiting to have children is also beneficial to achieving a non-hierarchical marriage. Many couples who did not wait wish they had, but most egalitarian couples waited many years before having children. A father from Pennsylvania, Ben, relates:

We were married for six years before our daughter was born.
During those six years we really got into an egalitarian living
situation, although I don't think we had any role models. As
a matter of fact, we've looked very hard to find some and
felt frustrated because not only can't we find any role
models but we have some difficulty in finding professional
couples with children who manage to stay together. When
the woman gets pregnant and the baby arrives, the woman
stays home and gets a lot of pressure to do so from her
husband.

Studies indicate that young couples often function equally
until the birth of the first child causes the woman to drop out
of the work force. The presence of children under twelve makes
role-sharing more difficult.[15] It has been repeatedly shown that
the curve of marital satisfaction drops when children enter the
family and it climbs when they leave. The unequal roles of
traditional mothers and fathers are not conducive to marital
happiness. In reaction, younger egalitarian couples delay childbirth and often opt for an only child.

Political Ideology and Feminism

Role-sharing is influenced by sex-role ideology, as well as by the
woman's income and the age of children.[16] Political and spiritual ideologies strongly influence some couples. An Illinois couple dedicated to the Catholic Worker peace effort have "a common philosophy."

Ours is a nonviolent perspective that is probably at the root
of us. It's a very human way of trying to deal with life, both
the personal and the political. Out of the commitment to
nonviolence comes work for justice and peace and personally trying to live according to those values.

Will, the pastor of a church in Texas and his wife, Hallie, are
supported by their denomination's efforts for inclusive religious
language, as in including female imagery in describing deity and
in expanding "the brotherhood of man" and "God, the Father."

The couple report that feminist awareness at church sensitizes them to related issues in their domestic life.

The ideologies of the sixties and the anti-Vietnam movements made women and men more radical. Susan, a poet, describes the war's impact:

> The Vietnam war touched me a lot. That was a beginning for me. The war was much more in the forefront than women's liberation literature; in examining the culture I had to look at what I was doing as a woman. So that was the beginning of a deep change in my sense of myself.

Working for or belonging to organizations such as the American Civil Liberties Union, Common Cause, or Planned Parenthood made other women more politically radical. This activism carried over into struggles for justice at home.

Before the civil rights movement and feminism had entered her life, a young fiancée told her husband-to-be that they would have a 60/40 relationship, that he would make the important decisions and she knew she would agree with him. Soon, a combination of the realities of living together as a married couple and a dedication to civil rights ideology changed her philosophy to belief in a 50/50 marriage. Her husband supported her change. Although many sixties male activists continued to ask women to do the typing and serve the coffee, others were compelled to put their beliefs into practice in their personal relationships, if they did not want to appear hypocritical. Some couples found political awareness a great influence in their marriages; it was illogical not to practice equality between themselves if they advocated it for others.

Other women grew up in politically leftist families in which they inherited a keen sense of justice. A Connecticut woman, for example, was influenced by her uncle, a radical priest involved in civil rights struggles. Her Irish Catholic family invited black people into their homes from the time she was very young. Her sense of her family's going against the grain spurred her on to civil rights work, the peace movement, feminism, and an equal marriage.

The women's movement changed the life of many women who participated in consciousness-raising groups and read feminist books. "My life has changed since I've done a lot of feminist reading and had more interaction with feminist people. When you're isolated in the system you tend to bow to it," Iris explains. Some wives do not support the more radical aspects of the women's movement but almost every woman acknowledged that the movement gave her support in her decision to combine a career and motherhood. "I'm put off by the screamers," states a data processor, "and yet I feel that somebody has to do some screaming because there are *not* lots of men around who think that sharing the workload is a logical thing to do." Some women were neutral about feminism until they experienced discrimination firsthand. In Pittsburgh, a woman's employer told her he would not promote her to a higher position because it would place her above a man and he was not going to ask a man to report to a woman boss. Partly because of her outrage, she decided to go to law school, where she met her husband.

A similar story is related by a pharmacist: During her first year in pharmacy school an instructor told her and the two other female students they were out of place in professional training. The women proceeded to earn the three highest exam scores. After she was practicing pharmacy, customers made unfavorable comments to her such as "Where is the pharmacist?," "Are you sure you're a pharmacist?," and "I've never seen a woman pharmacist." Her personal acquaintance with sexist bias led to her feminism and to a role-sharing marriage.

Laurel, a California technician, describes her conversion to feminism:

> After college, I had a personal experience where I was a victim of sexual discrimination and that made the women's movement seem a lot more relevant and applicable. I can think of a particular winter that I feel was the winter of my radicalization. I read *The Feminine Mystique* and started reading *Ms.* and switched from thinking that feminists were all bra burners and loser-type women to appreciating what it was about and feeling like a believer. It felt like a major

change in attitude. I realized my fullest potential in it and that was part of falling in love with Steve.

The women's movement gave women pride in being female and a new appreciation for other women: "When I was trying to be one of the men," says a physician, "I thought being a woman was nothing. Then I began to see women as valuable, worthwhile people." Being a member of National Organization for Women and participating in a mental-health support group helped a Texas woman find a sense of self-worth. Before that she based her value on having caught a good man and being a dutiful wife and a mother. One college student realized she kept getting involved with men who treated her poorly, as her father had treated her. Feminism gave her the foundation to reject unequal treatment. Another woman also changed her orientation to men because of the women's movement. Before she was a feminist, "my identity was going to be determined by the man I married, instead of what I wanted to do. My whole expectation about sex roles has completely changed."

Two generations of wives were encouraged by the women's movement to have equal relationships at various stages in their marriages, older women during established marriages and younger women before their marriages. Women's exposure to feminist books in the early sixties had a dramatic impact on established marriages, often leading to heated confrontation with their husbands and sometimes divorce if the husbands reacted too rigidly. An example is Syril, a Colorado draftswoman, who divorced her first husband:

> I read *The Feminine Mystique* and I was furious. I felt I had bought the whole tamale—if only I had read it five years sooner. There I was with no job skills and three little babies, a husband who was a real manipulator and only saw his side of things. I took about six months until I got out of the marriage, took my kids with me, started working, and went back to school.

Other women struggled with more flexible husbands and made the transition from traditional to more egalitarian roles.

Annie, a store owner, relates that feminism turned her life upside down:

> We were very traditional until 1975, when I read Betty
> Friedan and found out that I was not the only person who
> was unhappy with nameless problems. I began to analyze
> my life and what I wanted to do and then the changes
> started fast. I could no longer put up with being isolated in
> a house with small children. We went through some big
> changes. There were a lot of late-night discussions, a lot of
> arguments and tears and harsh words, but we kept at it.

A Washington, D.C., woman read *The Feminine Mystique*
in 1966 as she was taking care of her children in her suburban
home, having given up her career to move for her husband's;
she thought the book was her life story. Reading it, coupled with
consciousness raising in 1971, affected her very strongly. She
felt she had arrived home when she met other women who were
feeling the same way. At first her husband did not understand
what she wanted because they had fulfilled all the middle-class
dreams—a suburban house, bright children, a dog and cat—but
he was willing to learn, and their marriage survived.

Feminism gave women the reinforcement they needed to step
out of customary female roles: "Everything that was incoherent
crystalized. Before that, I knew what I wanted but didn't think
of it in terms of the larger circle," states a physician. A businesswoman appreciated the support the women's movement offered
for combining career and family:

> The women's movement made me less worried about doing
> things in a nontraditional way. I've had crap from relatives
> and neighbors and adults all my adult life about what I'm
> doing wrong; it's wrong because that is not the way males
> and females act with one another or that is not the tradi-
> tional way. It used to bother me a lot until a wider variety
> of lifestyles was being recognized.

Raye, a mother of three, dropped out of graduate school in
1960 because her Freudian therapist convinced her that it was
not feminine to be career oriented, that her ambition grew out

of neurotic feelings of competition with her husband, and that motherhood should be her major source of satisfaction. She felt guilty about her restlessness with staying home with three children, until she became a feminist. (The Freudian view that a career woman suffers from penis envy and a masculinity complex can still be found in bookstores today. Such books as The Power of Sexual Surrender by Dr. Marie Robinson [1959] are worth reading for a look at the psychological propaganda generated against career-oriented women.) The women's movement provided a counterideology that gave Raye the incentive to return to graduate school and become a director of a counseling center. Her husband accommodated the strains of her long-distance commute to graduate school in a neighboring state.

Feminism removed pressure and guilt from an Idaho medical assistant who prohibited her husband from doing housework when they were first married. She thought it was not proper, even though she disliked doing it all and even though he wanted to share it. Because women are trained to serve and be self-sacrificing, she found it guilt-provoking to step out of that female role. Couples receive support from groups like NOW. A husband reports that it means a lot to know there are other couples out there like them. Their NOW activities "made a major difference, to let me feel right about my feelings," his wife adds. Wives shared their feminist readings with their husbands. Some husbands took the initiative in suggesting that their wives learn about feminism.

Younger couples who got married after the women's movement was prominent reported that everyone they knew went through the consciousness-raising stage, so an egalitarian ideal existed for them. In Michigan a young couple were influenced by the woman's feminist mother, who raised crucial issues about male-female relationships. Before they got married they talked about specific tasks such as who was going to cook dinner and stay home with the children. Entering into a permanent relationship when they were used to hearing discussions about equality helped in their role-sharing.

The feminist practice of keeping their premarriage names

helps some wives retain a sense of identity uninterrupted by marriage. Thirty-seven of the egalitarian wives I interviewed do not have the same last names as their husbands, compared to two in a group of seventy-five traditional couples I surveyed. Several women adopted their husbands' last names, but felt so uncomfortable they changed back to their own names after about a year. A husband commented that he fell in love with a woman who had her own name, not his, and was glad for her to retain her original name. One couple combined their last names with a hyphen, so they both have the same last name, as does their son. Susan and Philip Suntree made up an entirely new name that suited them both. Couples with different last names either give their children hyphenated last names or the father's last name. Giving a daughter her mother's name and a son his father's is another possibility.

The women's movement also has supported women's and men's freedom of choice regarding sexual preference. Of the two lesbian couples I interviewed one couple was from California and had children from each of the women's previous marriages. A younger couple in Washington have an infant son conceived by one of them through artificial insemination. If they have another child, the other woman will bear it. Having a lover who treated her lovingly and equally astonished one of the California women who had been unhappy in her marriage:

> I suddenly realized that here was a person who didn't act in all the old grasping and manipulative ways, and it was a stunning realization for me. I just assumed that as a woman, this was my lot in life. It never occurred to me that there would be an alternative unless I were another type, like a wealthy and eccentric woman or a hermit. But for a normal, run-of-the-mill woman, this is what I assumed had to be.

The lesbian women reported a lack of tension and a strong feeling of ease with each other, since they understood their partners' conditioning and values.

An earlier study of thirty-one role-sharing couples in Madison, Wisconsin (by one of the interviewees, Linda Haas), reported similar findings about influences on the wives: a working mother, a postgraduate education, growing up in the 1960s, establishing a career before marriage and viewing it as highly important, waiting to have children, and the crucial impact of the women's movement (reported by two thirds of the wives).[17] These factors seem pivotal.

Personality Traits

In the determination of a person's potential for succeeding at an egalitarian relationship, personality type is perhaps as significant as background and attitude. Sandra Bem designed a useful instrument that tests for androgyny, the integration of traditional male traits, such as self-reliance and strong opinions, and traditional female traits, such as cheerfulness and a yielding manner. Androgyny describes unconventionally flexible individuals who incorporate various traits rather than only sex-typed traits. Bem correlates androgyny with high self-esteem, maturity in moral judgments, and flexibility. The least anxious and most creative people are those who score androgynous. Those who score sex-typed, highly masculine or highly feminine, are more often characterized by anxiety and low self-acceptance.[18] (One study found androgynous people to be the best parents, producing androgynous children,[19] although those findings were refuted by another researcher.[20])

Four test results are possible on the Bem scale: androgynous (high masculine and feminine), undifferentiated (low masculine and feminine, often considered the least favorable), feminine (high feminine, low masculine), or masculine (high masculine, low feminine). When Bem's scale was given to egalitarian and traditional couples it proved to be an accurate predictor of the division of work within the family. Chart I illustrates the results. Bem's test was taken by eighty-nine egalitarian couples and by seventy-five traditional couples. (See Appendix 3 for a more detailed description of the study.) The couples fall into four categories: seventy-one egalitarian husbands and wives whose

[] = MALE

■ = FEMALE

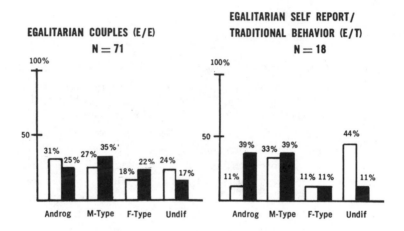

EGALITARIAN COUPLES (E/E)
N = 71

EGALITARIAN SELF REPORT/
TRADITIONAL BEHAVIOR (E/T)
N = 18

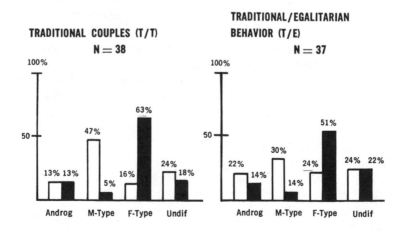

TRADITIONAL COUPLES (T/T)
N = 38

TRADITIONAL/EGALITARIAN
BEHAVIOR (T/E)
N = 37

time spent in housework and child care is within ten hours of their spouse's time on each task (E/E); eighteen egalitarian couples whose actual behavior is more traditional in that the women do more family work (E/T); thirty-eight traditional couples who in practice have an equal division of family work (T/E); and thirty-seven traditional couples who in practice have an equal division of family work (T/T).

E/E wives fell into categories in this order: masculine, androgynous, feminine, and undifferentiated. They have more masculine scores than their husbands and fewer androgynous scores. Of the E/T wives, many were also in the masculine category but they scored more androgynous than those in the first group. As one would expect, most traditional wives scored feminine and were paired with husbands who scored masculine. Thus the majority of women scoring masculine and androgynous were role sharers and the majority of feminine women were in traditional marriages.

It appears that in order to assume some male roles and give up some female ones, a woman has to have some masculine traits. The high correlation of masculine-scoring women with feminist beliefs occurs because masculine traits are necessary for career achievement: To be "yielding" is not conducive to advancement or to insisting that one's husband participate in family work. One study found that girls who reject the traditionally feminine role have higher intelligence scores than feminine girls and that masculine traits in both women and men are associated with mental health.[21] A study of the Bem scores of 369 middle-class women in Los Angeles found similarities between androgynous and masculine women and between feminine and undifferentiated women. Masculine-scoring women were more liberal about women's roles than were androgynous women and they were less satisfied with their marriages, but both types were well educated, were employed, and had high self-esteem. In contrast, the feminine and undifferentiated women were more often homemakers. Feminine-scoring women in another study are also least in favor of wives working full time.)[22] The feminine women in the Los Angeles study seemed better adjusted than the undifferentiated ones, they were more satisfied with their marriages, and they had higher self-esteem and were less introverted. But androgynous and masculine scorers had higher self-esteem and were more extroverted than the other two types.[23]

Perhaps egalitarian wives are more deviant than their husbands and require greater personal strength to defy convention. To achieve, to do, to strive are part of the male ethic, so men who combine dual roles are proud of their success and do not feel guilty about devoting time to their careers. In contrast, in *The Female World* Jessie Bernard describes women's values as love and duty. The female role calls for serving, doing for others, compliance, "stroking." It is "inherently nonegalitarian." [24] For a woman to succeed at combining a career and family, she has to reject traditional feminine values and integrate some masculine ones. A lawyer trying to balance her cases, her two children, and her relationship with her husband will not succeed if she is too compliant. To forge a new identity takes strength of character. A comparison of egalitarian husbands and wives shows that women are more often fueled by anger than are men (who are directed by logic) possibly because we live in a society that values men more than women. To rebel requires a tremendous amount of energy to swim against the current. Anger or indignation at injustice or unhappiness in a traditional relationship can supply the impetus to change. Women are trained to express their emotions, which among feminists leads to pioneering new relations between the sexes.

3
Egalitarian husbands

"What strikes me is how few men are in any way prepared to share fully in a relationship and in the running of a household and the raising of children. I'm struck by how difficult it is for them, unless they are extremely motivated to get those skills and do it."
—A Connecticut husband

He and his wife have two young children. Although they are college graduates, they have chosen to share a bus-driving job in order to have time with their family and to engage in work for peace through the Catholic Worker movement. They share a large old house with two single women. His political commitment is a major influence in his dedication to shared family roles.

If it is difficult for men to be equal partners in family work, the backgrounds of men who have equal marriages are worth examining. One husband feels thousands of women could step into his wife's shoes but very few men could replace him.[1] His wife, a teacher, agrees, "The key is not me; it's Don." Other men ask him how he manages to do most of the cooking, share in the care of their daughter, and attend law school. It is difficult to replicate what he does, he believes, since other men "need to see it on TV or read about it and there is nowhere to do that." Another wife agrees that men are less willing than women to be in an egalitarian marriage. Because we live in a society where men have more power, they have more to give up; men have to be willing to put their privilege on the line. She feels it is a rare man who will try equality for a while and not quit when it "gets hard."

Parents: Positive or Negative Examples

Many egalitarian men are not threatened by strong women because they have an achieving mother whom they respect. The isolation and small size of the family mandate that the parents shape the child's views about the gender to which he or she belongs. A man with a manipulative mother is often suspicious of women, while a mother who helps her son establish self-esteem produces the expectation that women are pleasant people. It is not surprising, as studies found, that husbands of achievement-oriented wives often have close relationships with capable mothers who work outside the home.[2]

Probably the single most crucial factor contributing to an egalitarian man is his mother. A lawyer in Maine, Cathy, observes about her husband, Paul, also a lawyer:

> I really do believe that when you look at a man's mother you see a lot how he relates to women. I was struck by the fact that his mom is a very feminine woman and very competent and intelligent. I really like her a lot. She is no wimp at all. She is very confident, although she has no career.

As a result, Cathy's husband is comfortable with her being a "racehorse," ambitious in her job. In contrast, a man whose mother catered to him reports he had difficulty recognizing his share of responsibility during the first several years of his marriage.

A Cincinnati businessman's mother was the central figure in his family; she worked as an accountant and church organist. As a result of his respect for what his mother accomplished, Len wanted his wife to be a career woman: "The thing that turned me off most was the type that preferred to stay at home," he explained. His wife is an English professor and published poet. Raised by women, Greg, a North Carolina dentist, feels he has always accepted men and women as equal because women were his authority figures. One man's mother supported her family after her husband died and provided an image of an individual who survived on her own effort. Many working mothers encouraged their children's independence by teaching them skills, such as cooking, so they could help with housework.

Other men reacted against their mothers' lack of identity and resolved to select a wife with a firm sense of self. A Wisconsin psychologist explains that his mother lacked a strong self-image and did not contribute effectively to his family. "Somehow from a relatively early age I decided the problem was that she had no real self-identity." Thus he decided he wanted to marry a career woman. Neil, a physician, thinks his mother was abused because his parents both worked but when his father came home he rested while his mother continued working until late at night. A lawyer views his mother as a bright woman whose life was totally wasted. He decided never to marry anyone like his mother, and he achieved his goal when he married a woman who is also a lawyer.

Such men want to have a more active role with their children than their fathers had with them. A Texas scientist explains:

> When I was growing up my mother was the keeper of the family. If you wanted to talk to my father you'd wake him up off the couch. He was a tremendous guy but he stayed out of my life more than I wanted him to. My mother was the disciplinarian; if you had a question, you went to her; if you needed money, you asked her. She taught my brother and me how to cook and iron. I always thought that if I had children I wouldn't want to be to them like my father was to me. I would be involved in their lives.

A Florida father made "a very conscious decision" to spend more time with his children than his father had spent with him. His is a typical reaction of husbands who are actively participating in child rearing. Men react against their fathers' roles in other areas as well. A psychologist, who views his father as a benign dictator, rejects his father's patriarchal style as one that does not fit him.

Some men's parents contributed equally to household management and child care. An Indiana sociologist's parents worked in an aircraft factory and shared domestic tasks; his mother did the home repairs. She taught her children to cook as soon as they could reach the stove burners. Laurel, a California technician, sees her in-laws making joint decisions and working together—they were both marines during World War II—and feels their influence was a positive one on their son.

One psychologist, Al, grew up in a Jewish immigrant neighborhood where all the men shared housework because their wives worked outside the home. His father, for example, did the shopping and made breakfast. A construction worker in Idaho also observed that his father did not put women into a narrow role. His father scrubbed the floors and did other housework. As a result, "it was almost unthinkable for me to assume that women did one sort of job and men another." Stewart's mother and father worked, cooked, and did housework when they got home. Because he grew up in an untraditional family he thinks it was easier for his wife "to go on thinking she was an equal human being" after their marriage. The impact of living closely with only one adult woman and one man is enormous and is an argument for raising children in extended families of friends or relatives. Also remarkable is that a negative example can be as influential as a positive one, and much more influential than having a neutral one.

Even if their parents did not share housework, many boys divided tasks equally with sisters: Both boys and girls shoveled snow and did dishes, for example. Some boys had only brothers (about 20 percent in my sample) which meant they had no choice about performing all kinds of chores because there were no sisters to do "female" tasks. Some egalitarian men came from families with two to five boys. Victor, a physician, reports:

> Because I come from a family of five males we were expected to do house cleaning and cooking in addition to masculine tasks like working in the yard and learning to fix things. We were expected to clean our rooms, do the dishes on a rotating basis; and that wasn't considered feminine.

Some men who had younger brothers and sisters took care of them and learned parenting skills. About 65 percent grew up in families with more than two children, as did about 64 percent of the wives in the study. Another study found that young men who favor nontraditional sex roles tended to come from large families with sisters.[3]

Other influences that led men to share family work were the need to take over housework following the illness or death of their mother or first wife or growing up in working-class families that could not afford hired help. Philip and his twin sister cooked their father's meals, for example, because their mother was out working at dinnertime.

Avoiding Training into a Macho Mold

Some husbands feel they escaped the traditional socialization into rigid male roles. "I was left to my own devices. I sort of grew up and they provided a place for me to be," notes a California businessman who was the youngest child. Clinton, the youngest child of sixteen children in a poor North Carolina family, also felt distant from his parents. A restaurant owner, he later encouraged his wife to run for local office because he always wished everyone could have the opportunity to achieve his or her goals, perhaps because his parents did not spend enough time with him to teach him their prejudices.

A youngest son, born when his mother was forty, views his birth order as significant:

> You know how the first child is always the image that the parents want and the second child is a little farther, and the third child is . . . Well, I was the third child and last child. I grew up so free. I was kind of an afterthought. The family didn't put much pressure on me to do anything.

As a result, his wife characterizes him as having a lot of tolerance and sympathy for the underdog.

Most men are deeply influenced by the cultural expectations for proper male behavior and find it hard to free themselves from their conditioning. It is a difficult process, according to a Pennsylvania psychologist:

As a man it has been really difficult for me to let go of my male conditioning even though I was coming from a place of wanting to and at the beginning thinking it would be easy. I didn't expect that I would have leftover feelings that would get in the way of my doing what I wanted to do, which was take care of my children half of the time and be a nurturing father and share in the housework. I found that a lot of my male socialization got in my way and I really had to deal with that. I talked to other men about it and examined myself.

A characteristic of many egalitarian husbands is their view of themselves as nonconformists. "I challenge traditional thinking. I tend not to accept the given. I don't assume that everything should be the way it is," states a physician. As a hospital administrator, he has appointed a majority of women administrators; he likes and respects women. Another husband described himself as naturally rebellious although he is now mayor of a large city. Several men considered themselves hippies during the 1960s. One of them, operating an air-conditioning business in Massachusetts, says he consciously worked against everything he was brought up to accept, including sex roles. A lawyer states, "I never grew up being very much of a cultural stereotype. I have always been somewhat aloof from the prevailing culture."

An Arizona anthropologist's questioning of tradition began in early adolescence:

> I think the first day I went to junior high school I became intensely aware of how all of a sudden there was this intense sex-role thing happening all around me but I wasn't aware of why. I spent four years trying to figure out what the hell it was that was going on around me and then figured out that what it was was a lot of crap.

He was also offended by the way his friends' fathers treated their wives in contrast to the respect his male relatives gave their spouses.

The rebellion against the traditional male provider role is caused in part by not wanting to feel solely responsible for a wife's well-being. A Michigan husband explains:

I always wanted a woman to stand by herself so I wouldn't feel like I had to support her. The macho syndrome has always turned me off. I think it is a very phony kind of philosophy, a symbol of insecurity in a person. The feminist movement is important because it tends to negate that the guy has to be all-persuasive and omnipotent.

Others didn't fit into traditional male behavior, not because of any conscious rebellion but because they were not successful at pursuits such as sports or did not have aggressive personalities. Victor explains:

I might be a very open-minded male who thinks that the women's movement is great and say I support it, but really my unconscious would be sexist if I felt more aggressive in those roles and fit in better as a child, but I never did. So I more naturally fit into the role that I do now. I grew up really resenting that I was supposed to fit into a masculine mold that wasn't how I was. I was an outcast of the four other boys in my family. If I was a traditional male as a child, I would not be who I am today. I wouldn't have had to ask those questions and come to grips with it.

Another husband describes himself as abnormal, a shy adolescent who did not date in high school. He still does not fit in with his male peers who drink a lot while he abstains. High school was also difficult for Wilt, an accountant, who found it hard to match the standard masculine role, such as excelling as an athlete or being tough:

Any time macho roles came up, I felt uncomfortable in that I couldn't do it, I didn't want to do it, I didn't like it. Boys were supposed to be tough hard men, and that was hard. It wasn't a lot of fun having to be tough when I didn't feel tough.

Their lack of popularity as adolescents did not impede their adult achievement. Many of them are successful professionally, so macho critics cannot judge them as being ineffectual. Rejecting the rigid masculine role model made these men able to empathize with their wives' struggles with limiting definitions of femininity. An interviewee, a sociologist who thinks of himself as being traditionally masculine in some ways, points out the interesting continuum of men who are role-sharers. Some reject masculine traits and some build on them, seeing themselves as independent, active, secure leaders of social change. He took the initiative in his marriage by insisting that both he and his wife support the family and try out various tasks. Masculine pride can be applied to new settings, he suggests, to fight for changes in sex roles. Another husband who aims for the "perfect" equal marriage is also an example of applying male aspirations for success to developing a better family life.

Living Alone

Most of the role-sharing husbands lived alone for some period during their twenties and learned to take care of their domestic lives by themselves. They believe that being on their own was vital and that it is foolish to go from mother to wife without space in between to learn independence. Some men learned home economics in a class, in Boy Scouts, in military school, or in the Army. Survival necessitated their learning how to cook, mend, and clean, and they do not let their skills grow rusty even in marriage. Delaying marriage and children is also beneficial in that as men get older they have less pressure to prove their masculinity through competition and career achievement. Many men in their thirties make a transition to more emotional expressiveness.[4]

A Previous Marriage

One remarried husband suggested that he needed a first marriage for practice in how to have an equal second one. Other couples suggested the importance of living together before marriage, although research has indicated that it makes no difference to marital success or to more egalitarian roles.[5] Men who had previous marriages with traditional wives reacted against the distance created by separate roles. They found it boring not to be able to have lively conversations with stay-at-home wives. One husband said he was lonely in his first marriage because he and his wife had little to say to each other. His wife was unfulfilled and, as a result, he did not respect her. In contrast, his second wife reports that she is very different from his first wife and that it changed his self-image to marry a lawyer.

A California man, Philip, describes the distance he felt from his attractive first wife. He married her when he was a college student. When they became parents of a son, she did not work outside the home.

> I was married for seven years in a very traditional relationship and was divorced and swore I would never do it again. It was a no-growth situation and I felt like I was in a rut. It was unfulfilling and too lonely. We didn't get a chance to share anything real. She didn't really want to be part of my world and I didn't want to be part of hers. So we got to be like two strangers and just drifted apart. It was a pretty traditional American disaster.

He also felt victimized by being the sole wage earner.

> The roles were so defined that if I had a job and the job terminated, it was necessary for me to be the number-one breadwinner. I would have to go out right away and find almost any job. I have taken some really awful and humiliating jobs.

His second wife, Susan, taught the same subject he did in a community college. She shares many of his interests in poetry and folklore, as well as their children.

It gets tiresome trying to play ball with yourself, explains another remarried husband. He's thrilled that his second wife, a feminist, catches the ball. He got tired of being solely responsible in his first marriage and enjoys being able to share. His wife has four adolescent children from her first marriage and is putting herself through college by working as a secretary. She learned independence as a single parent and applies it to her second marriage.

A computer scientist, Clay, describes how he felt bored with and used by his first wife:

Before she had children, I wanted her to work because I was working and would come home to a bored housewife who was looking to me for her source of interesting things. Women who have something that they do that is important to them are more interesting than people who hang around waiting to hear what you do.

Men like me have resentment for the woman who lives in their house, drives their car, eats their food—all of which is paid for by the man. I felt used. Women talk about being treated as sex objects, but men are treated as security objects. I'm not your meal ticket—I am a person. I want to feel we're equal or I'm going to feel ripped off as a security or identity object.

As a result he feels reluctant to have another child with the woman he lives with, a therapist who has not been married and who would like to have a baby.

An engineer in his third marriage felt unappreciated and manipulated by his second wife, who practiced the kind of tactics taught in the best-selling books *Total Woman* and *Fascinating Womanhood*, which teach women how to appeal to men. He felt she was devious, and he has found genuine happiness in his present marriage because he and his wife respect each other as equals. One husband describes his former wife as a prime example of the Phyllis Schlafly school of relationships. He disliked being excluded by her from household tasks. Reading feminist books such as Betty Friedan's *The Feminine Mystique* and Marilyn French's *The Women's Room* helped give form to his desire to share with his present wife.

When an older man has a second marriage with a younger woman, he is sometimes more cooperative about doing family work because he is no longer so competitive at work and he appreciates his wife's achievements. One such husband reports that he feels very lucky that he met his third wife, because she fulfills his image of an ideal person. Other couples found the age difference contributed to the man's willingness to share. A remarried woman, who believes her husband would have no qualms about being First Man if she were the president of the

United States, thinks her husband is secure because he is eighteen years older than she. But three men who are about eight years younger than their wives are also egalitarian. Age differences were not a factor for most couples. The man's unwillingness to be a success object or to treat women as sex objects to be pampered is more important. Egalitarian men feel exploited by the traditional male role and modify it to include two providers in a family.

The Wife Who Insists on Equality

Some husbands in egalitarian marriages had no particular personal history that directed them toward sharing tasks. Rather, they went along with the strong feelings of their wives, as one Colorado husband, Ted, explains:

> I think there are a lot of men, like myself, who don't feel that they're doing anything out of the ordinary. It just happens that the woman he falls in love with decides to assert herself, and that's fine. I've met a lot of women who think they're liberated but can't really carry it through. Maybe there are more men who are receptive to this than there are women who are willing to assert themselves. By the same token, there are women who know what they want and go out and get it. If Judi would have been a Suzie Cream Cheese, we probably would have had a different relationship.

Judi is an actress, whose first marriage taught her not to be submissive. In contrast, wives in some traditional dual-career families "crowd out" their husbands from family work, such as child care. One study found that husbands spend less time with their children when their wives work outside the home, as the woman monopolizes child care when she is at home.[6]

A Michigan husband, Michael, states simply that his wife is a very strong woman and that is the reason they share roles. It is easy to be lazy and let someone else take care of the work, observes Tom, a Montana wildlife biologist. He adds, though, that he could not live with his conscience if he behaved like men he knows who don't lift a finger around the house or are ignorant about how to take care of their children. Tom has never lived with a woman "who would put up with that b.s.," so he has not had a chance to try it.

Some couples started sharing after their marriage was well established. In those cases, the wife underwent a major change, often encouraged by participation in a feminist group or by reading feminist books. The husband, who thought he fulfilled his main duty to be a good provider, usually was bewildered by the change. One such husband explained that "I had to grit my teeth and try new things. She felt very strongly about it. It really wasn't as bad as I had suspected." He is a Washington, D.C., physician who did not have any models for equality: It took his father two weeks to learn how to operate a washing machine after his wife was in an accident.

Since role-sharing means the man must give up some leisure, it naturally provokes resistance. Many arguments about sharing housework occurred before some men changed. "We had some real discussions about the whole thing," says Will, a president of a New Jersey company. It took a while, for example, for him to get over the belief that he was helping with his wife Cleo's job when he did the dishes or laundry, although she shares management of their company with him as well as the care of their son. It is a slow process to undo a lifetime of separation of men's and women's duties and responsibilities.

Logic and Fairness

Numerous role-sharing husbands state that the reason for their lifestyle is its logic and fairness. They define themselves as rational, a stereotyped male attribute that can be put to good use in breaking out of rigid roles. A young technical writer with one child gives an example of this orientation:

> I looked around at what my relatives and people around me were doing in terms of traditional roles and I didn't think

that it made any sense, or that what they were doing was based on any sort of logic or reason. I've always been a big person for having everything around me make sense and be explainable. My family tended to think that the woman should be at home and I could never see a reason for that.

Currently he and his wife are moving from Ohio, despite his well-paying job there, so that his wife can complete her college education. His relatives think that is an unwise reason to move, but the couple are doing it nevertheless.

Some wives who struggled to get their husbands to do more housework successfully used the argument that fairness was the principle at stake. Since the men prided themselves on being fair, they conceded. Ron, a Washington co-owner of a business explains that his marriage began with very traditional roles; even though his wife was the wage earner putting him through graduate school, she did most of the housework and all the cooking. She finally pointed out that her workload was ridiculous. He recalls:

I had a lot of respect for my mate and the argument made so much sense that I couldn't say anything but "okay." I had a nice deal going; it was a little painful at first to come home from a day of work and actually organize and prepare a meal and do the dishes. That was quite a change, but it made so much sense that I didn't have any argument against it.

They now manage their business together as well as share the care of their three children.

A sense of fair play also made the president of a company, married to an IBM saleswoman, realize that "if she was going to be beating her brains out all day to earn money, it was only fair" that he contribute at home. He enjoys the income she earns and wants to make it comfortable for her to keep on working. The thought that some women put up with coming home from work to do all the housework makes one husband, Victor, feel sick to his stomach. He and his wife are physicians, and his wife's equal education and earnings give her status.

Also, as professionals they could afford to take several months off from work when their young son was born. Their having a housekeeper also relieves tension.

Applying the golden rule is part of the fairness applied by husbands who want a companion rather than a maid or a mother. Steve, a California attorney, states that he could not stay home and take care of four kids, so it is not fair to expect his wife to stay home. He refrains from sitting down with the "boob tube" after she works all day as a data processor. A psychologist has his version of empathy for his spouse: He could probably live with an arrangement where his wife did all the housework, but

> I'm also objective enough to know that if I was in that situation I certainly wouldn't put up with it. I look at it pretty logically. I believe in sharing. I didn't want to marry a mother, I already had one and I had no intentions of being a daddy to a wife. I wanted a companion and friend. I feel a big part of friendship requires sharing. To have an equal partner you treat your partner the way you want to be treated.

Appealing to a man's sense of logic and fairness is one of the best tactics a woman can use to point out the rationale for shared roles, since men are usually trained to rely on their reason rather than their emotions.

Political Orientation

Working in the civil rights or peace movement sharpened some husbands' sense of equity, and they resolved to practice at home what they preached to others. A few husbands are socialists or had socialist parents. Men who were politically active in the anti-war and racial integration movements of the sixties sensed that justice for minorities carried over to women's issues. The decade of the sixties had a major impact, sometimes indirectly through the influence of older brothers and sisters. Many couples became more liberal and more antiestablishment because of their rebellion against cruelties perpetrated by the U.S. government during the Vietnam war.

A couple who were in college in that period explains that while they were not campus leaders or activists for peace, just being students then was enough to make them critical of authority. He contrasts his political sense with that of younger teachers recently out of college who seem unaware politically and uninterested in issues such as the Equal Rights Amendment. In contrast, the husbands (and wives) in my survey of traditional couples were more likely to describe their political orientation as conservative or moderate. (Current polls of bright teenage students find them increasingly conservative, socially and politically, which raises the question of the probability of equal marriage among young people not influenced by the sixties.)

The women's movement made many men think about sex roles, fair division of labor, and role models for their children. They read feminist books and a few joined men's groups. A Louisiana husband, David, describes his conversion to feminism: "Like Paul on the road to Damascus, the intuition swept over me with enormous power of understanding the problems of women in this society." As a result, he spoke on talk shows, convinced a woman sitting next to him on an airplane to buy a dishwasher to save her time, aided his wife in her candidacy for political office, and shared equally in child care.

Some husbands view sharing roles as a political act, as does Art, a Pennsylvania psychologist:

> The movements of the sixties and the seventies had a profound influence on me. I was really influenced by feminism. I went through a revolutionary personal change in the early seventies and got in touch with my nurturing side. In getting together with Cathleen I wanted to explore that further and being a half-time parent was a way to do that. To be really close to my children felt wonderful. I want to acknowledge that there's a political decision involved. I think the nuclear family is a real disaster and that the ideal human condition would be some sort of tribal existence. In spend-

ing so much time with my children and in home tasks, I think I'm making a political statement about that.

A Canadian wife describes her husband as a better feminist than she is in practice. While she had done more reading about it and he does not explicitly identify himself as a feminist, she is more likely than he is to slip back into stereotyped ways of thinking. She sometimes feels guilty, for example, about not doing enough "woman's work" but he never seems to feel uneasy about doing "women's work." After exposure to feminism, a sociology professor in Colorado realized he was exploiting his wife in many ways, although that had not been his intention.

Feminist principles made sense intellectually to liberals; making changes at an emotional level, however, is very difficult, as Jack, a business owner, explains. He and his wife spent a year intensely discussing changes they should make in gender roles:

> It was really work and during that time I came to like and respect Annie. The political concepts I could understand, because Annie knew me well enough to be able to put it into areas that I could see in my family, like spending more time with my boys. The emotional takes a long time. You have to be politically committed before you become emotionally committed. It is a lot easier to be macho crazy than it is to be a feminist male, because you are bombarded hourly with all the television commercials, *Playboy*, etc. It is a lot easier to say "Yeah, that is the way it is" than to try to change.

Older husbands who started out traditionally were afraid they would be labeled henpecked if a neighbor saw them changing diapers or doing dishes. They have recently found more support for sharing. The women's movement has made domestic involvement less threatening for men.

Not being white, Anglo-Saxon, and Protestant was a factor in some men's egalitarian attitudes: "I'm probably more sensitive to fairness and shafting" because of identification with the oppression of Jews, explains a Delaware market researcher. A wife traces her husband's attitude to "a lot of sympathy for the underdog that comes from being Jewish and the Jewish leftist position." A Jewish heritage was also an important influence for a Washington psychologist because of its humanitarian and intellectual orientation: He describes his male relatives as temperate and reflective. One man whose father is Chicano felt that he was taught a sense of duty to family and a gentle manliness emphasizing involvement, respect, and obligation to women and family, contrary to prevailing views about machismo. An Asian-American and a black husband also emphasized that family was central to them, partly as a protection against the dominant culture. Even though there is an emphasis in black families on the male as the head of the family, in reaction to the myth of the black matriarchy, in practice studies show that roles are shared more than in white families.

Additional influences on men's awareness of equality are their education in a liberal college environment,[7] their practicing a helping profession, or their belief in a religion whose members are involved in social action. Although one man's family was conservative, his exposure to radicals at Oberlin College changed his political orientation, which carried over to his attitudes toward sex roles. Being a history major and reading about social reform movements in the United States had a liberalizing impact on an Ohio business president. One man traces his openness to new ideas to his work as a newspaper reporter, while some therapists feel their training in sensitivity to others has made them more egalitarian husbands. Men in Unitarian, Quaker, Catholic Worker movement, or Protestant denominations, which deal openly with sexism, learn awareness of equality issues.

Being Secure

"I have a fundamental premise that people who are bigots and people who want to keep women in their place at home are afraid of their own inadequacy." This statement is perhaps the most revealing of the nature of egalitarian men; they have strong self-images and do not need to control their wives.[8]

A woman seeking a role-sharing husband should avoid men who are constantly proving their manhood to an invisible jury that never lets them relax except when they are numbed by television or drinking. Role-sharers do not have an image to defend because they are content with who they are. Several men spoke of the social pressure to maintain a masculine image and recalled how they rejected it; a man who is insecure about his image will likely stay away from cooking, sewing, and changing diapers, according to a New York television engineer.

Being secure allows flexibility; it doesn't restrict activity to traditionally masculine or feminine behavior. Several husbands sew for their families because they like the technical challenges of sewing, while traditional men would be afraid to be seen operating a sewing machine. Other men enjoy cooking or are fascinated by learning about birth. A California geologist, Steve, relates why he likes to get involved in all aspects of daily life:

> My hunger is to understand as much as I can, which means experiencing it myself. And for that reason I find it important and very satisfying to go through all the steps in making something happen; understand it, get a feel for it, and get my hands dirty with it. We planned the wedding and the birth much the same way: We had the birth of the kid in our bedroom.

Being a middle-class, well-educated professional is different from being a blue-collar worker. Betty, who works in a Texas factory, describes her male fellow workers as seeing their wives' main function as taking care of them, so they forbid their wives to work outside the home except for minor employment such as selling cosmetics in their spare time. The men would never dream of doing housework and they give Betty "a lot of slack" for working. Social class is a strong determinant in attitudes toward sex roles, but the desire to keep women as nurturers crosses class lines. A hard-hat worker who admits helping his wife with family work is frowned upon at work as a scab. Blue-collar men do not have a monopoly on that tactic, however: A business executive on vacation with other couples reported the other men razzed him when he did his share of domestic chores.

Egalitarian husbands' definitions of masculinity include being nurturing and open about emotions. Since they accept themselves, they can also accept a woman for her honest self and do not expect her to fit a stereotyped feminine image. Their wives frequently describe them as easygoing. Maddy, a Wisconsin teacher, relates that her husband, Don,

> is totally non-threatened. He's absolutely not a macho man. He's not the type that carries his ego on his shoulder and waits for somebody to knock it off. He's calm, easygoing, gentle, and sensitive. Don bakes bread for ERA fund raisers and his masculinity isn't at stake. His brothers consider him a pariah in the family because of his support for women; but due to his strong sense of self, he doesn't bend to their pressure.

Another woman, an attorney, describes her husband's confidence:

> I think it's easier right now for a woman to assume nontraditional roles than for a man. Chuck is extremely strong in his ability to say, "I do not need traditional trappings or role models to feel good about myself."

Men who are continually anxious about their masculinity clearly are going to find it difficult to be in a 50/50 marriage. (Yet masculinity is so tied to performance that uncertainty in young men is almost inevitable; a student who read this manuscript pointed out, "I'm continually anxious about my masculinity but I'm not 'macho.'")

Growing up in America makes most men fearful about proving their maleness, as Herb Goldberg spells out in *The Hazards of Being Male* and *The New Male*, which describe how the traditional male role emphasizes performance, competition, and denial of emotions, causing stress-related illness.[9] Male fears that get in the way of equal relationships are explained by Clay, a New York computer scientist:

I don't feel I'm a faggot if I live with a woman who does
some tasks that men are supposed to do. I have a very strong
sense of having worked through things that men are normally worried about because of our culture. Men are se-
cretly afraid that they are gay or can't perform and are
going to be lesser human beings. As boys we grow up admiring maleness and set yardsticks for proving that. Many
men are threatened by women who want to be self-directed.
I think they are threatened because they consciously or unconsciously worry about themselves.

If a man does not need his wife to make him feel superior,
he can appreciate a partner who will challenge him. "One of
the worst things in the world is to spend your life with a half
person, a woman who will only reflect you without any aspirations of her own and be dependent," states David, a Louisiana
writer. His wife is an administrator and a feminist, and she is
active in politics. A man who is comfortable with himself will
not need his wife to diminish herself to make him feel important.

Personality Types

In addition to a man's background, his personality type is an
indicator of the role he will assume in the family. According to
their Bem scores (see Appendix 3), more androgynous men are
found among the truly equal couples than in any other group.
One androgynous-scoring man, David, describes himself as "in
touch with the woman that is in every man." He finds this adds
to his creativity as a writer as well as to his empathy with women.
The scores of egalitarian men who do not do as much family
work (E/T) as E/E men are much less androgynous and much
more undifferentiated. Perhaps those men do not have the psychological strength necessary to carry out nontraditional roles.
Undifferentiated men have lower self-esteem than other types
of men and they have less intimate relationships, according to
two studies.[10] Androgynous men have higher self-esteem than
undifferentiated men, and they are more autonomous and less

conventional than other types of men.[11] Unconventional men are able to have more intimate friendships and reveal more about themselves than conventional men.[12] Androgynous fathers are more loving with their children than are masculine fathers, and they are also less firm and less directing.[13] Androgynous people have the most liberal attitudes about women's participation in professions.[14] If all these findings are put together, one could make the equation for men that self-esteem = unconventional = androgynous = intimate = egalitarian. It appears that a woman in search of an equal mate has better chances of success with an androgynous man.

In contrast, most traditional men are in the masculine category, although those who share family work (T/E) have higher androgyny and femininity scores than purely traditional men (T/T). More college men who score masculine believe a wife should take primary responsibility for child care than do college-age androgynous men.[15] Thus my Bem score results and other studies concur that there is a difference between egalitarian and traditional men's personality types. Most androgynous- and feminine-scoring men share family work with their wives, while most masculine-scoring men do not. The attitudes reflected by their low femininity scores seem to impede nurturing activities.

The men, rather than the women, made the difference in each group whose practice is different from its ideology. Egalitarian women's scores are high masculine and androgynous in each group, but the men's are much different—the egalitarian men who do not share equally in practice (E/T) are more undifferentiated and less androgynous. The traditional women's scores are also similar, but the traditional men who are equal in practice (T/E) are lower in masculine scores.

What to Look for in an Egalitarian Husband

Another way of defining the backgrounds and attitudes of egalitarian couples is to compare them with traditional couples. The results of questionnaires filled out by eighty-nine egalitarian and

seventy-five traditional couples indicate distinct differences between the groups (see Appendix 2). The majority of egalitarian
couples had working mothers while over 60 percent of the traditional couples' mothers were homemakers. Traditional wives
hold fewer professional jobs than egalitarian wives, although
there is no significant difference between the husbands' jobs.
Egalitarian couples average fewer than two children and traditional couples more than two. Role-sharers are more liberal
politically, more disapproving of traditionally defined masculinity and femininity, and more approving of feminism.

Comparing the egalitarian couples who are equal in practice
(E/E, seventy-one couples) with those who are more traditional
in their actual division of family work (E/T, eighteen couples)
indicates many similarities. The only significant difference is
that the more traditional couples (E/T) are younger, in their
early thirties, while the egalitarian couples are over thirty-five.
Fewer of the women are professionals but they are working outside the home. The lack of attitudinal differences points to the
importance of the Bem scores in indicating a person's likely
behavior. Comparing traditional groups again indicates similarities. Fewer T/E women are homemakers which may lead to
more equal division of family work.

The woman's occupation seems crucial: in the other studies of
role-sharers by Haas and DeFrain the wives were also highly
educated women working outside the home. It makes sense
that women with solid incomes have more equality. Haas also
found that three fourths of the husbands did not view their own
career advancement as very important. The men value family
life. Overall, there do seem to be distinct patterns characterizing
role-sharers, both male and female.

The factors that seem to be most important in the makeup
of a role-sharing husband are his androgyny score, his feelings
about his mother, and the degree to which he accepts himself
rather than attempting to match a masculine image. The mainstream culture pushes men in a direction opposite to that followed by egalitarian men, so such men are hard to find. The
most practical steps a woman can take in selecting an egalitarian

spouse are to delay marriage until both she and her potential spouse are older, to observe him with his mother, and to ask him specifically about his beliefs about having a working wife and sharing child care. What would he do if she received a desirable promotion that required moving to another city? Would he get up with an infant and change its diapers in the middle of the night? Would he stay home from work with a sick child? Would he take responsibility for remembering that a baby sitter needs to be called? To radically change an adult's attitudes is almost impossible. That is, if a man responding to such questions hedges or says the questions are trivial, a woman should be wary. Detailed discussions of probable events in a marriage need to occur at length before any long-term commitment is made.

The facts that some husbands in my study initiated role-sharing and that some traditional husbands were able to become role-sharers when their wives initiated it offer hope that change can occur. Men have much to gain in equalizing the provider, initiator, and decision-maker responsibilities and gaining a partner rather than a subordinate follower.

Role-sharers, male and female, are similar in the self-confidence that permits them to oppose norms of appropriate behavior. Some gained their confidence from supportive parents, others from overcoming childhood difficulties with parents or with acquaintances, others from being academic and professional achievers. Some avoided the usual training for femininity or masculinity or rebelled against it. Androgynous personality types might be indicated by that rebellion against customary restrictions on sex-appropriate behavior.

4
Staying together

We kiss a lot. But it is not me walking up behind her and giving her a peck and then it turning into symphony orchestras going up in the background. It's just two human beings who like each other.

—*A Wisconsin husband*

Sharing the operation of their small record business and the care of their two sons leads to closeness between them that did not exist when he was responsible for the business and she was at home with the boys.

The Myths

Like the crowd admiring nonexistent garments in "The Emperor's New Clothes," our society bases marriage and parenthood on pretense and illusion. Since most of us have no training in relational skills such as disclosing feelings, problem solving, negotiating conflict resolution, and knowledgeably handling sexual matters, we fill in our ignorance with myths. Fantasy about marriage is provided for girls by childhood stories, toys, and games, Barbie and Ken dolls, jump-rope rhymes that predict the initial of their honey bunch, romance novels, ballads, and television soap operas and films. Boys sneak sessions with *Playboy* magazine and read superhero comics. They know they are supposed to prepare to be providers but do not think much about becoming husbands and fathers. Elementary school children in progressive Berkeley, California, schools were asked to describe a typical day in their life when they are thirty-five. The boys talked about careers, not family, and the girls the opposite.

As the divorce rate indicates, many people do not have objective information about how to select a compatible mate. They get married because they are sexually attracted, feel lonely, think the timing seems right, or simply accept being selected. They believe their spouses will make them feel complete and resent them when they inevitably fail. Add to unrealistic expectations about marriage and child rearing a crying baby interrupting sleep every three hours or teenagers acting out negative feelings, and it is surprising the divorce rate is not higher. The rate of divorce climbs as women's salaries increase, a fact that seems to indicate more couples would divorce if it were economically possible. Some stay married because of the expense of establishing two households, religious beliefs prohibiting divorce, or inertia. Clearly, we need to know more about the dynamics of successful male-female intimacy.

Love is the subject of innumerable songs and stories, but we know little about it. Romantic love, infatuation, or falling in love fades, according to egalitarian couples. While it lasts it is exciting but uncomfortable. Researchers label these different emotional states passionate and companionate love: The former is characterized by anxiety/relief and elation/pain, and the latter is based on deep affection.[1] Mature love is based on friendship, respect and commitment—three words often repeated by the couples in my study. Many of them were aware of the unrealistic nature of American myths about marriage and parenthood.

Annie found it useful to read the *Intimate Enemy*,

> where George Bach talks about the expectations that we get from parents, church, movies, TV, the media in general. I began to say, "Yeah, he's right. That is all baloney. That is not real life." Through reading and talking to people, I began to form thoughts about what is real life and to think about what love really is to me. What do I want out of a relationship? That is where I got the ideas that I have now. I can't watch old movies on TV because they are so fake and I think "How many years was I fed those lies about how I was going to feel and how it was going to be?" Hey, it isn't that way for anybody. I don't care if you are rich or poor, it's not real. So I slowly began to build real models.

She also gave up illusions:

> The biggest myth is that the other person is going to auto-
> matically know what you want and do it for you. I still
> sometimes expect Jack to know what I want and say what
> I want him to say at that moment. It's really hard, but I
> think I am getting a lot better at learning to express my
> needs and my wants and knowing that there are going to
> be times when we just don't get along. I think another
> problem with the romantic love idea is that the people
> don't really communicate in the romantic movies. People
> just kind of come together. There is very little day-to-day
> nitty-gritty stuff, or if there is it is treated in such a way
> that you think, "Wow, they really handle those things
> well." Nothing in life is like that.

Several of the women I interviewed have a Cinderella complex,
and they wish their husbands would sweep them off their feet
and bring more excitement to the relationship; one wife said that
she still has an image of her husband as a knight on a white
horse. She sometimes gets upset when he does not match her
ideal. Another wanted to be pampered by her prince, to be
taken care of and to live happily ever after. She realized, though,
that white horses are really dirty animals and her husband is not
going to ride one, although occasionally she still feels mistreated
when he does not read her thoughts and gratify them. A Missouri woman in her twenties who was waiting for her hero realized she had to give up the idea of looking for someone to carry
her off. She realized that she could go wherever she wanted to
go by herself. No longer does Cinderella have to wait for the
prince to achieve womanhood. Most wives did not expect the
thrills of courtship to last and are pleased with the comfortable
familiarity that replaced it.

Some couples who married in their early twenties had to
struggle with unrealistic fantasies about their proper role as
husband or wife. Their illusions had no connection with the
reality of daily living. One such husband, Kenneth, who is probably typical of many young bridegrooms, believed he should be
a superhero:

My initial notion was that I would be sort of Batman. I would be kind and strong and take care of everything and never complain. I always had that romantic dream, even as a kid—that was the kind of husband I wanted to be. But internally after six months I knew that it wasn't working. But I didn't know what else to do, so we decided that marriage counseling would be a good place to find a better basis for how to relate to each other.

His wife, Marge, had her own fantasy about marriage:

If we only have a good enough relationship then life will be all golden clouds forever. It doesn't work that way, though. We began to recognize that it doesn't matter how beautiful your relationship is, you're not always going to be happy. One of the very useful things that they teach in Marriage Encounter is that all relationships go through romance, disillusionment, and joy, and then back again. That has been a very helpful concept for us.

Another husband, Dave, thought he should supply all his family's financial needs and "present this macho image that I was the man of the house." His stereotype ignored the reality that his wife was a nurse who wanted to work, that they needed the income she earned, and that she was a strong-willed person. A counselor gave him encouragement to feel good about sharing responsibility and wage earning. One husband, who was influenced by the My Fair Lady image, believed that the superior male's duty was to develop and mold his young wife into the full-blown woman of his desire. He changed his view after his first wife left him.

The marriage illusion dictates that the wife should take care of all the family work. Even though his wife worked outside the home, Andy, a company president, would come home from work, head for the couch, and read the newspaper, expecting his wife, Clarissa, to do everything. They had some angry discussions and Clarissa developed an ulcer before Andy's myth of the superwife was dispelled.

A Colorado wife had naive goals for her first marriage:

Initially you want everything to be romantic. You want checkered tablecloths on your table, and an apron and a frilly dress when you cook the dinner, and candlelight. I think friendship is a much bigger part of love for me this time than it was before. I cannot in my wildest imagination think of myself being married to or romantically involved with any man who is not truly a dear friend. I want romantic times, but I don't want all times to be romantic. That would just drive me crazy. I can't be bothered with that.

The trouble with the image of the aggressive prince and the passive princess is that he gets worn out taking care of her and has a heart attack and she gets depressed with living vicariously and takes mood-elevating drugs. Couples who waited till their middle and late twenties to marry or who married for a second time were not as saddled by romantic myths. A study found that second marriages had a higher level of satisfaction,[2] probably because of the growth away from the unrealistic expectations young couples bring to marriage. A typical mature assessment comes from Richard, who says,

I had always had a view of marriage that there were ups and downs and disappointment and happiness. I was never going to be your prince coming down on the white stallion to carry her off in the sunset. I was never that much of a sentimentalist to think that could happen. To me a marriage takes someone who is bright and hard-working at keeping a relationship going.

Another husband realized "the fantasy girl" did not exist and that he wanted a real person who was solid and pleasant. One woman's reality check was to think about what it would be like to see her fiancé every morning for forty-five years. Marriage is not very romantic, an Indiana couple noted. (A survey of married couples in the Southwest found that wives preferred sewing to having sex with their husbands.[3]) The stresses of daily living and child rearing are not conducive to candlelight dinners and uninterrupted conversations. Yet the ideal of romantic love persists, perhaps so men and women will buy commodities designed to enhance romantic attraction, such as those portrayed in car or nylon hosiery commercials.

The Myth Makers

Most people did not see their parents' marriages as romantic and some in fact report that their parents' relationship was the opposite of their fantasies. What, then, are the sources of our unrealistic expectations about living happily ever after? The myth has existed for centuries in Western culture. The cult of courtly love developed in eleventh-century France, a pastime for leisured aristocrats who battled for their lady's favor when no other fields of combat were available. Love was not seen as possible or necessary in marriage. The adored lady was not to be sullied with sexual contact but rather worshiped from afar. Frequently she was married to another man. The medieval outpouring of adoration for the Virgin Mary, evidence in the splendid cathedrals built in her honor, also was directed at a woman who was inaccessible. Worshiping someone is easier than living with someone, struggling to understand or be understood, to compromise and negotiate. Putting women on a pedestal serves to confine them, gilding their cage.

The heroine in romantic novels of the eighteenth and nineteenth centuries was another version of the pure and innocent maiden for whom the hero performed his feats to be rewarded by her hand in marriage. The stories end with the assurance that the hero and heroine lived happily ever after, with no indication of how they dealt with daily life. A film such as *Love Story* has to end before the honeymoon glow dims. A wife whose favorite movie was *South Pacific* was angry that she was not taught what marriage really required. She thought that one enchanted evening your eyes met across a crowded room and bliss followed.

The romantic novels currently sold in supermarkets and advertised on television are big business, a major support of the publishing industry. In such novels, the couple typically decide to get married after one thrilling session of dancing together and a dozen passionate kisses. The hero in Sally Wentworth's *Summer Fire* (1981), for example, is fifteen years older than the heroine and their political views are opposite, but they do not discuss these disparities. In one incident he grabs her and tears off her blouse, a standard event in these novels, but the couple never discuss pleasing ways to communicate passion or the violation she must have felt. They fall in love in a month on the basis of their sexual attraction, his power, and her innocence. Of course the novel ends before they begin married life. In his analysis of American fiction in *Love and Death in the American Novel*, Leslie Fiedler notes the consistent lack of mature contact between men and women.[4] Novels reveal little exploration of daily male and female interaction, and the stories we have inherited do not prepare us for reality.

Films, television, popular music lyrics, and romance magazines and novels have formed our expectations for love in a cruelly unrealistic manner: "I was raised with romantic notions of Prince Charming who would save you," says a Texas wife. Couples report that popular songs such as "Today I Met the Boy I'm Going to Marry" perpetrate the magical love-at-first-sight theme. The implication is that love is a mystical, instant click. In that situation, the other person is merely a screen for the projections of our desires, as enchantment implies illusion.

The media takes the fairy-tale hero who rescues the victimized lovely girl—Cinderella, Snow White, Sleeping Beauty, Rapunzel—and resets him in the American frontier as the cowboy on his white horse or in the city as the young man on his motorcycle (the hero seems to need a vehicle to enhance his power). Girls are taught to look forward to their wedding day as the climax of their life and to look forward to cooing babies and an adoring provider husband who brings home lovely gifts and creates a perpetually happy family. An example of the impact of media myth-making is given by Sheila, an Indiana professor:

I was so unfair to my first husband. I had unreal expectations of what he should be and the things I should do. I was absurd. I was in never-never land. I allowed too much of self-identity to be tied up in him. If he wouldn't wear a belt on his pants I felt that reflected on me somehow, because I didn't have any sense of who I was or what a relationship was. I wasn't willing to allow him to have human failings.

The popular media's impact on Barbara, an Ohio wife, was to frighten her when she had periods of not feeling total devotion to her husband or passion for him. Now she realizes that cycles occur in marriages and that the myth propels people to divorce in hopes of finding the *right* person with whom one is always in love. Once the honeymoon is over, *Ladies' Home Journal* replaces *Seventeen* and *Bride* magazines; advertisements show men and women who are content because she makes him a good cup of coffee and removes the ring around his collar. A Washington family lived out the American dream:

I assumed that when I had children I would be a happy homemaker for the rest of my life and I never questioned that we'd have a lovely home and family. After I had my second child I was delighted. I wanted four, but after my third, I changed my mind. Then it started to get to me—cleaning messes and diapers. I hated housework. The kids I liked, but the housework I couldn't stand. Rob was great when he came home from work, but I was under the gun twenty-four hours and he for twelve hours. It was a hard time for me. I felt very uncomfortable being more or less dependent. He was a great guy, so why was I upset?

Most of the couples with lengthy marriages had to change their ideas about family as the total source of satisfaction for women.

Egalitarian couples were raised in the same cultural milieu as traditional couples. The difference is they do not expect their spouse to fit a stereotypical mold of wifely or husbandly behavior. They realize they are living with a human being and that a great amount of work and time is required to achieve the understanding that nurtures love.

Why Falling in Love Is Short-Lived

Falling in love is not rational, according to egalitarian couples. It is exciting partly because of the anxiety and tension of not knowing what will happen next. Will he phone? Will she agree to go out with me again? "You can easily be swept off your feet because this person deigned to give you attention and you're flattered, even if you didn't actually enjoy being with him," explains Judith, a California wife. Often when the bubble bursts as the novelty wears off, one looks at the former beloved and is astonished by how little is still appealing. Tom, a Montana wildlife biologist, explains:

> I suspect I put off getting married until I was thirty because I kept thinking that giant bells were going to come along and I finally realized it's a crock. That's never going to happen, or rather it happens all the time. I could fall madly in love with somebody on the street, who I never met. And it took me awhile to realize that nine hundred and ninety-nine times out of a thousand I wouldn't even like that person if I got to know her for ten minutes.

Many of us are love-junkies addicted to the excitement of beginning an affair, bridging the gap between two strangers, without any deep knowledge of the person we are attracted to: "I often fell madly, passionately in love and then I woke up out of it," Ted, a Colorado businessman, relates. His choice of words "madly" and "woke up" illustrates the lack of consciousness we associate with infatuation. "I had a lot of magic two-week romances," says Linda, an Iowa graduate student and secretary. She missed the thrill when she began living with her future husband, but she realized that

> what I thought was magic was actually discomfort with other people. You had to have a feeling of constantly not being at ease. I thought that was what I wanted. As soon as that was gone we felt so comfortable and I thought I can't really like this person because I'm too comfortable. I can talk to him too easily. It took me a while to get over that and realize what I really wanted.

While on a trip, she ran into several former lovers and felt the romantic tug at her emotions.

They were very good-looking, exciting men and I spent an afternoon with each of them. Coming back, Ben sat in the corner all the time reading books and for a couple of days I went around wondering what I did to end up with this one, where's all the fireworks and stimulation? Then I realized that I would have never been comfortable with those other men. There would have been constant friction. I would have been so unhappy, while Ben and I fit together perfectly. The other stuff was only fun for an afternoon at a time but I wouldn't want to live with that at all. It made me really appreciate Ben to have the experience of being with these exciting but rather irritating men.

Before they lived together, Ben had to struggle with the *Playboy* compulsion to have numerous affairs. As a married person he realized he could delight in sexual fantasies about other women, share them with Linda, and not act on them. Most couples agreed that monogamy was necessary to build trust and commitment in their marriages. Several couples experimented with "open marriages," but found it painful.

The glitter of falling in love is accompanied by tension; as one song acknowledges, falling in love leads to "pain and sorrow." Some couples were glad to have it end, so something more solid could be built, as a Colorado woman, Judi, describes: "I can remember that great passionate attraction for Ted, and thinking I would be kind of glad when that's out of the way so we could really talk and get to know each other." Another wife reports that holding hands and talking is nicer in the long run than the "passion when you first kiss someone and it's really bubbling."

Other couples agree that falling in love inhibits communication: "It puts pressure on you not to be really honest." In that state, you do not confront each other and you set up dishonest patterns that are hard to break, couples note. Physical discomfort, such as being unable to eat or sleep, having butterflies in one's stomach, accompanies it; so does fear of being rejected, the pressure of having to perform, to talk, to make an impression. One woman states:

> To me, the romantic love idea is you're presenting yourself to a person as just a part of yourself; particularly the women in this situation are portrayed as docile, quiet, sexual things. They don't have minds, they don't have intellects, they never argue forcefully for a point, they don't have strong opinions. It is not real . . .

The mother of Elizabeth, an Indiana physician, expressed this attitude when she told the teenage Elizabeth to make boys think they knew more than she did and not disagree with them.

The feeling of obsession with a lover, "the breathtaking titillation, can only occur with a new relationship," believes a Colorado teacher. Romance is a beginning but not a foundation, not something on which to build a lasting relationship. Studies have found that romance is half over by three months and usually lasts six to thirty months.[5] If people try to build marriages on such short-lived unrealistic ground, divorce often results. A Chicago store owner, Wayne, concludes:

> So many people have problems because they never get to really know each other before they get married. They become very infatuated with one another and in their desire to please one another they distort the way they really are. The woman goes to all these sports events with her fiancé and then when they get married she hates sports and he wonders why she never wants to go to sports events anymore.

When he looks back on his romantic involvements, Wayne is delighted he did not marry on that basis. He had objective criteria that his business executive wife fulfilled.

I asked Herb Goldberg and Warren Farrell about the effect of romantic love. Both are writers, speakers, and Ph.D's, the former trained as a psychologist, the latter as a political scientist. Goldberg states:

> I think romantic love can be destructive when people marry on the basis of it and have children on the basis of

it. If they would just enjoy each other and do it like a high and come down like you do with champagne, that would be lovely. It's a wonderful experience even though often unreal. The unfortunate thing is that it's given a reality it doesn't have. The romantic couple are often immature parents. The traditionally feminine woman is too childlike herself to give very much and the macho male is so performance oriented that he can't give very much to his children either, so you get a messy situation.

Farrell also observes that romantic love is oppressive:

> Romantic love in its present form leads to the oppression of women and men. It leads women into being seductive, manipulative, indirect, since they aren't allowed to be direct. Men learn that we should be overcoming. That forces us into a situation where we have to put our ego on the line. Almost any man who is going to be vulnerable by constantly putting his ego on the line is going to have to protect that vulnerability. It's easy to make women into sex objects, because very frankly it's a lot easier to be rejected by an object than it is to be rejected by a real human being. And that process I think destroys any type of real communication between women and men. But I think the absence of excitement in a relationship, a type of romance, a type of courting in a different form would be a sad sacrifice for equality.

Radical feminists believe that romantic love is the main tool in women's oppression. In contemporary society it keeps women feeding their energies into men while men create culture.[6] They also believe that separate roles in isolated nuclear families make women suffer, that male-female relationships are loaded with power issues that need to be placed in a class context rather than viewed as the individual problems of a particular couple.

When I asked radical feminist Robin Morgan about her own sixteen-year marriage to the poet Kenneth Pitchford, she commented:

> The consciousness that he has is extraordinary now because of the enormous amount of work I put into it, strug-

gling, raising the issues, explaining the issues, seeing it
didn't connect one way and trying another, feeling you
may be crazy or wrong. These struggles are political. It is
possible to seize control of destiny, out of love and intelligence. A high cost is paid, and commitment is required; it's
hard.

As partnership grows, a couple develop a bond of closeness
by going through challenges and joys together. Romance fades
with the close contact of living with someone day in and day
out. "Underwear hanging on the side of the tub is decidedly
unromantic, unlike thirteen or fourteen years ago," reports one
husband. Having to scrimp and save during the early years of
marriage does not provide a storybook setting either; one pair
of newlyweds, for example, had a $55-a-month apartment over
a furniture store in downtown Chippewa Falls, Wisconsin, next
to the "raunchiest bar in town."

Financial struggles, sickness, pregnancy, seeing the other person ill tempered or depressed, and having disagreements also
spatter mud on the prince's horse or the princess's gown. So do
the interruptions and the stress created by children: "It's hard
to be romantic when you're under stress. The last few weeks
my son has been a pain in the butt. You couldn't get him into
bed and he whines," says Tom in Montana. A marriage built
on illusion will crack when tested by reality if the partners are
not genuine friends.

Love

In contrast to fantasies about romance and family, love that
endures is defined by couples as "feeling comfortable and enjoying being in each other's presence." They define its characteristics as companionship, affection, the sweetness of intimacy,
deep closeness, being with someone you can talk with honestly
and openly, sharing life's passages. They find that love consists
of friendship, trust, concern, acceptance, support, being on

the same wavelength, and feeling good in the other person's company.

Most couples knew each other well before they married, so they did not feel let down by unexpected discoveries about their spouse after the honeymoon was over. Their love is based on intimate knowledge of each other. A few couples had been learning about each other since childhood. George Bach and Ronald Deutsch point out in their insightful book *Pairing* that intimacy begins when romanticism wears off, when trying to match an image is replaced by realistic appreciation of differences.[7] During their engagement one Iowa couple exchanged journals and letters written over a ten-year span. He found that "one thing I loved about Linda was that I was so comfortable around her, like being with a friend or a sister."

Love gets deeper and grows with experience, as Mary, a Washington woman who owns a business with her husband, explains:

> I think it's like a good friendship when part of the excitement of the newness of it wears off, but then it gets better and better because it becomes more realistic. It's based on something that's more real than what you originally thought and it gets deeper. As you get older, you build up all the good times that you have and they hold you closer and closer.

Love is deep caring, writes Erich Fromm in his classic *The Art of Loving*. One husband puts it this way: "I'm concerned about my wife. I want to see her develop, be a complete person, a happy person, and hopefully I can contribute to that. I appreciate the concern that comes my way from her."

Fromm points out that love is possible only if two people know themselves at the center of their existence and are able to communicate this self-knowledge. Love requires constant challenge; one proof of its presence, he says, is "the depth of the relationship and the aliveness and strength in each person concerned . . ."[8] Another writer defines love as "positive regard," such as respect and admiration, and the desire to nurture the other person.[9] These definitions of love make it clear that a marriage based on love requires mutual respect.

As they know each other more, trust more, survive difficult times with each other's support—a colicky infant, a disturbed child, health problems, the illness of a parent, taking a risk by moving to new jobs or starting a business—love deepens. An Ohio couple, Rich and Joan, picked an area in South Carolina where they wanted to live and risked making an offer on a house there before they had found new jobs. They discovered that "our relationship has really solidified by going out on a limb. We are pursuing what we want. Isn't it fantastic and scary?" Most had difficult periods in their marriage but instead of ignoring the problems or divorcing they went to a marriage counselor and talked about their disagreements. Their commitment is not only to work through difficulties but "to make the most pleasure for her as possible and she makes the same commitment to me."

An Indiana lawyer's main criterion for his spouse was that she would be a lifetime friend; she has proven her friendship by backing his decision to give up full-time work in a lucrative practice so he could become a writer. She now is the main wage earner and he spends more time with their children. Friendship flourishes between two equals who respect each other, and two authors claim "intimate marriages are always equal." [10] In traditional marriages based on role segregation, the couples often feel scorn for one another, by thinking "men are just big babies" or "women are so helpless." They keep secrets from each other and turn to same-sex friends or family for support.

Three traditional couples I interviewed separate their worlds and responsibilities. Two of the husbands spoke out against the Equal Rights Amendment. They believe that only one person in the family can have a full-time career. One woman has turned down promotions in her job, for example, because "we both can't have careers and raise children—it's not going to work." One of the wives whose children are grown wishes she had worked at a part-time job because "my life would have felt richer." Traditional couples' work at home is also separate, with the main responsibility for housework assigned to the wife. One husband helps with dishes or diapers when he is at home but considers it "not my job," just as taking care of the cars is not his wife's job. Traditional couples' personalities are also unlike. One couple, Louise and Roger, described their different qualities: He is an extrovert, while she is "nonsocial," he's aggressive and she is not. "He is definitely the stronger personality," states Louise. The advantage for them, according to Roger, is that "being different we don't have the competitiveness that a lot of people with similar interests have." The differences between traditional husbands and wives highlight the egalitarian couples' efforts to merge their spheres of activity.

Sociologists are conducting research that applies equity theory to intimate relationships. As applied to relationships, equity theory expresses individuals' needs to feel that what one puts into and gets out of a relationship is equal to what one's partner or other members of the group put into and get out of it. Inequitable relationships are stressful, even for the person who is getting more. Interviews with 500 dating couples found that the equitable couples are happier. A study of newlywed couples also found equitable marriages are happier. Couples tend to marry a person with similar physical attractiveness, intelligence, education, and mental and physical health. These attributes are part of the resources in a relationship: A man's attractiveness is a resource that benefits his wife, for example. Other resources that can be brought to a relationship are love, sex, status, money and other goods, services (such as housework), and sociability (such as getting along with in-laws).[11] In the past an attractive young woman married a financially successful older man as an exchange of resources, but their inputs were not equitable enough to produce mutual respect, trust, and friendship. It follows from this research that happy marriages are grounded in equity, which means that women need resources to match men's such as an education and a well-paid job.

A New York counselor, who lives with her lover, explains:

> The best thing about being egalitarian is that the relationship we have is extremely intimate and close, and it's because we share more than what I perceive traditional

couples share due to the respect we have for one another.
Because of that we share virtually everything in our lives.
That is very unlike most marriages and relationships that we
know of. We've only begun to realize that our relationship
is envied by a lot of people we know.

Researchers concur that women with integrated lives, combining a career and family, are more likely than traditional
women to enjoy activities with their mates and "to enjoy everyday activities." [12]

Similarity in backgrounds, religion, education, and class, as
well as delaying marriage, has been shown to be conducive to
lasting relationships.[13] "We understand where we're coming
from," states Hank, a New York physician, about his second
marriage, which is unlike his first one. His first wife, Debra, was
raised as a Catholic; he is Jewish. When she discussed her
guilt about sexual fantasies, her counselor replied that thoughts
were free. "They aren't for me," Debra replied, since as a Catholic
she had confessed impure thoughts." She was feeling guilty about
thoughts and I wasn't," Hank reflected. "I think that made a
difference in her attitude about a lot of things." A couple, both
raised as Catholics, agree that their expectations about marriage
dovetailed because of similar religious training. Yet a woman
raised as an Irish Catholic in a family where feelings were not
expressed appreciates the expressiveness of her Jewish lover, who
was raised in an outspoken family. For the most part, however,
spouses have similar backgrounds.

Results of Bem's personality test reveal that truly egalitarian
couples are similar—not more than 5 percent distant in any of
the four categories. This is in contrast to traditional couples in
which feminine women are married to masculine men, with few
androgyny scores for either gender. Egalitarian couples with
unequal family work (E/T) are also unequal in their scores.
The men are much more undifferentiated than the women and
the women much more androgynous, with the next frequent
category being masculine-scoring men and women. A study
found that masculine men do more child care if their wives

score high on masculine than if they score low on masculine, which shows that individuals' traits can influence their partner's behavior.[14] Perhaps if the (E/T) androgynous women had married men who were not undifferentiated their work would be more equal.

The combinations of scores among couples are worth noting. Almost half the traditional couples were masculine/feminine, compared with only three of the purely egalitarian couples. None of the traditional couples were both androgynous, unlike seven of the (E/E) egalitarian couples (see Appendix 3). (I also looked at combinations of astrological signs: 27 percent of the egalitarian couples and 23 percent of traditional couples for whom I have birth dates are married to a person of the same element—earth, air, fire, or water.)

Some couples have similar careers. They comment on each other's problems and concerns and share relevant readings. Two teachers in Hawaii learn from each other: "We're always comparing notes with one another." Others enjoy being in different areas and learning from their spouse about a new realm. When both individuals have careers, one person isn't growing and one person stagnating.

Even if one person earns double what the other does, the hours each spends working are considered equally important. Laurel, a California wife, appreciates that, although her scientist husband earns twice what she does, "The time I spend at work is as valuable and as much of a contribution and means as much as the time he spends. I feel that from him. It gives me a lot of freedom." A North Carolina teacher married to a college instructor points out, "If I felt he was superior to me professionally, I'd be in trouble. It's important that you feel like equal friends, peers who share in everything. That helps communication because there are no resentments." Respect for each other's work despite the amount of money it earns, even if one is a nonpaid homemaker, is a characteristic of egalitarian couples. For most traditional couples, the wider the gap in their earnings, the wider the inequality: The more the husband earns, the less housework he does.

A physician married to another physician in Washington, D.C., analyzes the importance of respect:

I think that the success in this relationship comes from a mutual respect for what the other does and stands for. He has provided support to me, but this is the key thing, it has not been a patronizing kind of support, like "Here is ten bucks, go do what you want to do," or "You want to go to medical school, go to medical school," "Go do your thing; don't bother me." He respects my accomplishments, respects what I think, is proud of what I do in a positive sense, and does not feel threatened by what I do. It's not simply an accepting of what I do and living with it. I think he is happy about it, feels good about it and I likewise. This kind of respect is what makes it work.

This is a typical statement about husbands feeling proud of, rather than threatened by, their wives' achievements.

Many couples emphasize that their marriage and family take priority over their careers. In the long run, parenting and accommodating their spouse's career are more important than keeping up with their colleagues at work, they state. One professor noted, "Each of us long ago recognized that we could have gotten much further ahead separately. We recognize that being married to one another meant making sacrifices for the sake of being together. Once we agreed to that, we didn't pay attention to what the culture defines as having value."

Pair bonding is enhanced by the flexibility and security provided by two incomes. The man does not have the burden of being the sole provider, wedded to his job. Men in egalitarian marriages have quit jobs to look for better ones, to retrain for another profession, to take time to do unpaid political and community work, or to be with their children. A teacher, Don, instead of having to grit his teeth and stay in a job that frustrated him, left to go to law school. His wife, an art teacher, is thinking about taking time off from teaching to work seriously at her art after he is a practicing attorney. Initially a man may feel flattered to support a clinging vine, but the vine can become suffocating as it multiplies. Initially it may be comforting to be taken care of by a sugar daddy, but that too becomes stifling. Women who work outside the home crave attention less than homemakers do.[15] Counselors such as Virginia Satir and Carl Rogers view a satisfying marriage as one that is dynamic, "in process" and observe that to live by rigid role expectations opposes growth.[16] Sociologists agree that the traditional division into breadwinner/homemaker roles is a major cause of marital dissatisfaction.[17]

Respect is accompanied by pride in the other's accomplishments: A man admires his wife's musical talent, and she appreciates his training with their son to run a marathon. Rather than feeling diminished by a spouse's success, these couples feel enhanced by it. Unlike many traditional men who enjoy feeling superior to their wives and feel they lose stature as a male provider if their wives succeed in their careers, egalitarian men feel there is space in the relationship for two winners. A New York husband, Nev, explains:

> A lot more people seem to be threatened by their partners, or they have to compete with their partners. The things she does are an extension of myself. I hear a lot of people compete with what their spouse does. I never feel like I'm in competition with my wife or my kids because I'm living their life with them.

Central to the success of role-sharing is that spouses like each other and are interested in talking to each other. Conversation is the activity they engage in most. It is striking how much emphasis they put on talking. "If you marry your best friend you've got lots of things you can talk about—talking is very important," a Colorado woman explains. Another woman, Simone, estimates that she and her husband have spent 70 percent of their relationship talking since they met each other. Couples enjoy bouncing ideas off each other. Louise, a New York woman, made a typical statement: "He is my best friend. I can hardly wait to get home at night to tell him everything that has happened to me during the day."

Coffee time after work is a daily half-hour a Michigan couple reserve for conversation: Their three boys know not to disturb them except in an emergency such as breaking an arm. An Indiana couple decided to get married when they found themselves engaging in twelve-hour conversations. Many other couples talk for several hours in bed before they sleep. One couple's usual talk time is while giving their infant a bath; others talk in the car after dropping a child off at an activity.

"You spend almost every day with this person, so they'd better be a good friend," is the common-sense conclusion of a California man. Each is enhanced by being with the other. Some report that they are opposites who help each other find a middle ground; often one is a calm anchor while the other is a dynamic catalyst. A Texas woman notes: "He would be dull without me. I get him going. He calms me down. I would have burned myself out years ago." Some wives described themselves as "hyper" or "a perfectionist" while their husbands are easygoing, as did one Wisconsin woman: "I consider myself a perfectionist; I felt more stress and depression before I married Slack than I do now and I think some of his personality rubs off on me."

Commitment is enhanced by mutual pleasure, according to Masters and Johnson.[18] What do egalitarian couples do for fun? Mostly simple at-home activities such as listening to music, watching TV, gardening, playing cards and word games, giving dinner parties, reading together, taking walks, riding bikes, or driving. They go out to dinner, to films, to the theater or dancing, and they participate in religious and political activities and attend their children's sports events. Some go camping, fishing, and skiing. Many couples go out together once a week and use that time to talk and plan; others found that going to a film costs more than twenty-five dollars, after paying for gas and a baby sitter, so they do not go out as much as they would like. Some make a ritual out of shopping together for food. If necessary, they will go to a store to get a carton of milk in order to have time for themselves. Others meet for lunch during the week or talk on the phone during the workday. They recognize that love requires nurturing and withers if it is neglected.

When asked about activities they do for fun, the couples

often laugh, because it is so difficult to find time to do anything as a couple. Many couples find most of their evenings filled with activities. A husband, Timothy, describes his feelings about finding time to play together:

> We both are so wrapped up in many things that we get our kicks out of politics, out of women's issues, out of careers. When we do finally take a weekend together, just the two of us, it's really a lot more like bells ringing and that sort of stuff. Then we say to ourselves, Why don't we do this more often? Why don't we just take a weekend off, go out to the show together and dress up to look nice for your partner? We say we have to do it more, and then we get back to our interests back home.

Adding "Tingle"

Involved with religious organizations, political activities, sports, children's lessons, scout groups, as well as paid work, couples struggle to find time together. "We get so involved we almost have no time left to play," says an Illinois man. He and his wife see themselves juggling four roles—an individual, part of a couple, a family member, and a worker—and they try not to let the couple role slip into fourth place. Fourth place is reserved for work: "We're not on the fast track," states a California woman.

Time with their children has high priority for egalitarian couples. Being parents is a bond in itself that deepens their commitment to each other. The younger men who were able to coach their wives' labor and birth were very touched by it. A carpenter relates that going through pregnancy, labor, and delivery of twins with his wife cemented their relationship.

Some try consciously not to give all their attention to their children but to save energy for the couple relationship.

> I think we've made our time together a priority, and sometimes I feel guilty about that. I'd think, "Oh God, here we go again, we're going to take off for the weekend on a trip

and they're going to have these big parties and wreck the house." But we still went. It was a real priority for us.

Many couples look forward to the time when their children have left home and they are retired from work. Some hope their lives will become more like they were when they were first married. The time before they had children was very important for their marriage, they note, because it provided a solid foundation of learning about each other, having fun together traveling, going out spontaneously, building a storehouse of pleasure to tide them over the stresses of child rearing.

Now islands of space together as a couple need to be zealously carved out. Sometimes this involves creating a romantic sexual scene, as one California pair does:

> I was crazy about Steve and I had a very strong partly chemical attraction to him early. That kind of heartbeat and not being able to eat or sleep that we had in the early relationship, that's not here, but the romance is, in that we take the time to create rituals, put candles all over the room. We go to bed early on Saturday night, or have dinner by candlelight or fix special little things for each other.

Evening is not a prime time for sex for a Wisconsin couple because they are tired after a demanding workday. They observe that many people treat sex as an obligation to be done once a week late at night, that many do not take enough time for it, and therefore it is not very satisfying. Saturday afternoon is their best time. They like making love in the daylight when they are relaxed and energetic. They put a Do Not Disturb sign on their bedroom door to ensure privacy. Another tactic to enhance intercourse is to delay sex, to spend the weekend together building up to it. "You start talking to one another. The old romance starts getting stronger. Then when you make love Sunday evening it's really nicer," according to Louis, a California computer analyst. Another couple kiss in their car or at their front door as if they were dating again.

Going away from home, doing a new or different activity, revives the "tingle" for some spouses. One couple travel to a motel only thirty minutes from their home to enjoy the pool, sauna, restaurant, and dancing. At home they go to bed at 8:30 P.M. so they have several hours together each day. Another couple acts on fantasies, such as making love in the Oregon forest. Just as their love for each other deepens, couples find sex gets better as they learn more about their partner. A husband jokes that there are two reasons he stays with his wife: "She bakes good cookies and she's good in bed. She's getting sexier as time goes on." A wife states, "As we know each other better we also know how to enjoy each other better and sex becomes more deeply satisfying, physically and emotionally." One study found that feminist women have greater sexual satisfaction than nonfeminist women and the greater the agreement between partners on feminism the more satisfied they are sexually.[19] If both spouses agree on the equality of women and men, the agreement seems to carry over to the desirability of orgasm for both and knowledge of the importance of clitoral stimulation for female orgasm.

A couple in Indiana make an all-night event of sexual play: They light candles, eat oranges and apples, turn on records. Going to their bedroom early is a routine for a Colorado couple:

> It wasn't like a conscious effort at first, it was part of our romantic sexual ritual. And it's developed from there. Whether or not there is a sexual follow-up, we nevertheless have the glass of wine and the quiet time talking together in bed. We seldom are interrupted at that point, as our children know they don't come in. We used to try to talk at dinnertime but you can't. There are still too many things going on. The business day is still too close. We talk about business then, or what the kids did at school that day, what you have to do that night or the next day. But I think it's great to set aside time.

It is easy to get pulled into a routine of maintaining the physical upkeep of children, house, yard, cars, appliances, and clothing. Traditional couples frequently discuss these physical demands—Did you pay the phone bill?—ignoring their deeper wants. One study shows that an average couple spend the incredibly small amount of seven and a half minutes a week talking with each other.[20] Egalitarian couples do not make that oversight.

Some couples add romance to their marriage by being physically demonstrative. One couple report they do a great deal of hugging in the kitchen while they are preparing meals and they enjoy eating popcorn together in bed. As a result, the attorney wife says she often sits in a dull meeting and finds herself lovingly thinking about her husband. These couples are also thoughtful, as an actress explains:

> When I call him and say, "My God, I got an audition with the theater," he comes home with a bunch of flowers. Or he comes in and says, "My test didn't go as well as expected," so the next day I've got a cake. Or he'll come and cook dinner, or I'll come in with something he wanted—a record or something. Those really romantic things are a surprise . . . and they're not often enough that we come to expect them.

As a result, she reports that "I still look at Ted sometimes and get this little welling up in my heart."

Being playful and exploring fantasies together also increase such bonding. An example of an imaginative exploration is described by a Colorado man:

> There is a time to be totally nonsensical: We have a fantasy that we stroke and walk across each other's body and describe the hairs on our arms or whatever, dumb crazy things. But I think it's the dumb crazies that keep the excitement. It's part of being childlike, creative and spontaneous.

These relationships work because the individuals involved do not have illusions about their partners. The couples most free of conflict were friends before they married and they talked over almost every possible issue. A pair who knew each other three years before their wedding felt they had gotten past the artificiality of many people who get married after six months and have not ever seen each other without their hair combed. Many of the younger couples lived together before marriage to "see what you look like in the morning." They advise great caution before making a long-term commitment because "passion can screw you up."

The contrast is striking between these egalitarian couples and traditional couples who enter marriage in a cloud of romance and wake up later to find they do not know or even like the person they are living with. The amount of time egalitarian couples spend talking with each other far exceeds the meager efforts expended on communication in traditional relationships. Egalitarian husbands and wives provide each other with information so they do not have to guess what the other person wants or needs. They have chosen to give their relationships top priority, to put effort into them, and evidently it pays off.

5
Housework

You can have it all. Why can't you have it all? Who says
you can't? It's hard work to have it all, but you can!
—A Colorado wife

She's an actress and her husband is in business. Married
2½ years at the time of my interview with them, they had
an infant; she had a good part in a play that required forty
hours a week of rehearsal and he was going to night school.
Since the interview, they had another baby and she is
doing less acting and finding it more difficult to combine
family and career.

Traditional wives have less marital satisfaction than their husbands.[1] Doing the family's menial work must contribute to their
frustration. A myth proclaims that women do less housework
today than fifty years ago because of the new labor-saving devices; but standards of cleanliness have increased and appliances
take time to be cleaned and repaired. Contemporary women in
fact do more housework than women did in the 1920s, in part
because they spend about eight hours a week driving, doing errands, and shopping.[2] A study done in the late 1970s found that
the amount of time women spent on family work was finally
declining, mainly in the area of cleaning and maintenance, in
part because of declining family size.[3] Most women in two-career
families, however, still divide family work along stereotyped
roles.[4] For example, in a 1980 study of dual-earner families in
Indianapolis, the husbands averaged fourteen hours a week on
housework and the wives twenty-three hours.[5] In only 18 percent of the families responsibility for home care was shared or
the husband had primary responsibility. In responses to my
questionnaire, even egalitarian wives indicated that they did

more family work than their mates. Of the thirty-six couples who were not equal in practice, the women spent 16½ hours a week on housework while their husbands spent 7.2 hours. The women spent 33.6 hours on child care and the men spent 14.8 hours. Other studies concur that working women get only slightly more help from their husbands than homemakers do (see Appendix 4).

Husbands who spend time in family work enjoy being home more than men who do not share it.[6] However, we are taught to consider the home and its tasks as a female domain, and women are more likely than men to view their home as an expression of their identity. Jessie Bernard explains, "The old fear that women would de-sex and coarsen themselves if they entered the labor force has been overcome; but the fear that men become de-sexed if they share child care and household responsibilities remains."[7]

How to Decide Who Does What Tasks

Egalitarian couples decide who does household tasks on the basis of who likes or dislikes a particular chore, who thinks it is more important, who has the needed skill, and who has the time. Gender is not the basis for determining who washes the dishes or mows the lawn because such chores are necessary to the entire family's well-being. A Michigan woman, Marian, explains, "You both use the toilet so you both clean it. It's not mom's kitchen; everyone uses the kitchen and everybody eats out of it, so we all pitch in to clean it." Josh, a physician in Washington, D.C., presents the male perspective:

> I think there has to be an acceptance that there are no tasks in the marriage or partnership which are inappropriate for the husband to perform. I can't circle an area and say, "These are things that I will not do," because there may be many times when it may be necessary for me to do them.

Except for those few tasks determined by physiology, role-sharing couples take tasks at face value, not overlaying them with stereotypes about sex roles. "Since Annie was a totally breast-fed baby, Jolene provided what went into the diapers and I took care of washing them," explains a Connecticut father. Progressive husbands recognize that the ability to wash diapers is not a sex-linked, genetic inheritance. Paul, a physician in California, advocates: "In terms of egalitarian-type relationships, I would suggest that people throw away the role models that they've had—forget about what's proper for a man or a woman to do. I clean toilets as well as my wife does."

The Roommate Test

Some couples use the roommate test to divide chores. They look at tasks in the same way as if they were college students of the same sex sharing an apartment. The image of walking in the other person's shoes is recommended by Stu, a California attorney in his second marriage. He asks himself if he would like to do a job. If he would not, why should he expect his wife to like it? Fairness means a sharing of unpleasant as well as pleasurable tasks.

A Washington couple, Rob and Margot, apply this test regardless of whether Margot is doing paid work or is a full-time homemaker. As she explains,

> I think that people should realize that the person at home is also working full time. Then, when the other guy gets home from work, you've both had a full day and from there on it's equal. Even when I was home and Rob was working, we took turns cooking. For people who don't manage to work out taking turns, if they can just imagine living with a roommate, it would be obvious whose turn it is and who is doing more work and what's fair. But somehow as soon as it's the opposite sex, especially when you're married, then that gets all thrown out and it's weighted in funny ways that you can't even define.

Derren, a New York male psychologist, warns:

The roommate test does not guarantee a completely smooth life. You're still dealing with two personalities, and roommates often fight. Egalitarian marriage does not guarantee freedom from conflict: It merely says that you cannot solve the conflict by invoking the phrase "I am the man."

The roommate principle seems simple yet is difficult to apply because the sexes are socialized so differently. It seems natural for women to clean up after people, because we see it happen so often. In the comic strip "For Better or For Worse" by Lynn Johnston, the wife sees objects to pick up all over the house. She yells, "I spend my life picking up after other people—and that's what they expect for heaven's sake!!!" Traditional women expect to do more family work and some even resist sharing it. A study of female professors married to professors found that they did more family work than their husbands—24.6 hours a week on housework compared with their husbands' 8.6, and 35.1 hours on child care, while their husbands spent 12 hours. Yet only a quarter of the wives thought their husbands were not doing enough housework and only 13 percent thought they should do more child care. One of the women explained, "Otherwise, how shall I be able to feel that I am the mother of the family?" [8]

A woman is taught to equate her success as a wife and her love for her family with being a good cook, hostess, and housekeeper, as television advertisements indicate. An Ohio wife felt ambivalent about her husband doing the laundry because she was afraid their neighbors would think she was not a good wife. A woman often notices imperfections in the house that a man might not see. "Even if you could write your name on the furniture, he just doesn't see it," states a California wife. In turn, the man's success is tied to the condition of his car or the outside of the house, while a woman might not notice a dent in the fender or that the lawn mower oil needs changing. As a Maine attorney explains, "when the lawn isn't mowed and the fences aren't painted, if the place looks like crap on the outside, people are going to blame me. If the house is messy and the dishes are unwashed, they're going to blame my wife."

Women, as well as men, need to learn new skills. Margot,

the woman quoted above, explains how she began to do repair work.

> When I started saying, "This is not fair, I do all of the housework," the next time the plumbing broke, Rob said, "I think it's your turn to fix the plumbing." And I said, "I don't know anything about plumbing." "I don't know anything about cooking either," he replied. And I quickly learned how to use tools and started fixing things. He's still a lot better fixer than I am because he's patient and thinks things through, but a lot of things are just plain dumb old work and you *can* learn them.

When Dick, a manager, and Katie, a bank vice-president, are struggling with awareness of what needs to be done, they find that Katie falls into the role of remembering the household tasks. Dick explains:

> I hate to admit it but I'm ready, willing, and able to do anything I'm *asked* to do. If Katie says, "Hey, I'm bushed, will you cook dinner tonight?" I'll say sure. But the point is, she's the one who has set up what we are going to eat in that the chicken is defrosted. So I do have to admit that the executive responsibility is much more Katie's, although execution-wise I think it's pretty close.

Katie adds her perspective:

> Sometimes we both look at each other and say, "Why have we gotten into this pattern?" We're both living here, we both eat, we both should think in the morning to take something out of the freezer. But I have a tendency to do that more and Dick has a tendency to think that I will, or not even think about it at all. Part of it is I'm more obsessed with the house and Dick's more laid-back. I think that's socialized. Little girls are supposed to have everything in order . . .

Michael, a husband who is more conscious of what needs to be done around the house, describes his changes:

> I feel that I've come a long way in the last three or four years. When Johanna started working full-time four years

ago the baby-sitter responsibilities were hers, the cleaning responsibilities were hers, the cooking responsibilities were hers. Yes, I helped but I always let her know, *I'm* doing the dishes tonight. I'm *helping* you out. I thought I was really into this fairness routine, not realizing that all the responsibilities were hers and I was only helping out when I got the chance. Now I don't feel when I change a load of wash that I'm doing her a favor. It's just something that has to be done and we each have our own things that we have to do.

Egalitarian couples do not see the woman as automatically responsible for housework and child care and as owing gratitude to her spouse for his assistance. Husbands don't *help* their wives; rather, they make their fair contribution to the household. This may seem to be a minor distinction, but in fact is a major one, because the equal sharing of tasks distributes the rewards and burdens of responsibility, guilt, and praise. Scott, an Indiana husband who is aware of the importance of attitudes toward housework, states, "For the male there has to be an understanding of sexism. If the understanding is missing, then his help is going to be token and not fundamental."

A beneficial by-product of sharing labor is that children learn to do the same. A two-year-old child in Cincinnati delighted her parents when she asked Santa Claus for a vacuum sweeper "just like Daddy's." One couple shopped for a broom for their son but found they were all pink, with pictures of little girls on the package stating "For Mommy's Helper." Unfortunately toy manufacturers have not caught up with these vanguard families who share housework. As a result their son now has a pink broom, but since there is nothing inherently sex-linked about color, they feel his sweeping ability will be unaffected.

Assigning Tasks Rationally

If task responsibility is not determined by tradition, how is it allocated fairly by egalitarian couples? The simplest way is the use of personal preference. One couple rate their feelings about each task on a scale of 1 to 10. In one family the man does not like to do laundry, so the woman does it and he cleans the bathrooms because she does not like that job.

Another factor determining who does a particular job is the value each person assigns to the task. Each person is in charge of those tasks that are most bothersome to that person if they are not done. Each person is in charge of those tasks that are most important to that person. Russell explains:

> We realized several years ago that I'm the one who is fussiest about how clean the kitchen needs to be, so it's my task. I clean it up. Then we don't get into me criticizing someone else's work. We split up tasks pretty much along the lines of everybody has their own thing that they choose in a positive way. For example, I like to grocery shop and Nancie doesn't, so I take that one on.

If everyone dislikes a chore, it gets shared. Tanya states:

> There are certain things I just despise doing, and certain things he despises doing that I don't mind doing. And those we can do for each other. And there are some things everyone despises, and those, you have to take turns.

Flexibility is an advantage of role-sharing. Tasks can be traded when one person becomes bored with a job or interested in learning a new skill. Bill paying is one job that frequently gets passed back and forth.

Competency is another basis for deciding who does a task. Gene, a Michigan husband, states, "You have to realize that your partner has worth and value. I am not good at budgeting, but Connie is. We make use of our various talents." Even if the husband is more skilled in carpentry and the wife in baking, for example, some couples believe it is important to try to learn all the useful skills and then revert back to traditional tasks if it is expedient. A woman who helped her husband with beekeeping discovered she liked it and took over that duty. She feels that until you have done a task at least once you have not been challenged enough.

One man, now an optometrist, took a sewing course in junior high school and became a skilled tailor, so altering clothes has become his job in the family. His wife explains that if a garment requires precise measurement, it is not her job. She recognizes that each person has different skills. When he does the laundry, it turns out gray, so she takes over in that area. As a business manager, she is also the financier in the home.

The time during the day when each person is home also determines task allocation. One man straightens up the house in the morning because he leaves for work later than his wife. A new job meant a long commute for Grace, a Washington, D.C., wife, so Ira, who got home an hour and a half earlier, became responsible for weekday dinners. "We didn't starve," he reports. Another husband is in charge of dinner because his wife, a nurse, had her shift at the hospital at that time. When a promotion changed her work hours to the day shift, her husband was threatened, not by her promotion but by fear that she would invade his kitchen and would plunder his whisks and spatulas. They did not want to end up in divorce court arguing over custody of the blender. Open-mindedness is the key, they conclude, and he retains supremacy in the kitchen.

Flexibility also applies to extended periods of time when one spouse has an especially demanding work schedule; during a wife's medical residency, her husband did most of the family work. In another family, when the wife went back to college for three years, her husband had dinner waiting for her each night when she came home from the university.

Making a Contract or Chart

Some families find written contracts to be useful, assigning specific tasks and specific days to do household tasks. The contract system helps take the burden of responsibility and guilt from the wife's shoulders, as Derren explains:

> There are certain tricks you can do like making a list of jobs
> in the house and assigning who does which. Sometimes it's

so the husband will remember to do his task, but it's often for the woman so she will not feel guilty when the task is not done. When you see the dirty bathroom faucets, you can feel nauseated and you can feel repulsed, but you don't have to feel guilty. The list is there; it's the guilt that you want to get rid of.

An Illinois couple, Barry & Karen, has a chart that they revise at the beginning of each school year. Each task has a point value based on how difficult it is; dinner is five points, while watering the plants is one point. They aim for equal points. Barry does the dusting, vacuuming, laundry, dishes, and dinner salad, Friday night dinner, and the lawn. Karen cooks the dinner, shovels the snow, and so on.

An Iowa family's chart is divided this way: Bob's tasks are to vacuum, wash and put away the dishes, carry out garbage, clean the cat's litter box, wash the diapers, clean the bathtub, mow the lawn, shovel the snow, and feed the cats. Linda's tasks are to dust, clean the kitchen, mop the floors, fold the diapers, wash and fold the baby's clothes, brush the cat, bathe the baby, change the sheets, and clean the sink and toilet. "It was exactly 50/50 until I had to trade some off to get rid of the litter box," Linda reports.

A family with three teenage daughters set up a schedule when the mother complained that she was feeling terribly frustrated about being the maid. They picked certain days for each person to clean the kitchen and do the dishes. She explains:

> Greg and I have Saturday. If someone walks out of the kitchen on Monday without doing the dishes, I may go back and do the dishes, but they have just gotten Saturday, the worst day. The kids each get two days and we get Saturday. I do the grocery shopping except when it's convenient for Greg on his way home. Each person does his or her own laundry; changes her own bed; cleans her own bathroom; each person has a Saturday chore which involves vacuuming and dusting. Each person chose what he or she was willing to do according to his or her ability. We can change this any time with anyone who's willing to trade.

A Colorado family with three children organize tasks by week: Each person is in charge of cleaning the kitchen every fifth week, including washing the dishes and mopping the floor. Cleaning another room for a week is also assigned to each person, plus responsibility for his or her own bedroom and laundry. Another couple in Ontario divide their home into zones that are switched every three months.

The benefits of an organized system are described by two husbands. The first reports:

> We've made contracts the last two years, written contracts about whose jobs are what. That way you are clear-cut about what you're doing and you don't seem to get as resentful or overwhelmed at what you think you have to do. We've had some struggles over it too. It's evolved; it didn't just happen.

The second husband states:

> I want to stress that as a man it was really hard for me to appreciate what kinds of tasks there were around a household and child care. Dividing it in a mechanical fashion and being responsible for half of it was helpful to me to find out how much there was and to feel fair about it. At the beginning I often felt I was doing more. When we divided it rigidly, then I could feel assured that I was doing half.

One woman, Faith, found that a contract relieved her of being a nag, a role she could not tolerate. She and Matt used to talk about how terrible it would be for their children if they got divorced over an issue like housework. Faith kept feeling set up to harp at him until they designated specific duties.

Administrative work is time-consuming and when making a schedule some couples find it important to give credit for the list making, organizing, phone calling, social-secretary work, and general remembering. The toughest part of domestic life, relates one female administrator in Pittsburgh, is that "I feel like an endless list maker. My head is crammed full of trivia and then when I suggest something that needs to be done I feel guilty and angry at the same time." One couple designed a coupon book with ten pages. The husband gets a coupon each time he initiates a task. If he does not use them in a designated time span he owes his wife $100. Another man and woman take responsibility for buying gifts, sending birthday cards, and writing thank-you notes to members of their own family.

One wife's first step toward role-sharing was to give her engineer-husband the floors to clean. He said, "Tell me when they're dirty and I'll clean them for you." But she insisted, "No, I want you to be in charge of them. I want one little area in my head that doesn't have to be responsible, something that I don't have to be at all concerned about." Derren, a New York psychologist, underscores this point:

> The thing we discovered over the years is that the important thing is to divide the executive responsibility, being in charge of thinking of what needs to be done. A lot of couples who claim to have an egalitarian division of labor have divided up the physical labor but the wife still often complains that she feels hassled, and the reason is that she has been left the task of remembering what needs to be done. For example, if the husband cooks every other night, is he the one who has to plan what to cook and remember to take it out of the freezer that morning or is the wife still doing that?

How to Involve a Reluctant Spouse

Most traditional husbands are reluctant to take on domestic tasks even if they say they believe in sharing. One husband's comments typify some men's avoidance of housework:

> Having heard what Jean has said about housework, I have to say that I don't have any consciousness about having resisted. It's not in my frame of reference to notice what the chores are. I'm not very good at recognizing what should be done in terms of housework.

A widely reprinted humorous article titled "The Politics of Housework," by Pat Mainardi, describes some of the tactics men use to resist taking on more work. Some of the standard lines are, You'll have to show me how, We used to be so happy, We have different standards, You can't make me do it on your schedule, and It's too trivial to talk about.[9] Another line that might be added to the list is You're compulsive, as in "I get on my wife's nerves because I don't do things as compulsively as she would like." As one husband stated, we all would like a wife who gets our slippers and paper while we watch the news after work.

How does a woman encourage an uncooperative man to do his share? Carol relates:

I went on strike. Gary got very upset. He said, "We have a problem here. The labor is on strike." I said, "You've got even a bigger problem because the labor is not only on strike, but 50 percent of the management is. And you do not have a model for that."

A psychologist, Sarah, advises:

How do you get him to do things he doesn't want to do? One of the most basic answers to that question is you must stop doing them. The task isn't always to get him to do them, but is simply explaining what you will do and what you won't do: "I will make dinner four nights a week, but I will not make dinner the other three. I will clean the toilets on these weeks but on no other weeks." It would be nice if people simply agreed and went about it nicely with all good intentions and good faith; but at some level, I think, men don't change until they must. As long as they think they can just play the game forever and never really have to change, I don't think they do.

The woman is trying to get the man to do more than he normally does. She has to be more serious and selfish about it and make clear that this must happen. I don't want to be in that kind of relationship where doing his share of the work is the price to pay for being in a relationship with him. You're special. Think of yourself that way. I don't think egalitarianism happens because you ask for it politely. It happens because you will have it no other way.

Power is entwined with the allocation of domestic chores. Sarah's husband, Derren, explains that the power issue is a deep one:

> I don't see people divorcing because one person won't do the dishes, but if what's behind that is a struggle over power, not over who will do the dishes or rather who gets to decide, then that could well mean going toward divorce. The woman has to be serious about it. It's not something that is frivolous. I think often men do not take it seriously until that stress is really there. Women have been socialized to hold their relationships together, to not rock the boat. Only when the woman is going to say, "Okay, I'm going to have a career with or without you," then something may get done. Many women are financially dependent and cannot do that, but the main point is that this has to be serious and can't be something you agree to disagree about.

If a woman has economic independence, she has the power base to demand a shared domestic workload. When the woman in a long-term relationship returns to paid work, she has to make trade-offs to share family work, although changes are not easy after years of traditional role division. After a wife in Washington, D.C., went back to paid work, the burden of being solely responsible financially for the family lifted from her husband. As a result, he was ready to share in housework. But making the actual changes is often difficult for both spouses. One husband reports that his wife would make out a shopping list for him and he would spend an hour in the supermarket. "It was a feeling of helplessness. I'd never done it before." She adds: "I think he reacted also with a certain amount of defensiveness—feeling attacked and uncomfortable initially. At the same time, he became quite a hit on the block. In the child-care center the kids adored him—Daddy was a real treat."

The difficulties involved in making changes in family work are described by Judith, a North Carolina wife. She and her second husband separated for six months before they sorted out the role changes necessitated by bringing together two sets of children from previous marriages. Judith explains:

We've had a tremendous struggle in order to figure out ways that suit everybody, where everybody doesn't feel oppressed. Initially, I did too much of it primarily because I was not good at identifying my own needs. I was part of the old mystique that anybody who's superwoman can do it all. I was absolutely terrible at identifying when I was frustrated. I simply didn't do it; I felt it, but I didn't sit down and say to everybody, "Hey, gang, I'm not responsible for running the show." I was taking the responsibility for everybody's happiness. It wasn't just physical things, it was emotional things. If things weren't going well, I saw it as a defeat. So it's been more of an internal liberation for me.

When I went back to work, that's when the crisis came. That's when the deterioration in the family setup occurred because I just stopped doing some stuff. He and I agreed to live apart and sort things out.

While we were separated, he lived in squalor and chaos. So now when I have a need for aesthetic harmony and beauty in the house, he's more than willing to say, "By God, I didn't know I had the need, now I know I have it too, and I'll be happy to hang the pictures and paint." He wants to do it and he even takes the initiative. Living apart made him realize how hard it is to remember to do the laundry— and he had one child with him during the six months whom he had the total responsibility for. He was hassled to death —no longer was there somebody to take over the homework or to deal with the emotional crises. He had to do it all. So he has a whole different perspective now. Now we share.

Getting Help

Another aspect of the mechanics of housework is getting assistance from other family members or from outside sources. Children are a close-at-hand resource, but motivating them is a major task. Eve and Randolph, who have three children, did it this way:

The kids had major responsibilities for household chores. We had a point chart system where there were three columns and different chores got different numbers of points. The only reward the kids got for this was not falling behind. And whoever was behind on the list didn't have any option but to do whatever chore was up on the list. When the kids were in sixth grade, they were doing fairly frequent meal preparation. I believed that each should be able to put a complete meal on the table. It didn't have to be anything elegant—Hamburger Helper, a vegetable, plus a drink made a meal. There were some things the boys got paid for. It depended on how much of my time and energy it took to get someone to do the job. If it took a lot of my time and energy, then they didn't get paid.

Another wife does not believe in paying children to get jobs done. Robin states:

I feel very strongly against paying for chores. My philosophy is that we're five very capable people living together. There is no reason why one person should be the servant of the other four. A reminder usually works. If it comes down to the very worst of things, someone will ask me to take her somewhere, and I'll say, "Gee, I'm sorry, you have to stay and do your chores." That works. I think they're unusually responsible young people. At five years old, we gave them alarm clocks and told them it was now their responsibility to get up in time for kindergarten and that they should make their beds before they left.

A Colorado family with three children adds more work if a job does not get done:

If the kitchen is not clean enough for the person who takes over the job, or if it gets done after "a screaming fit," then that person has the kitchen responsibilities for another week.

Other families get young children to work by giving stickers when tasks listed on a chart are completed.

Couples who can afford it hire outside help to clean. Many families hire a person once a week for a few hours. Some raise the feminist issue of reluctance to hire a woman for such a traditional job. One couple hired male college students to do housework and were pleased with the results. That is certainly one answer, but perhaps the most significant issue is paying the worker a fair wage. Some include grocery shopping and cooking dinner among the paid tasks. Hiring outside help cuts down on arguments over who is going to clean, it allows needed time for relaxation and for the children, and it creates a paid job. That raises the issue of economic-class distinctions: dual-career couples realize they can afford to hire housecleaners, pay for child care, have two cars, and take time off work, all privileges providing flexibility not available to low-income workers. Some husbands would like to spend more time on family work but can earn so much more than their wives that they feel compelled to work full time and hire outside help.

A few families have a live-in housekeeper. In addition to the expenses, however, problems can arise with having another person in the household. Two physicians in Washington, D.C., with a live-in housekeeper said that it is difficult to find someone who is permanent and healthy. They and their friends with housekeepers live from one crisis to the next, often spending months searching for a new housekeeper.

Others have received help of another kind from books about efficiency techniques, some of which suggest buying and addressing all birthday cards at the beginning of the year and marking the date of mailing where the stamp will go; having a central information center with yearly and monthly calendars and a message center with phone numbers, medical information, and appliance guarantees; shopping by catalogue; entertaining on a large scale once a year; and making daily and long-term lists, then prioritizing them, delegating and eliminating tasks.[10] Appliances can also be time-savers. According to a Louisiana husband, the three secrets of a happy marriage are a dishwasher, clothes washer, and clothes dryer.

Lowering Standards

One way of coping with housework is lowering the standards of how a house should look. Studies show that working women spend less than a third of the time on housework spent by homemakers.[11] One woman in Michigan remarked that her house would never make *Good Housekeeping*. Jill, an Illinois wife, relates that their friends are amazed at all they accomplish: "Frankly, one of the things we do is that we neglect the house," in contrast to women whose evenings are filled with housework.

An older man in New York explains: "We're really pretty casual about our housecleaning." His wife adds, "The house exists for us; we do not exist for it." Another couple share the philosophy of not being a slave to the contemporary ideal of a spic 'n' span home:

> I think that basically our tolerance for a dirty house is higher than a lot of people's. We feel that you have to eat and have clean clothes. Beyond that we're not likely to get bent out of shape if the carpeting needs vacuuming or there is dust on the tables.

The lowering of standards is not difficult for some women, such as Pat, a Washington realtor, who says, "Housework has never been something I've taken great pride in. I'm neat but I don't care if the windows shine." A Colorado woman, however, explained that lowering her standards caused "a certain amount of guilt. Who we are as people seems to be tied up with how clean our houses are. Men don't seem to have that problem."

Bottom-Line Tasks: Cooking and Finances

Cooking dinner is a major task. Some couples have changed their standards in this area too, by using packaged foods, popping a pizza in the oven, or opening a can of soup. Other quick meals, like hot dogs, pork chops, steaks, and hamburgers, are also popular. Sibyl states, "The thing that we have sacrificed most in terms of normal family living is meals. They're always catch-as-catch-can. We no longer do normal kinds of very nice dinners." A vegetarian family in Colorado relies on cooking a big pot of soup or beans twice a week, another stir-fries vegetables and tofu.

Other families prepare dinners on the weekend and freeze them for the week ahead. A male optometrist explains: "We tend to cook in large quantities. When we make pot roast, for example, we'll make eight to nine pounds of meat at a time and package it. That way if we get home late, there is something that can be taken out of the freezer." They usually make two meals at a time of a main dish and freeze one. Andy, president of a corporation in Wisconsin, gives an example of his cooking one Sunday: For the week ahead he prepared a chicken, lasagna, ground-beef casserole, and a steak. Couples find that the use of a microwave oven and crock pots and reliance on frozen foods are time-savers.

Careful shopping is another important time-saver:

> Our refrigerator is full with leftovers and ingredients for a pretty fair selection of meals. We put a lot of effort into getting our food trip organized and efficient so that we only grocery shop once a week. As soon as we run out of something, we put it on the shopping list and buy everything on the list on Saturday morning. Planning got us over what was probably the low point of the day—getting home and trying to decide from scratch what to do.

Some families do a major shopping expedition together once a month or once a week. Some divide the task, so that one person does the meat shopping and the other buys dry goods. Adding items to the food list is everyone's responsibility in one Connecticut family. As Ann explains: "It's not like a traditional household where you say, 'Mom, why isn't there any peanut butter?' If you see that it's getting low, either you buy it or the next time Rich goes shopping, we have added it to the list."

Some spouses make chores into enjoyable rituals. One couple spend an evening a week in front of the television or fireplace folding clean clothes together; Barbara and Slack also shop for groceries together. Shopping is actually fun for them:

> If I go grocery shopping alone, it's a chore, but I really like the Saturday morning ritual of grocery shopping together. It's a good time to talk and make decisions together about

what to get and how much. All those stupid little things make it fun. We both enjoy food and eating a lot and that feels like a way to share that pleasure and share the responsibility for it.

Another task as difficult to delegate as cooking is budgeting and bill paying. Caroline, an attorney, comments:

It's very important that both people have some financial skills. They both need to know what a budget is, how to keep a checkbook, what a danger credit cards are, what a mortgage is, how the interest rates work, and what the money market is, because for many people financial matters are really a sore spot. It usually comes either from one party being in control and one party not knowing and resenting it or from both parties not knowing what in the hell they're doing and one or both pretending that they do.

Some couples alternate financial responsibility: "I paid the bills for a long time and it got to the point where Jeff was saying, 'What do you mean we don't have the money? Where did it all go?' So I said, 'Well, you pay the bills for a while and see.' So he paid the bills for a few years and I don't quite know how I got it back."

Some husbands and wives each pay separate bills, as in a New York household where the woman pays for the mortgage and child care and the man pays the other bills. In a Texas family, she pays for food, clothes, and medical bills and he pays for other expenses. They make adjustments several times a year if one has spent more than the other.

Some couples pool their money, have joint checking accounts, and pay bills together. Others keep their money in separate accounts and use the roommate format. One California couple divide the bills according to their percent of income. If one earns 60 percent of the family's income, he or she pays 60 percent of the bills. Finances are also divided for an Iowa pair, Linda and Bob, but since he has had better-paying jobs than she has, she owes him several thousand dollars. In another case, a prompt bill payer took over from her procrastinating spouse.

Heather pays all the bills, tells Thurlow the total, and he pays her half at the end of the month.

Money is a notorious source of conflict for couples. One Colorado couple came up with a solution to their frequent disagreements about how to handle their finances:

> Tim is more of a spender than I am. I'm too tight with money; he's too loose. The only way we can balance each other out is by having budget meetings once a month. Otherwise, I'm getting pissed off because I'm not buying things, which is my problem. I say, "We can't afford that, so I won't buy it." And Tim says, "To hell with it, I'm going to buy it!" The only way we can work it out is to sit down and say, "Okay, is it more important that you get shoes this month or that I get shoes this month?" We talk it out—where do we want our money to go, how much money do we want to go into savings, what are our goals, how much money will we need to achieve those goals, how important are the Visa and Master Card bills.

An Illinois couple, Melanie and Royd, found when they bought a house that society has not caught up with the idea of a married couple with separate accounts. Melanie explains:

> We had an awful time buying a house because the state could not cope with a married couple that had separate financial accounts. We wanted to buy the house jointly but had no joint assets. We had to incorporate as a land trust and we had to show the insurance company our marriage license to prove we were married.

Despite society's backwardness, role-sharing couples find their division of labor beneficial. When a wife is not the household drudge, she looks upon her husband as a help, not a hindrance, unlike many traditional wives who are relieved when their husbands are out of the house. Helen, an Illinois program director, relates:

> My boss is a woman who has to do all the housework. She, and a lot of other women I know, say, "Well, my husband is gone for the weekend so I can do what I want." I'm al-

ways shocked when I hear something like that because when
my husband's gone for the weekend I have a harder time.
I have to do all the work and all the dealing with the child.
I don't get to do what I want because what I want is to be
with him.

When housework is divided between family members, it becomes less burdensome and sometimes even a source of amuse-
ment.

6
Child care

It never occurred to me even for a few minutes that we would not have an egalitarian marriage. That was perfectly plain to me and to Arin. We had an egalitarian household for about seven years. It only changed when we had children.
—*A Washington mother*

She's a counselor, age forty-five, and she dropped out of graduate school to have three children during the era of the feminine mystique. Her husband is a psychologist, age fifty. Married for over twenty years, they went through a major transition when she went back to graduate school in another state. They still feel pressured, finding their time at home hectic.

I catch your eye as you walk
    thru the door
the children crowd around you and
    there is no room for me
Or I am the one returning and
    I walk into a tiny human
        flood of mania and grubby hands
I see you on that far shore I reach
    for you and smile or cry
Even when there is not time for
    romance or even a quick hello
I know you are there for me
    and I am here for you.
        —*Kathleen, A California mother*

She has three children from a previous marriage and her husband has four. They each work part time, she as a proofreader, he as a mental-health worker, in order to have time with their family, but they find it difficult to make ends meet.

Difficulties

Raising children together is a bond between a couple and an "enormous responsibility" that requires that couples work out difficulties in stressful periods in their relationship. It is "a shared endeavor that we work on together. There wasn't anything between us that was so shared before," a father of one child says. "We have roots together. In a new relationship you would never have that again," an Ohio wife feels. Another father describes his feeling for his son as a "first real example of total, unconditional love. It's phenomenal." A mother states, "We both adore the process of raising our child who is so much fun to be with." Children give one father "a sense of identity, fullness, roots." Having children is definitely the acid test of an egalitarian relationship. Those that succeed in avoiding the established roles of absentee father and primary caretaker mother are touched by their shared endeavor.

A common theme voiced by parents, however, is the stressful impact of children on their lives: "The burdens of being a parent are enormous." A conspiracy of silence exists about what parenthood is like in an isolated nuclear family. "I don't know why I was never told that you'll go crazy with your child and you'll hate it sometimes and want to throw him off the cliff. I didn't know that mothers felt that way," explains a mother of three. The myths about parenting promise that it is fun and gratifying, while the reality is that it is often hard, frustrating work. Children are romanticized as sweet, cute, and loving when they are often difficult. Studies routinely show that couples with children at home are less happily married than couples without children at home.[1]

My experience was parallel to that of the interviewees'. Previous to my pregnancy I had read widely about women and the family and then about the detailed mechanics of birth, but I found no books that described what it was actually like to be a parent. (Since then, useful books have been published.[2]) I had heard that being a parent restricted one's spontaneity and that your life would never be the same, but not much more than that. I was not prepared for the torture of sleep deprivation, of being awakened every three hours around the clock for months by a nursing baby, or the nerve-racking colicky crying every day around dinnertime.

When I talk about some of the difficulties of parenting, it is as if I have spoken a heresy or revealed an embarrassing—although common—practice not to be discussed in polite company. The media presents us with images of cooing Gerber babies; it ignores temper tantrums, messy diapers, the pains of teething or illness. Similar to many couples, a Florida couple thought a baby would be "like having a cute cuddly pet," but they soon discovered their misconception. Our society segregates children so we do not have much contact with them, unlike many other cultures where children go with adults to religious rituals, parties, work, or to child-care centers at work. (The Asian-American couple I interviewed always take their children to gatherings with other Asian-Americans.)

In every aspect of our life children are separated from adults —housing areas, schools, religious schools—so it is not surprising that unrealistic fantasies fill the vacuum created by ignorance. "Before you have any children, you have an idealistic notion of what it's like. Then when you get involved in a day-to-day, nuts-and-bolts involvement with a child, the idealism disappears," explains an attorney, a father of one. Laura, a frank mother of a gifted daughter, relates that if she had known what motherhood was like she would never have had a child.

The myth is that children make a marriage more enjoyable and will shore up a shaky relationship. "Whoever said 'Have a baby to solidify a relationship' is off their rocker," comments Blake, an Arizona anthropologist. The reality, as Jessie Bernard has described in The Future of Marriage, is that the happiest married people are those without children or those whose children have left home. Childless marriages are also more equal, the husbands more supportive of their wives' careers and more helpful with domestic work. The more children a couple has, the less the father helps.[3]

The new baby takes away from the primary relationship, states

Terry, a new father, who is surprised at the jealousy he feels. Another father who felt displaced by his new daughter had hostile fantasies about her for a while. Couples whose children have left home report being closer now that they have more time together.

This is not to deny that parents love their children, are proud of them, and feel enriched by them, but to point out that children cause stress in a relationship. "You're no longer number one," stated a woman whose son proceeded to illustrate her point by wetting her pant leg. It is much easier to be egalitarian and happily married without children. But the only study I found that did not report a drop in marital satisfaction during child raising was one that interviewed Nebraska parents who shared child care at least 60/40.[4]

Being a parent is difficult because of the loss of free time, as Katherine, a Pennsylvania mother, explains:

> I think that both of us thought parenting would be much easier than it was because we're both strong feminists and we had such agreement that we really wanted to do it equally. I don't think either one of us expected how hard it would be. A lot of that has to do with the way most people are raised and how isolated parenting is and also with being poor, too. When I think of the different stages we've been through since we've lived together, the times when we've been close to breaking up and the adjusting, it's amazing. I think that sharing the household tasks and everything is progressively harder the more children you have and the younger the children are. There's a lot more work.

Roger, her husband, gives his perspective:

> I wanted to share the children with Katherine completely, but I was unaware of what an impact that was going to make on my life. I don't think I had a realistic appraisal of the amount of time that fifty percent care of the child meant. I experienced a lot of resentment over loss of freedom. It took a long time for me to sense what I was getting back out of it because I experienced child care as not doing anything. When I was taking care of the children, I had a

lot of impulses to be doing other things at the same time, to relegate child care to a secondary place. That created a lot of tension for me until I saw that I could appreciate really taking care of my children.

Another father said succinctly that chores such as changing diapers "took up a hell of a lot of my time." A first-time father discovered that

babies take so much time, even though they sleep a lot. When they're up, you're feeding them, or changing them, or walking around with them to calm them, or playing with them. We adopted the philosophy that we're going to get the important things done. We're going to get the laundry done and the food made, and everything else is either going to get done in half-assed stages or it just won't get done.

Other parents noted there is no way to realize the amount of time it takes to parent young children until one experiences it. A toddler wants all his or her parents' attention and "that means that it is impossible to do anything else in the evening," Tom, a Montana father, explains. Instead of coming home from work, unwinding and talking over the day, parents of hungry children must prepare dinner, feed and bathe them, and attend to a bedtime story accompanied by struggles over going to bed. By then the house is in disarray and needs to be straightened. Never-ending messes are aggravating, and pets often add to the chaos. Parents are exhausted since "you're trying to do so much in a short period of time," after work and before bedtime.

The interruptions of young children are also stressful; the mother of an infant was surprised to find it took her two hours to get the dishes washed because of her baby's interruptions. I remember being glad if I could get the dirty clothes washed as my one achievement in a day with a newborn. One mother of a toddler describes her experiences:

It's frustrating to always be interrupted in whatever I do. I never get to finish anything, which means that often I don't start because I know I get so irritated when I get interrupted all the time. Also, when you're exhausted from a lot of sleepless nights, it's easy to get on each other's case because you don't want to beat up the baby. I was probably a fairly realistic person but I was still romantic about being a mother until I found myself wanting to throw him into the wall because he'd awakened me about sixteen times.

Interruptions and demands are continuous and have to be dealt with by parents, unlike childless couples who can choose not to cook dinner, can go out spontaneously, or can put some task aside until they feel like coping with it. Paula, a Maine attorney and mother of two, explains:

One of the most difficult things for achievement-oriented people in dealing with kids is that you make up all these mental lists about the things you want to do and it's hard to see your children in a daily way as sort of an achievement. You don't get much of a sense of achievement out of diapers and cleaning up a mess, and the constant interruptions make it very frustrating. With kids you are never sure of unbroken time. I would look forward to nap time and find myself being resentful or angry if they didn't take a nap on schedule. You just never know and don't want to start anything—you are interrupted one hundred and fifty percent.

Another attorney refers to the "crossfire" of interruptions from a child, which requires being able to juggle several things at once. Caroline was brought up by her mother to be able to "replot constantly what was going to happen next, in order to keep all the plates in the air." In contrast, her husband finds the crossfire enraging, although he is learning to cope with it. Because their office is at home, the problem is more acute now that their son is old enough not to need afternoon naps.

Another source of frustration is that tasks take longer: Getting in a car to go shopping requires gathering up the young child's paraphernalia at the proper time in his or her sleep cycle, for instance. Once there, you cannot "whiz through the store because the person with you is taking two-inch steps. That's hard." Finding time to be alone or to have uncluttered space, "a clean place without a bunch of dirty clothes piled there where I could sit down and read a book" can also be difficult to obtain. Studies concur that "role strain" is not caused by a woman's combining a job and marriage; rather it is connected with having a child.[5]

In addition to the daily frustrations involved in typical child care are additional ones caused by sickness. Don was a law student when his son came down with chicken pox, an ear infection, strep throat, and scarlet fever all at once, during exam period. If a child is too ill to attend a day-care center, or if a baby sitter gets ill, cannot travel in snow, or is late, who stays home with the children? Behavior problems such as hyperactivity add to stress. One couple's second child did not sleep regularly until she was five years old. Her mother reported, "She just about drove us crazy, literally. That's another reason we got into therapy. We didn't get to sleep for five years." Another baby cried, it seemed, all the time; it was awful, her mother reports. She feels that if she had a second baby, with the same behavior, she would have a nervous breakdown.

Parents' recreational activities are restricted by children. One has to plan ahead to get a baby sitter, and the expense and inconvenience of transporting a sitter also puts a damper on seemingly simple activities such as going to a movie. Couples travel less because of the difficulty and expense of finding a baby sitter or because working parents feel guilty leaving their children to take a vacation. Some couples find it difficult to play tennis or jog together because one must stay home with the children while the other exercises. One Michigan couple had to hire a baby sitter so they could work in their garden together. A man and a woman become more dependent on each other. "Before if Sue wanted to do something, she could do it without affecting me. Now if she wants to go out, I have to stay home with our son," a father reports. Couples also have less money available for recreation: To raise a child born in 1979 to age eighteen could cost $134,414, according to the Department of Agriculture.

Career advancement can be slowed down by children; Glenn, an executive, for example, turned down a desired promotion that would have taken too much time away from home. Working mothers bear the burden of guilt about not being with their children, because of traditional attitudes that primary responsibility for nurturing children should rest on the mother's shoulders and that a woman has "greater sensitivity to her emotional environment." [6]

Marie, a Quebec professor who has two children, sees her life as

> well rounded but it also means I'm not going to be a leader in the field. I can't be as high-powered as I know I have the capacity to be. You can have two people doing medium well, but you can't have them both—unless they don't sleep—absolutely dedicated to their profession and be good and happy parents.

Role-sharing fathers also give priority to their children: Jim, a West Virginia community college teacher, has sacrificed research time because he feels it is not worth losing a night with his daughters. One man gave up a time-consuming job: He reports that the reduction in income is worth the gain of more time together. "It's so much better having less money and having Sam around than it was having gobs of money and never seeing him," concludes Ginny, a Minnesota wife.

Pregnancy and infants often interfere with sexual intimacy. Some men feel threatened as their wife's body changes from being associated with sexual pleasure for both of them to existing for the growing fetus. Nursing continues the obvious bodily changes. Some nursing mothers report a reduced interest in sex because of hormonal changes, fatigue, changing feelings about their breasts, feeling overweight and unattractive, or experiencing a love affair with the new baby as primary.

The mother of a newborn reports that she gets her "snuggling needs" met by the baby. Lauren, another new mother, explains:

> Between pregnancy and breastfeeding and all the attention and energy going into child care, I don't have much energy for a sexual relationship. Sunday afternoons in bed with cof-

fee and the paper and lovemaking hasn't happened in a long time. I think that sex had a lot to do with that kind of time that we used to be able to spend together. We're not getting that nurturing and I'm looking forward to that coming back, both in terms of my hormones and in terms of time, with the child growing a little older and more independent and having a smoother schedule.

The more attention children demand, the less is available for one's spouse. Parents of young children often find the needs of an infant overwhelming. It is like getting hit on the side of the head with a golf club, reports one new father. Nick, a father, explains:

It's always hard to find time to talk with the baby screaming. We just don't get that much time alone to work things out. We feel lack of time alone to become centered and know ourselves so that we have something to communicate. When we're off balance we run into each other.

How to raise children also causes disagreements. If both parents are involved in child care, then there are two opinions to deal with, not one, explains one father. How to handle their three children causes the most disagreement, reports Sam, a Cincinnati teacher married to a therapist. Sam defines their tension spots as

how to discipline the children and the stress of not enough time to ourselves. Now the kids are older and staying up later, so by the time they go to bed, we have about half an hour before we pass out. We both have those human-service jobs that drain you out.

Children also lead to greater involvement with grandparents. Some couples feel unpleasant pressure from the older generation to act in traditional ways, such as not to leave an infant at a day-care center. One couple facing this conflict decided to move away from the grandparents. A wife realized that instead of confronting her mother who was pushing her to stay home with her children she was dumping her bad feelings on her husband.

Disagreement over how many children to have—none or one or more—is a deep fissure for some couples. One husband wanted more than one child and his wife did not; one wife wanted a child and he did not (although they later had a second child because he was so delighted with their first-born). A study of 226 professional women found that the birth of a second child was much more of a barrier than the first was to working outside the home.[7]

Two professors worked out a system of child care that became more difficult with the birth of their second child, as Sarah, the mother, describes:

> I don't think we got less happy as a couple, as people, as a family, as anything with one child. We really loved having one kid. When Emma was very young, we alternated care for her by day—the caretaking is so continuous we wanted it for one day at a time. When Emma was a little older, we switched to a system of weeks where one was in charge of Emma for the week and the other one was in charge of meals. Then you switched. Every other week with respect to Emma, we're off. Being off for a week was really nice. It meant you could play the traditional "daddy" role; you could play with her whenever you wanted to but when you got tired you could go in the other room and read your newspaper. So for us having one child, while it cut down our spontaneity, life was still easy, fantastic. We had lots of time to ourselves as individuals because you had this whole week off where you could choose to spend as little time with the kid as you wanted.
>
> When we had two kids, that was really the big change in our lives. Our system is that one of us is in charge of Emma for a week while the other one is in charge of Jonathan, then we switch for the next week; not switching being off and on, but being on for different children. So that means that we lost our time off. We have found that each day is very full. You've been busy from the minute you woke up until 8:15 at night; you haven't had time to sit down and read the newspaper, watch the news, to relax and listen to a record—nothing. So, with two children we have found our lives very, very hectic.

Parents of three boys add that two nights of soccer practice a week are multiplied by three, so juggling their schedules becomes complex. Researchers have found that fathers spend more time with their children when there are fewer than three of them,[8] so it behooves role-sharing couples to limit the number of children.

Children create friction that aggravates any pressure points in the adults' relationship, so "kids will destroy your marriage if you don't have the foundation," Jack, a father of two, believes. He adds that with preschool children "there's tension. You cannot relax when you have a kid in the house." Another father observes: "A lot of couples with a seemingly egalitarian lifestyle have a child and that changes it. They go fairly traditional. It's a cutting edge." Couples advise waiting to have a child until a marriage is well established and couples know one another's sore spots.

Parents find that teaching their children nonsexist, nonracist, nonviolent values is difficult in the face of countervailing messages from television, toys, schools, playmates, and grandparents. A Pennsylvania couple's parents are shocked, for example, when the mother leaves her sick child to go off to work, despite the fact that it is her husband's day to take care of the child. She regrets that their parents cannot understand the security she feels knowing that her son will be well taken care of by his father.

Television cartoons teach children violence and provide stereotyped role models: Males rescue females and figure out solutions, as Popeye does for Olive Oyl. Children want to watch cartoons because their friends do; some parents prohibit television and some discuss its content with their children.

Toys reinforce stereotyped sex roles. Although one family has never purchased a doll for their three-year-old daughter, she has twenty-seven given to her by friends, along with tea sets, pots and pans, and other toys preparing her to be a homemaker, while her brother gets building toys and chemistry and doctor sets.

Couples are surprised at the impact of the dominant culture. In a St. Louis family in which the husband does most of the

cooking, their nine-year-old son will turn to his mother to com-
pliment her for the good spaghetti dinner even though his father cooked it. Kate and Mark noticed a major change in their
son's attitude toward stereotyped sex roles when he entered
public school. They believe the culture influences children possibly more than parents do. Kate suggests that feminists need
to give much more attention to studying and thinking than
to child rearing.

Not only do parents have to struggle with outside pressures,
they also have to sort out their own ingrained sexist attitudes.
One New York father, Victor, realizes that he plays rougher
with his son than he would with a daughter. He knows he and
his wife are giving their son messages about male and female
roles that they are not even conscious of, because "we work in
the fabric of society. We're stuck and can't be out of it as well
as we think we can." Another couple point out that it is impossible to make a quantum leap in one generation. They hope
their children will make refinements on their parents' example.

Dividing Child-Care Tasks

Child care is the family work most likely to be shared by contemporary couples, although even wives with careers retain
more responsibility and fathers tend to engage in play activities
while mothers do maintenance duties.[9] In contrast sharing
mothers expect equal participation from their partners. An
Iowa mother states: "It goes against my grain if people say I'm
lucky because Lenny helps with the twins. I'm not lucky. I
wouldn't be around a person who wasn't like him." Egalitarian
men do not look upon time with their children as baby sitting
for their wives.

Egalitarian couples, rather than believing that women are
innately better parents, regard parenting as a learned skill. They
see other men supporting their children economically but not
emotionally. They are amazed at how little time fathers in

their neighborhoods spend with their children. Some couples observe female friends monopolizing children, preventing the fathers from being closely involved. Some couples report that their own child is closer to the father than the mother, that the father is more patient or better able to calm a baby, is more relaxed with their child, or spends more time with the children. Some women, however, found it hard to give up being the primary parent, as their mothers had been. Betty, a California mother of four, reports that her ego is hurt by seeing her children go to their stepfather with problems, but she realizes she could not have a career and also be the primary parent. Elise, a mother of two, describes "a twinge of feeling threatened, especially when it seemed like he was doing a better job than I was, because women are supposed to be natural mothers and all that rot."

Sharing responsibility for children also requires that women give up imposing their own standards. An Indiana husband permits his daughter to engage in activities his wife thinks are dangerous, but she realizes her way cannot prevail if they share child care equally. Many couples found they had different beliefs about how bundled up a child should be to go outdoors or what activities are appropriate; most resolved the conflict by agreeing that whoever was with the child is in charge. Being responsible gives the right to set standards as Sarah explains:

> With respect to our kids, we don't handle them the same. For example, I used to let Emma drink milk in bed after she brushed her teeth, while Derren didn't do that. The kids have learned that mommy and daddy do things a little differently in disciplining, too. Derren was a little more likely to smack a kid on the behind and I instituted the system of timeouts—having to go to your bedroom or the bathroom to be alone for two minutes. We found it constraining to have to do it the way the other person wants it or the way that we would both decide, so we've given each other lots of freedom. When you're in charge, you do it your own way.

Paul, a father who shares equally in the care of his son, formulated his own philosophy of child rearing. He treats his son "as I would a creature from another planet, a Martian who dropped in from outer space." Paul believes a child has his or her own personality and intelligence, equal to his or her parents', but needs to be respectfully shown the customs of this planet. A child is not a blob of putty to be shaped but is distinct at birth. "I try to give as much responsibility as you can to a three-year-old kid. I don't see myself as father with a capital F, with a son with a capital S, and my wife with a capital W, all of us in our predetermined roles."

Couples who began their marriage before the women's movement became a societal force underwent upheaval before the father began to share child care. Before the change to equality in the family, the man viewed his contributions to child care as helping his wife. The primary responsibilities for child care were viewed as the woman's duty. A Texas husband reports that he knew his wife would hear the children crying in the night so he did not worry about them: "I could do what I wanted to, but Jean had to do it. That's the biggest change I went through in awareness."

One father fell asleep on the couch when he was supposed to be watching his sons. "Frank didn't realize that they didn't know enough not to go out on the street. He didn't know they needed to be watched," Ethel, his wife, relates. As a result, he did not develop a close tie with his boys. Ethel explains:

> When my son was about five I had a copy of a magazine and on the cover was a man holding a baby. My boy said, "I don't like that cover—men don't hold babies." It just about broke my heart. Frank doesn't kiss them or hold them or carry them to bed. He will wake them up and shake them and tell them to go into their bed to sleep. It really makes me sad. What he does is roughhouse with them, so they get the feeling of love and contact, but they won't kiss him.

A father in his thirties reports that he is still more of a helper than a real partner in parenthood because he does not keep

track of his daughter's food supply or clothing needs. He notices that the floor mats in the car are dirty and washes them,
but he "can't seem to make a mental note of when she needs
clothes." Another father observes:

> Lots of fathers will give their child a bath every night and
> even put the child to bed. But does he remember that to-
> night is bath night, or, if he fixes the meal, had the child
> had a vegetable at noon, or had the child pooped that day?
> It turns out that it's not the physical labor which really
> drags you down. You can think while you're engaged in
> physical labor. The thing which really clutters up your head
> is the executive responsibility of remembering.

In a truly egalitarian household both parents participate in selecting and directing baby sitters. A New York couple, Victor
and Gerda, both tell the baby sitter what needs to be done.
"In fact, we sometimes tell her different things and that's
embarrassing."

Other couples alternate preparing children for school and for
bed—one takes charge of bedtime while the other washes the
dishes. Whoever is doing a household task is free to do it with
full attention because the other parent is giving attention to
the children. Aiding at nursery school, taking children to medical appointments, and attending parent-teacher conferences are
also alternated. Some parents alternate or divide staying home
with a sick child, one missing work in the morning and the
other in the afternoon. One Indiana father, who takes his turn
at appointments with the pediatrician, reports that the little
kids ask their mothers, "Why is the daddy here?" Parents also
share school activities like being room parents or attending PTA
meetings.

If one parent decides to stay home full time to care for the
children, the other egalitarian parent shares child care when he
or she is at home. A couple in Nebraska, Ellen and Wayne,
share equally in family work because they consider the woman's
job as full-time mother as time-consuming as the man's. Part
of her work is taking their daughters to weekly lessons: four

violin, two piano, and two gymnastics. Ellen decided to be at home with her two daughters because they could not find good child care that was nonsexist, that provided natural foods, and that offered adequate developmental programs. She was the one to give up her job as a social worker because Wayne can earn three times as much as she, despite the fact that she has taken more graduate courses. Ellen explains:

> Our society is simply not geared for shared parenting. In Europe parents can both work half-time and be home half-time. Here one must choose between raising one's own children and pursuing one's career. I have chosen a ten-year sabbatical rather than let someone else raise my children in a typical American middle-class, sexist, violent, consumerist, capitalist, inhumane, racist, anti-intellectual environment! Meanwhile I worry about what I'll do with my career in another five years. But where would I find a feminist to provide a nonsexist environment for my daughters, age three and six? Who would find nonsexist books, and change all the library books they hear read, and call the animals "she," and make sure they call public servants mail carriers, police officers, fire fighters, etc.? And who would carefully build their self-images, self-confidence, and self-love so they can someday do anything their hearts desire? It's the hardest work I've ever done, totally all-consuming, draining, and exhausting. It's also the most rewarding: It's great to see them growing so proud and secure.

Ellen and Wayne believe that her child-care work is important, so she should not be expected to take on in addition "the lion's share of demeaning, unsatisfying, boring labor" required to maintain a household. Wayne takes care of morning responsibilities, getting the children dressed and fed, and is in charge of child care from noon on Saturday to noon on Sunday. In the evening after he gets home from work he gives the girls their baths and helps one daughter practice her violin for an hour. He cooks and washes the dishes on Thursday, Friday, and Saturday. He puts the laundry away and does his own ironing, and neither of them does much housecleaning.

Advantages of Shared Parenting

American children spend very little time with their fathers—twelve minutes a day. Studies report that fathers interact with infants for thirty-eight seconds a day and with one-year-olds twenty minutes a day, much less than the thirty hours a week they spend watching television.[10] If children spend all day with their mothers, they learn that "women are meant to wait on people, to get dinner, to sweep, and pick up things; that men are made to bring home things," according to Charlotte Perkins Gilman.[11] More than eighty years ago, Gilman also pointed out that mothers will love their children as well or better when they are not in hourly contact with them. A contemporary Quebec social worker/professor confirms that she feels real pleasure when she is with her baby because she is not with him all day. Benjamin Spock, author of *Baby and Child Care*, reflected in an interview on his own mother's role. He concluded that "my mother would have been less exacting, less demanding of her children if she'd had other interests." Studies concur that working mothers are less overprotective and their daughters are more achievement oriented.[12]

Some mothers who felt duty-bound to stay home with their young children realized that it was not beneficial for anyone. After several years, Claudia, a Louisiana mother, became aware that she was looking forward all day to going to the supermarket without her son. She felt like she was going crazy staying home, a feeling reiterated by other mothers. Another woman described her feelings of restriction and isolation as being nailed to the ground; she realized too that her bitterness was not good for her children. Both women felt they were better mothers when they were working outside the home. Lois, a New York administrator, relates her experience:

> I felt an obligation that one of us should stay home with the children. Obviously, at that point it seemed the logical choice that the woman do it. I wasn't resentful at first. I was really bored until my last two years when I took classes at the college and did a lot of volunteer work. That was

probably the worst period of our marriage. When our marriage had a rocky point, it was because I was so bored I knew I had to get out of the house.

A pastor whose wife was temporarily a full-time homemaker found that it "about drove us both nuts." A wife who was a full-time college teacher until a move to another state reduced her work to one course a semester finds that her situation is a major source of conflict. She feels frustrated that her training and experience are "going down the drain," although she is glad to have time to spend with her two daughters. She feels her husband misses out on parenting them. He is tired when he comes home and does not feel like doing much, while she feels stuck at home all day and wants help and adult activity. Unfortunately, many young women romanticize staying home with babies, according to an Indiana professor's observation of her students.

Role-sharing couples (like other dual-earner couples)[13] devote their time at home to their children, so they probably have more interaction with them than do parents in more traditional families, in which the television might blare from morning until evening. The child of a full-time homemaker was reported as saying, "She yells and hollers at me and talks on the phone all day." Wives who previously were not doing paid work often filled up their time with volunteer work and "the children resented that." Working mothers spend more time reading to their children and planning activities to suit their interests.[14] Studies show repeatedly that the children of working parents are as well adjusted as others and are more independent.

Advantages for Children and Parents

When children see parents performing various roles and tasks, the same flexibility is open to them. Children of both genders learn to cook, sew, build, and repair; an Ohio couple take turns driving so their sons can see women at the wheel. "Mommy's a good driver," their son commented. When a three-year-old boy went to visit his aunt he asked if he could play in her sink. He said, "Look at me washing dishes, now I'm a daddy." His aunt "damn near lost her teeth" because "that role stuff really works." The parents of a son report that it does not occur to him as unusual that his mother fixes the plumbing or his father bakes the bread.

A lesbian couple with sons are attempting to teach them to be self-reliant. Juanita states:

> They think that a way of having love demonstrated to them would be that we do everything for them. And if we suggest to them that they might want to make their own peanut butter and honey sandwiches, they take this as a rejection. But I think they're learning that you can get lots of good feelings from being self-sufficient and doing your own things.

Being involved in the adult life, such as going places with parents, gives children independence and models of achievement. A poet takes her daughter to poetry readings, for example. "She sees me up there and really gets off on that. I'm her woman's image," the poet explains. An attorney takes her seventh-grade daughter to city council meetings and on business trips, unlike her husband's first wife who was always at home with her children.

Children learn to make decisions and take responsibility when they are given tasks to do and when they share in family problems and successes. Marlene reports:

> We treat our kids very much as peers and share a lot of concerns we have. We told them we are broke this year and don't know how we are going to pay for Christmas so don't ask for any expensive gifts. They are really cooperative and take a lot of that responsibility. Earlier we wanted to go to Florida and didn't know how we were going to finance the trip; Brad, who was only eight at the time, came up with a way to finance it. If we go someplace with the kids, it's like going someplace with friends and we stick around together. They are two of our closest friends, although we are clearly the mother and the father. We have mutual respect.

Many parents report how expressive their children are as a result of having two adults giving them a lot of attention and discussing concerns with them, as well as having contact with other children in day care. "He's vivacious, friendly as can be. He's absolutely not shy about other people. People stop me and say how cute and sociable he is," a father states. A mother describes her five-year-old as

> very independent and self-confident. She tends almost always to be the leader in play situations. She plays well and seems to have very well developed social skills. I think that is a lot from having been in a day-care situation; also the fact that she is treated as a third member of the family. She gets choices that are appropriate for her age, such as what clothes to wear.

Another mother, Gloria, reports that her son is an incredible child and has a tremendous vocabulary because her husband spends a lot of time talking with him. From his birth "we had an agreement that this was half his kid and half my kid."

Some children are so equally parented that they call for "momdy" or "mommydaddy" or alternate calling for one parent or the other at night. They view fathers as involved in child care: While playing house a three-year-old boy told the doll's daddy it was his turn to get the crying baby. As a result of their father's shared parenting, two boys see their father "as a person. He is not someone who disappears in a suit and comes back and maybe takes you to a ball game or tells you he is tired and he doesn't want to talk to you," their mother states.

Children in egalitarian families develop unprejudiced attitudes. A family with two girls recently adopted a nine-year-old boy whose adopted mother describes him as a dyed-in-the-wool sexist. His remarks provoked comments from his sisters such as: "Girls can do anything but be fathers and boys can do anything but be mothers." "Dad cooks better and cries louder than mom," and "Mom keeps the hammer in her desk, right next to the budget." Their mother reports that their remarks are based on their observations rather on what they have been told and that they don't suspect yet that others put limitations on what girls or boys can do.

Children whose fathers participate in school activities are admired by other children. The sons of a father who went on school field trips were delighted because the other children told them, "You have such a neat father." They were impressed that there was a father along. Another boy proudly tells his friends to come over because his father makes great cookies. The teenage children of a Texas couple, however, do not know of other egalitarian parents and tell their parents they will never get married because they will not be able to find anybody like them.

Fathers benefit from the close association with their offspring. A Wisconsin father related that he would like engraved on his tombstone, "He was a neat father." He didn't become involved in spending time with his sons until they were ages three and six, when his wife entered into partnership in their business. Since then, he has experienced "a revelation. I'm getting to know my kids again. I am a born and bred parent."

Another father describes his seven-year-old daughter as his pride and joy; he is her confidant and pal. A sense of enjoyment comes from knowing your own child, states a Connecticut father. A sports writer explains that he wants to be part of his son's upbringing, an active part of his life. When his son had to be hospitalized, he felt: "Nobody is going to tell me that it's the wife's job to be in the hospital with the kid and I go to work. I'm going to the hospital; and if you don't like it, take your job and shove it." He adds that, as distasteful as changing diapers and maintaining a child may be, there is a lot of fun in the overall care. He is a part of that, in contrast to traditional husbands who sometimes play with their children and help them with their homework but avoid mundane tasks. An Iowa father who cleans up his sons' messes feels that being involved in the total maintenance makes him appreciate the nice aspects all the more "because of going through the hassle first."

Sociologist Lillian Rubin hears many men saying that next

year they will spend more time with their children, until they realize their children are gone. Sadness and remorse result. Rubin explained in an interview:

> The bondedness between mother and child does not exist between father and child. Even though the mother's bondedness may come with many troubles and trials, it is nevertheless an eternal bond. The father doesn't have it, and he begins to suffer a depression or remorse and sadness.

She believes that the empty-nest syndrome is more painful for fathers than for mothers, and that the fathers who share in their children's upbringing will not have to face the mid-life crises traditional men experience.

Both spouses benefit from the joint understanding of the difficulties of being a worker and a parent. One father, after spending all day at home while his wife took her turn working at their business, realized that "you've spent six hours, done not a goddamn thing, and you're exhausted." Mental health is preserved if the man is not burdened by being the sole earner or the woman by being with preschool children twenty-four hours a day. When fathers share in parenting, women can move ahead equally in their professions, in contrast to women who fall behind men in their careers when they take years off to do child care in their critical twenties. Men who choose to spend more time at home with their children while their wives work find the social pressures difficult. Bruce, an Ohio father, for example, took his sons to the playground on weekdays. The mothers there thought he was "weird," so they would not let their children play with his sons. His wife's colleagues thought he must be henpecked to stay home with his children.

A mother who spent some months at home being primarily responsible for three children notes: "It's so boring and yet they're so entertaining. At the very same time those things are true. But if you don't have anyone to share it with you, the boredom just smothers you." Her husband agrees that the role of a woman or a man who is on duty all the time with children is unsatisfying. He thinks it is an unhealthy way to live and does not see how women do it. (The fact that American women take 70 percent of the tranquilizers consumed may say something about how they cope.) A more workable arrangement of child care is demonstrated by a Colorado couple who took three months off work when their baby was born. When one got tired the other took over. The husband took the baby out of the house when his wife wanted to take a long nap. Neither of them felt burdened, and the bond between them deepened. They did not experience the stress of other new parents, "not because we're such special people but because our situation was right. If every couple had the opportunity to be off together for the first three months of their baby's life, probably there would be less postpartum depression." Working parents are given this opportunity in Sweden, where nine months paid parental leave can be split by both parents.

The traditional division of labor is bypassed by role-sharing couples, so men are not strangers to their children and women do not undergo the agony one mother experienced before she went back to work. Ethel remembers:

> The kids were little and I had one pulling one way and one pulling the other way and was trying to boil something on the stove and the washing machine was buzzing and he would sit down and read a magazine. He didn't notice how I was feeling. But I didn't make a point of it, I allowed him to not notice.

In contrast, a mother with a two-year-old who started throwing herself on the floor screaming morning after morning became nearly hysterical herself. Instead of blaming her, her husband suggested that she share his bus-driving job so they could alternate being away in the mornings. His solution worked well for the entire family.

When both are working outside the home, it also adds interest for both of them. A dentist explains:

> I'm sure if she stayed in the house and cleaned up after the kids she'd be a bitch all the time. And I would be too. But she comes in and she says, "I'm exhausted, but I've had a

great day. Let me tell you about it." Sometimes I'll come in right after work and we'll sit till seven o'clock talking about what we've been doing.

A school of thought currently in vogue holds that the major cause of the tension between the sexes is the mother's role as primary parent. The solution to better relationships is to share parenting. Warren Farrell explained in an interview that the absentee father has an insidious effect on his son. The boy looks up to his father but does not spend enough time with him to know him well. So the boy imitates a male *image*, such as that provided by sports figures or super heroes on television. He has a mystique about his father away at work, combined with a feeling that he is not worthy of his father's attention. He tries to get more of it, which carries over to his adult life. It is the cause of men continually seeking ways of getting approval, Farrell believes.

The sociologist Nancy Chodorow, author of *The Reproduction of Mothering*, emphasizes the difficulties caused by mother-monopoly of parenting. In an interview, she explained that daughters develop more connectedness to people than sons do, since boys are expected to break close bonds to their mothers in order to become men. The mother also experiences her son as an other, more separate than a daughter. The advantage for women is that they learn empathy and close connection to others. The disadvantage is that they may become "too much embedded in relations and not able to be separate enough." Since men have to repress identification with and attachment to their mothers, they "feel uncomfortable with being in touch with their emotions."

In a heterosexual relationship men can replicate their first relationship, with the female partner replacing the mother, but women look to their children to re-create the mother-child bond. "It may be that men are looking for mothering in a way and women become the mother in relationship to men and children," Chodorow suggests. "It is very hard for people to learn that women are people with their own legitimate needs and wants and that mothers are people."

When women are seen as primarily responsible for parenting, they are blamed for their children's problems, without adequate consideration of the influence of the father or children's peers and social institutions. This inflames Western culture's denigration of women.

Nancy Chodorow traces the development of the blame of mothers to the nineteenth-century idealization of women's role as mother, to Freud, and to the preoccupation with momism in the 1950s (as in the smother-mothers in the novels *Portnoy's Complaint* and *Generation of Vipers*) and the resurgence of mother-blame in the more recent *My Mother/Myself*. The role of fathers is rarely studied. Studies of dual-career couples find that women bear the emotional costs, the guilt, and the anxiety about the family. The expectation that mothers spend most of their time with their children is the norm that works most strenuously against dual-career couples. Men can be more objective about the family because they are trained to view their major role as provider.[15] Since young children are so dependent on the mother to gratify physical and emotional needs, her power becomes almost mystical. The father is more distant and he appears human, rational. Both sons and daughters blame the mother and resent her for not giving more, explains Dorothy Dinnerstein in *The Mermaid and The Minotaur*. Their feelings transfer from mother to other women. The fear and resentment of women, documented in books such as Wolfgang Lederer's *The Fear of Woman* and H. R. Hays's *The Dangerous Sex: The Myth of Feminine Evil* or in neo-Freudian analyst Karen Horney's essays, can be avoided by men's involvement in equal parenting.[16]

Child Care

The trend for young women is to not interrupt their careers for lengthy periods after childbirth: A study of 815 dual-career couples showed that the median time off for childbirth was twelve weeks.[17] The typical pattern for the couples I interviewed is having a paid baby sitter in the home or bringing the baby to a sitter's home, although some have found good infant-care centers with a two-to-one staff-infant ratio. Many parents find that a home setting provides flexibility. If the parents are delayed at work, the sitter can give the child dinner; a center that closes at 5:30 or 6:00 cannot. When the child is a toddler, he or she then goes to a day-care center or nursery school. A few fortunate couples live close enough to grandmothers who are willing to provide child care. A neighbor or a student is hired to do after-school child care for school-age children.

To find a baby sitter for an evening is difficult. "One of the pains of my existence is to have to find a baby sitter," one mother laments. Some parents avoid the expense by joining a baby-sitting co-op. A few hire a live-in housekeeper, with the resultant freedom not to have to be home at a certain time, but with the problems of expense, loss of privacy, and irritations over different styles of housekeeping and child care. Some housekeepers are efficient at running the house but are not good with the children, and others are warm to the children "but crummy in every other way." Several couples loaned cottages in their backyards to young couples in exchange for child care and found it worked well until the young couples tired of the job.

Housekeepers are expensive. A couple in Quebec pay their nine-to-five housekeeper five dollars an hour, and they wish they could afford to pay more. Two professors who in 1979 paid more than $10,000 to their sitter feel it is important not to exploit their employee and to pay for an educated person to teach their children. They suggest parent cooperatives for parents who do not have a lot of money to spend on child care.

Having children in day care during the workday requires that parents be able to let go of the idea that only parents can give quality care. Anthropologists such as Margaret Mead have pointed out that children thrive from contact with many caring adults and that North America is unusual in its emphasis on mother-child exclusiveness. Cross-culturally, mothers who have sole responsibility for children do not like it as much as mothers who have help, Nancy Chodorow points out. An Ontario, Canada, mother appreciates that children at the day-care center love to play with her baby and that they provide him with more attention than she would if she was with him all day. "We're not uptight about a third person having love and intimacy with our child," states a physician. A mother who initially felt she was supposed to stay home with her children now thinks it was unnecessary. If she could do it over she would have gone to work when the youngest was four, she says.

Some parents are able to interchange work and child care. A study of Nebraska couples who shared parenting (the mothers averaged 54 percent of the child care, the fathers 46 percent) indicated that 67 percent had flexible work hours.[18] But their main problem was also job inflexibility. Work structure dominates issues of shared parenting. Some parents who work at universities take a child to the office occasionally. A woman who works in her family's business took her first child with her to work until he was two. The eight employees gave him attention when he wanted it, but the mother felt more tense because "I knew sometime he was going to start crying and want food or be waking up." Some days she had to leave early because he was too demanding. A father who works at home as a writer and part-time lawyer states, "It's not like I'm only here when I'm tired and mad. It's a good relationship." Spouses who own their own business sometimes alternate times at work and at home with the children. For a summer, one father worked from 5:00 A.M. until noon and the mother from noon until 6:00 P.M. They enjoyed the amount of time they spent with their son. The father took him swimming in the afternoon but he felt uncomfortable being the only adult male at the pool. He also felt guilty about not being at work in the afternoon even though he had accomplished a lot in the morning. "I felt like I should wear a sign around my neck proclaiming, 'I've been working since five this morning,'" he said. Two chiropractors have a room in their office for their infant and school-age daughter. Because they own their own practice, they can take afternoons off to be with their children.

Most parents do not work for progressive corporations that

facilitate combining work and parenthood. Men have to struggle with work associates who think they are deviant because their priority is their child rather than their work. For example, Steve, a newspaper reporter who works at night, has an employer who

> likes to talk with pride about how when his kid was born he didn't even leave work. When he found out it was a girl he was pissed off. There are times when he would want me to stay at work overtime but he knows that I'm going to hit him with my kid is going to wake up at eight in the morning and I'm going to be there. He doesn't understand why my wife isn't doing all the child care.

Some parents have found that working different shifts (typical of almost 25 percent of American working parents) facilitates sharing child care. It also prevents dinnertime from being hectic, as it is when everyone arrives home at once, tired and hungry. It is easier if one arrives home in the afternoon and gets dinner preparations under way. Some parents alternate going to work late in the morning to get the children off to school. The disadvantage of working different hours is that parents do not see each other enough: "We both go through a period of depression when we feel like single parents," reports a nurse who does shift work.

Stages of Child Rearing

Most of the younger couples in my study began sharing parenting when they attended prenatal classes, visited their gynecologist together, and had a husband-coached birth. The fathers who were present at delivery described a close bonding with their infant, and they resent the fact that books do not discuss father-child bonding. Egalitarian couples also share in nursing the infant. Most of the fathers get up and change the baby and burp it and put it back in its crib after it has nursed. A new father states, "I think we've got it worked out where we're both up as long in the middle of the night." Laurel felt relieved about his equal commitment to infant care because

I've seen so many examples where theoretically there was an egalitarian couple, but the woman ended up doing everything, staying with the child and taking the responsibility for child care—like it was her job to get a baby sitter if she wasn't going to take care of it. None of those fears have come to pass. I'm amazed at how equal an effort we're putting in.

If one father, Curtis, did not get up voluntarily, his wife says she "would a lot of times wake him up too, even if he was trying to ignore it. I figured misery loves company. If I was up, why shouldn't he be?"

Some nursing mothers pump breast milk and freeze it so the father or baby sitter can feed it to the infant. Nursing does put more restraints on the mother; an attorney remembers trying cases in court with milk leaking inside her clothes; other mothers rush home or to a day care center at lunchtime to nurse or have to reduce their working hours. A father who took time off work to be with his baby brought her to his wife's office at noon to nurse.

Parents concur that it is most important for fathers to participate fully in child care from the time of their infants' birth. Usually neither parent knows much about babies, but it only takes a few weeks of spending most of the time with the infant for the mother to become an expert. Derren suggests that sometimes the mother leave the house to encourage the father to become an expert too:

> He can be very self-conscious about it and what will happen is that he will constantly be asking for advice as if she's the expert and if there's only one right way to do it. If he's a reasonably intelligent adult, there's not much he can do wrong. It's better if the woman will not continue to play the role of expert. It's not good for her to sit and watch. She should go out and even stand in the backyard if necessary but he'll do just fine. Otherwise both of them will fall into the trap where he will do the physical labor but continue to rely on her for decisions. Any mother or father knows when they first have an infant that they don't know exactly what to do.

A physician concurs that the early months establish an enduring pattern that is difficult to change: Once the mother-child bond is created by spending time together it is very hard for a man to break into that relationship. Some fathers managed to spend equal time with their newborns during the day. One found a three-day-a-week job, several carpenters did not take jobs in order to stay home with their infants while their wives worked, and one father took a three-week leave, then worked half-time for three months.

An atypical set of parents did not find their life changed much by their infant, because she was an "easy" baby. They were both working part time, and they were accustomed to spending a lot of time at home. In contrast, a woman who was at home full-time when her boys were young describes how she

> wasn't able to even think clearly because I was too exhausted from all the work. There was never a coffee break, never an anything break until they were old enough to know not to go out in the street or to put small things in their mouth— I was never off duty for a minute.

When two parents and a baby sitter are sharing time with an infant, it does not become a burden for one person.

It's a "hell of a lot easier to be egalitarian when you have a twelve-year-old than when you have an infant." This was the consensus of parents in my study. Research indicates, however, that ages six to fourteen are the worst time for marriages.[19] Studies also show that husbands help most when children are under three (or no children under 18) and much less when children are between three and eighteen.[20]

As children assume more independence, the load lightens in some ways for parents, but one parent of an adolescent daughter reports, "It's harder than I thought—due to the slamming doors" and similar outbursts. One woman's twelve-year-old refers to her as "humdrum." Demands arise such as making sure children are transported to lessons, religious instruction, meetings, sports, and school activities and that they get homework done. An Illinois father describes a typical after-work scene:

I got into my running gear, drove my son to his music lesson, drove back to the railway station and managed to only be three minutes late for my wife's train; she dropped me off at the corner and I ran eight miles the long way home. She went to get Dan and then we all converged on the house.

Parents find their burden lightened (and their worries increased) when their teenagers learn to drive and when they can leave them alone for a weekend knowing they can cook and take care of themselves. Teenagers also can buy their own clothes and supplies.

Having an older child and a much younger one is a boon, since the parents have a built-in baby sitter. A California couple, Susan and Philip, who have a fourteen-year-old son and a three-year-old daughter appreciate the help their son has given them. They compare the different stages of adolescence and preschool:

> We have three adults at the table now. So when he goes into his childish side, he's so big to be a child. He's like a raging bull. Paying for his lessons is expensive and takes a lot of energy taking him to them. He takes just as much energy as the baby because when he needs attention he needs it fully. But it isn't all the time. He can fix his own dinner and likes to. He enjoys his own day if we go away for a day or two. So it's a different cycle than with a little one, but it's just as intense.

Stepchildren require a different kind of adjustment. Living with stepchildren requires "marrying them too. The three children have been the most difficult area of our relationship," states an Idaho stepfather. When Doug's two daughters go to visit their mother, he realizes how the focus of his attention shifts back to the woman he lives with and how being tired from taking care of the girls dims their relationship.

Combining two sets of stepchildren happens frequently (in the United States one out of every six children under eighteen is a stepchild), and role-sharing parents in such second marriages find it difficult. A teacher recalls her experience:

the hostilities between the two sets of kids—it was my house everybody moved into and my children were terribly resentful and jealous. I didn't realize it because I was so concerned about the new children feeling out of it because it was our house. Oh, it was just a mess—it took me a while until I fell apart under the pressure.

Another couple had six children from previous marriages all living with them. It took some adjusting. A couple who had daughters from their first marriages, one of whom lived with them, found it easier not to do activities with both girls at the same time.

Tanya, an attorney with one daughter, married a businessman with four children. She had seen that a lot of second marriages did not work because of misunderstandings about children, so she made it clear to him before marriage that she was not going to be mother to his children. They were welcome to visit often, but "a lot of the things I do I can involve my daughter in and she can go with me but I couldn't do that with five." They view each other's style of parenting as foreign. Tanya encourages her daughter to express her opinions, which he considers "lippy," while she considers him authoritarian. But they do not aim to change each other. (They are one of two couples who have separated since I interviewed them. The other separation also involved a second marriage, in which the man had had a very traditional first marriage.)

Two parents whose children from previous marriages all live with them decided not to make a distinction between "my kids and yours." They do not feel obliged to answer a child's question immediately but take time to consult each other if they think it is important. A father in Wisconsin provides an example of new parenting responsibilities: He attends his stepson's parent-teacher conference along with his wife and her first husband. Whatever degree of closeness is adopted between child and stepparent, couples agree that policy needs to be discussed before marriage.

Couples try various forms of shared custody: A Canadian family had the father's daughter with them two or three days a week, and the girl spent the other days at her mother's home. She found it inconvenient, so she now alternates by year. Her parents live only a mile apart so she can go back and forth as she pleases. A divorced egalitarian couple now share custody of their two daughters, who spend Sunday afternoon to Wednesday at one parent's house and then move to the other's, which is in the same neighborhood. Costs of child raising are shared in proportion to their incomes.

Egalitarian couples agree that having children is the single most difficult factor in role-sharing and that one child is easier than two. Their solutions are to divide up child care equally between them and to pay for outside child care. Their children seem to flourish, to be independent, and to be leaders.

7
Resolving conflict

CAUSES AND SOLUTIONS

"If you suppress yourself for the other it always returns to haunt you."
—A Colorado wife

She is thirty-seven, an attorney. Her husband, also thirty-seven, is a teacher. They have a two-year-old. Their major conflict occurred when they had been married for six years and she decided she wanted a baby and he did not. After two years of negotiating, their son was born; both were so delighted they are expecting another baby soon. Like other couples, they report they deal with conflict by talking a great deal.

Sources of Disagreement

Lack of Peer Support
A major area of conflict for many egalitarian couples is the tug-of-war between the demands of two careers and family responsibilities. Time pressures or role strains are created when two people work in a social system designed for the male worker with a stay-at-home wife to take care of his creature comforts. Every worker would appreciate a back-up person to be social secretary and hostess, to chauffeur the children, to be home for deliveries and repairs, and to cook, clean, and mend. Egalitarian couples do not have that kind of unpaid support service. In addition, they face conflicts found in most marriages over money, time management, parents-in-law, sexuality, different intimacy needs, and child rearing.

Traditional couples who have numerous role models and societal approval face less pressure. "Trying to grab things out of the air is not easy, and conflict is inevitable in trying to work out new role relationships," explains Blake, an Arizona anthropologist. Researchers agree that role-sharing is more complex, more tension producing, and more strenuous than traditional marriages, because of the lack of guidelines and the work overloads.[1]

Conflict may occur more often when two assertive, competitive people are involved than when one spouse is submissive and passive. Having a defined sense of self "sharpened our struggle and the tension in our differences," reports Doug, a California husband, but he goes on to say that working through conflict has also led him and his wife to closeness. Role-sharing is not a path for the faint of heart.

All the traditional sources of conflict are heightened for egalitarian couples by lack of support. They often are criticized by their families, neighbors, acquaintances, or business associates. A 1980 poll of adult family members found that a majority believe the family suffers when both parents work.[2] Both women and men have to muster strength to cope with opposition and guilt. Women especially are made to feel guilty about not being the sole caretakers of their children and for having less-than-immaculate homes. But men feel pressure to conform as well. Marv, an optometrist who decided to give more priority to his family than his career and to accept his wife's career as the most lucrative one in their family, needed a counselor's encouragement to "help me deal with my guilt about doing something that was not traditional. I knew it was the right thing to do, but I felt pressured not to do it. The pressure was as much internal as any. I was worried about what people would say."

Miles, the husband of a pharmacist, found it took strength to cope with his wife's success. His wife, Shirley, explains:

> I think he is very special. There aren't a lot of men who back in 1971 could stand a wife who was an assistant manager of a drugstore for a big corporation when there were only two women in the chain. People would ask him, "How do you like your wife making all this money?" I think the men who are managing to adapt to us women should get more praise than they do.

Male friends pressure role-sharing husbands not to set an example that traditional wives can hold up to their spouses, such as doing cooking and dishwashing at dinner parties. Female friends may feel jealous and resentful. For example, a female physician married to an attorney reports that some of their women friends who "put up with their husbands' demands on them for years saw Lou participating and shut us out for a while."

Some spouses find it difficult to live differently from their acquaintances, as Annie, a Wisconsin business owner, relates:

> We feel like pioneers oftentimes—it is very, very frustrating. I get to the point where I am at a loss, because everywhere I turn I see people who are *not* doing what we are doing. They are doing the traditional thing or they are not married, period. They are single. We come across a problem and there is nowhere to turn.

The institution of marriage itself can be a source of inequality and conflict. Couples warn of the pull into rigid roles. The marriage ceremony with the father giving away the bride and the minister introducing the new Mr. and Mrs. John Doe can set the tone for male superiority. The wedding day gives the bride her "day of glory," but, as one St. Louis woman put it, "she is queen for a day because she's going into a life of drudgery," like sacred virgins being prepared for a ritual sacrifice. A Kansas husband warns that when a couple start being husband and wife, the roles can dominate their identities as individuals.

A Missouri husband, Max, suggests that couples recognize that marriage is traditionally unequal. His wife, Kelly, wonders if it is even possible for women to develop complete confidence and wholeness within marriage. Her own conflict about marriage began on her wedding day, when she realized that was the big moment of her life, while her husband would often be in the spotlight, especially because he is a pastor. People who had known them well before their marriage treated them differently afterward, when they viewed her as Max's wife. She realized that Max felt free to interrupt her stories and correct them, diminishing her credibility. If she had done the same to him, it would have been called nagging. Max commented regretfully, "I couldn't have done it on my own. I had to have the support of a society that looks down on women." Max also appears more stable than she does because he is less sensitive and less reactive to emotional problems and as a man faces fewer of them. Her income, for example, is half what he can earn. Kelly concludes that people are trained not to see and to hide from the real impact of marriage. Their solution is to establish a ground rule of respect for each other and to be active in women's and men's groups that help them analyze sex roles.

Another source of conflict is the high divorce rate, which is discouraging to some couples who see many of their friends separating. One husband explains:

> You can get caught in the stampede of being more the exception than the rule. If there is a better life out there with somebody else maybe one should go out there and look for it. Plus when you are high-powered people you search for things which might not be practical to search for in a relationship.

Training the Sexes to Be Opposites

The frequency of divorce and the gap between husbands and wives is illustrated in current novels. In *Marriage Voices* by Benjamin Barber (1981), the wife leaves her husband although they love each other and have two children. She has looked to the family for her identity and her husband has looked to his work, supplemented by affairs with other women. At age thirty-nine she tells her husband, "You talk about us, but us is you, Tom. Not me and you together, just plain you." She needs to be more than his wife and the mother of his children.

In Marilyn French's popular novel *The Women's Room* (1977) spouses share only their suburban homes. The housewives and their husbands have almost no common interests. Women turn to their female friends for support. When Mira, the heroine, is divorced by her physician husband, she enters graduate school at Harvard where, although men and women share more interests in an intellectual environment, they still do not mesh. None of the female characters has a successful permanent relationship with a man. French's second novel, *The Bleeding Heart* (1980) is a more sympathetic treatment of a man involved in an affair with a woman, but in that book, too, Victor is what his name suggests. He views relationships as power struggles and cannot trust or nurture an equal relationship with a woman. The heroine believes love is at the center of women's lives but not of men's; men want to be "stroked" but not to stroke in return. Our society trains women and men so differently that it is amazing any of us manage to build bridges of understanding.

Some egalitarian couples feel that they are considered deviants violating norms of proper behavior. A father who was a homemaker for a while heard the question raised, "What does he do all day at home, try on his wife's underwear?" His behavior was seen as perverted since it did not fulfill male training. His wife explains that stereotyped portrayals of men and women as two different species "prevents thinking we could have some type of common understanding." According to a construction worker, men and women are in two armed camps. He hears husbands make remarks about "the bitch, she's a pain in the ass," and in return the wives criticize "the bastard."

Sociologists agree that men and women live in separate worlds. Jessie Bernard in *The Female World* shows that they have different values, language, economics, and ways of behaving.[3] (My first book, *Women's Culture: The Women's Renaissance of the Seventies*, shows that women's creations and organizations are different from men's.) The sexes are raised very differently. Boys are taught to be achievement oriented, to prove their masculinity by scoring in sports, in accumulation of money, and in sexual conquest. Male performance can be measured in amounts: his car's horsepower, dollars in his bank account, notches on his belt to mark sexual conquests. Emotional expressions of tenderness or empathy block conquest. Male magazines show men surrounded by expensive possessions and numerous young women, but not by their wives or children.

Girls are taught to succeed by being attractive and well liked and by marrying a good provider. Winning too much at sports or games or doing too well in science and mathematics courses can label a girl unfeminine. A well-known study by Matina Horner showed that girls are taught to fear success as unfeminine.[4] The theme that girls should hide their talents is stressed in contemporary teen romance novels in which adult women do not have paid jobs ("making a home is my career") and appearance is stressed above any skill or intellectual interest. One young woman hides her library books from her friends, for example, so boys will not think she is a bookworm. I was advised not to get my Ph.D. because it would threaten men. One of the egalitarian wives found an entry in her journal written at age sixteen, in which she had noted that a woman should stand behind a man in order to get one. It is time that these limiting definitions of womanhood begin changing.

To be skilled at relationships requires sensitivity to others' feelings, thoughtfulness, and valuing emotional interaction. Women are taught these traits as survival skills to please a man (father, employer, husband, or son) on whom they are economically dependent. Men are taught that interpersonal skills leading to intimacy are feminine and therefore trivial and boring. To be labeled "like a woman" is an insult. Coaches and military instructors tell their groups of young men not to be a bunch of girls, sissies, pansies. Boys insult each other by saying, "You woman" or "You fag."

Thinking like a man means to be logical, while thinking like a woman is to be scatterbrained. Many men, including some egalitarian husbands, have confidence in their abilities to think objectively and numerically, while women feel comfortable analyzing relationships and nurturing them. As Sheryl told her husband:

> Most of the time when I think there is something to talk about, you don't think there is. I guess you talk about things when you're aware of them. [To the interviewer:] I try to drag things out of him.

One husband observes that he tends not to confront his feelings: He thinks that they will go away or that an issue will eventually resolve itself without needing to be talked about.

Lillian Rubin explained in an interview that girls do not have to sever their identification with their mothers, and they are raised to focus on social situations. Rubin describes women "like radar homing in to the emotional side of things." A man is taught to deal with issues objectively and rationally. When a wife says to her husband, "Why don't you talk to me?" he replies that he is talking, that he doesn't know what she wants. But he does not respond to the emotional content of their exchange. The result, according to Rubin, is often "no language with which to cross the barrier." As the woman becomes frustrated, she gets angrier and the man dismisses her as hysterical. An example is given by a New York man, Nolan, who describes himself as intellectually oriented and his wife, Becky, as emotionally oriented: "To accommodate that in our relationship is always a task." Rubin concludes that we need to find new ways to train children for new family roles.

These differences in emotional literacy also cause men to fear women's "expressive power" over them, according to researcher Joseph Pleck. Pleck explains that traditional men experience emotions vicariously through their wives. Men also depend on women to validate their masculinity, to be their symbols of success, to mediate for them and provide a refuge from male competition.[5] Psychiatrist Pierre Mornell concurs that men's search for approval is a full-time job. Because of their emotional dependencies men fear women's power and want to control and diminish it. Mornell found that "husbands intuitively knew their wives were better in relationships and could dominate and destroy them if they got too close." Men are not prepared to be emotionally active; in their work, for example, they are on "automatic pilot," doing what is expected and suppressing emotion.[6]

The differences begin at birth, when a boy gets blue clothes and is praised for being strong and active while a girl gets pink clothes and is described as cute and delicate. Boys receive approval for being active, girls for being pretty. Schools segregate boys and girls in different lines and different games. A teacher punishes a boy by making him sit next to a girl, and each sex thinks the other has "cooties." Until recently, school readers showed adult women mainly in the kitchen wearing a frilly white apron. Women were rarely shown at work outside the home; they were not shown doing anything as active as driving cars. If they did paid work, it was as a nurse or teacher. In textbooks boys did the interesting and adventurous activities such as building racers or being astronauts, while girls in dresses and bows watched with their hands held passively behind their backs. The result has been that adult males and females are seen as having different personality traits; those of women are analogous to children's traits—dependent and expressive—and those of men to adult behavior—active and assertive. These limiting stereotypes are often reinforced by therapists and marriage counselors in working with clients.[7]

After years of training to be opposite, we seem to be able to connect with each other only through sex. Opposites attract, but they cannot live together, points out men's liberation leader Warren Farrell. A study of college students, however, found that the majority of girls first engaged in sexual intercourse to please their partners rather than to satisfy their own sexual desire.[8] Misunderstandings result, because boys are taught to score ("Did you get to third base?") and girls to believe in romance and valentine-card sentiments. Girls want tenderness and talking and boys want to get down to business. If either sex feels differently—the boy wants to cuddle and the girl to initiate sex—they often feel uneasy about stepping out of their "proper" roles.

Sexual conflict occurs when the woman wants emotional intimacy to precede sexual intercourse and the man expects intimacy to follow sex. This is often the case for traditional couples. Friction can especially occur when young children prevent a couple from having time together. A Kansas wife related that early in her marriage her two babies made it impossible for her and her husband to share with each other except in bed. Her husband's ideas of what they should share there were different from hers, and they both felt frustrated. In a similar situation, Art, an Indiana husband, states, "Lisa says she can't have sex unless there is full emotional support, like icing on the cake, and I say you can't have a full emotional relationship until you have physical communion. We've had that basic difference since our first date." Art wishes she would initiate sex more often. Lisa finds as she gets older that she can be more flexible, more able to engage in sex even if she knows their daughter will wake up soon or "he hasn't given me twenty-five hugs in the last two hours or said the right thing when I told him my supervisor was driving me crazy. We compromise." One unusual husband states that it is more important to him than to his wife to take time to create the right setting and emotional closeness preceding intercourse. Differences in expectations about sex require discussion and, often, compromise.

A frequent source of discord is that the woman has greater desire for emotional intimacy not only in sex, but in the relationship in general, a finding that is true for 95 percent of the friends and clients of psychiatrist Pierre Mornell. He describes a typical scenario in his book *Passive Men, Wild Women:* Both spouses arrive home from a day at work. He "tunes out," wanting to rest. She wants to "tune in," to share feelings about their day. His passive withdrawal to the television set makes her furious. He retreats further from her anger, and a vicious cycle is created.[9] Some of the couples I interviewed experienced this kind of frustration. One woman explains, "I'm the one the relationship is a lot more personal to and I'm more intertwined in it. I've had to struggle with him to get that because he is perfectly happy. He feels he knows me if he has breakfast with me and sleeps in the same bed with me."

A Southern woman plans to leave her marriage when her youngest child leaves home because her struggles for intimacy haven't produced satisfactory results:

> I decided years ago that the effort I was extending trying to make an emotional relationship was not going to pay off,

and it was not worth the effort. It took a great deal of emotional energy on my part to reach him and in two days' time
he had forgotten it had ever happened. So it was totally
frustrating. I will be much, much happier when I give up. I
gave up on the idea that he should provide all my needs. I
think it's unfair to expect that of any person, but I think
that two people can create and share a great deal of closeness. I still believe in that because I have friends—some of
them are very close—who believe in sharing.

Conflict between men and women is inevitable until they are
raised to have more similar definitions of achievement. Although
the middle class conveys a belief in companionship in marriage,
Jessie Bernard doubts that close friendship between spouses is
widely practiced. The fact that most American couples spend so
little time talking with each other seems to indicate a lack of
intimacy.

Work

Work pressures can particularly cause stress in a two-career
marriage. A Washington, D.C., accountant says that "being
satisfied with our working situation is important because when
we've been miserable with our working situations, life was hell."
Many couples agree that the never-ending demands of professional jobs that do not end at 5:00 P.M. add resentment to
the relationship and that irritations brought home from work
are a major source of friction. "I've been angry if he wants to
work late and he's been angry if I want to work late. We've done
more fighting about that than about anything else," says Cheryl,
an IBM saleswoman. After returning to work from being a
full-time mother, "I become very involved in my work and that
puts a lot of tension and stress on me which I carry home. That
makes things harder. The extra money I make is nice and that
makes things easier." A strain on a marriage can be created by
the demands of the career of the highest-earning spouse, often
the husband. An Ohio city manager with four grown children
looked back on his career and noted: "I think if I were to make
a change now it would be the amount of time I spent on the

job. There was a time when that was at least as important if not more important than the family, and I spent too much time away."

Difficulties can occur if the woman is more successful at her career than her husband even if her husband is very mature. Keith is an owner of a small business and Moira, his wife, is the manager of a Chicago branch office; he has needed to make

> some mental adjustment due to the fact that I can't seem to get my career going as smoothly professionally and finan- cially as she's gotten hers. But Moira is very good about that in not making me feel uncomfortable. It's just a private sort of discomfort that I feel although it is not really an ob- stacle. I think if we were younger and it was a competitive type of situation where jealousy and envy might arise, then that could be a much larger obstacle. But I think we're both at the point where we see that life has a lot of ups and downs.

Only one couple, professors in the same university depart- ment, mentioned competition in terms of their careers. Perhaps other couples choose not to recognize it. David Rice, a therapist, finds that dual-career couples experience but deny competitive feelings.[10] The high-achievement personality, as Rice charac- terizes it, is competitive, somewhat rigid, single-minded, and narcissistic. He concludes that competition is inevitable for two- career couples. Competition can carry over to arenas other than work, as a California social worker describes:

> We compete over whose goals are the most important, who does this or that best, who does more housework this week, and who is lazy. It's easy to compete with each other. I feel that competition in our relationship sometimes and it's destructive.

A Minnesota couple realize that they compete over the time and attention they give to each other, since work and children also make demands.

The most difficult work-related decisions for dual-career couples are those involved in a move for career advancement; moving to satisfy career needs is a severe stress, one that many employers and employees are struggling with. A study of forty-five dual-career couples in 1977 found that ten had made moves for the husband's career and none for the woman's.[11] "When it comes down to moving for the woman's job you find out what equality is," states a woman attorney. She is presently making such a move from Nebraska to Oregon, although her husband has no job contacts in Oregon yet. A husband who works in park management and whose wife is a pharmacist describes the impact of their move for his job:

> If we had stayed in Michigan, she would be in a better job position. I think there was a lot of resentment that she wasn't doing what she wanted to and I was. I was enjoying my job. She didn't know what was wrong except that something was wrong. It just wasn't fun up until this last year, when she got involved in activities with her colleagues.

Couples who own businesses together have their own particular problems. They like the flexibility that comes with being their own bosses and the understanding they have for each other's workloads, but they have to struggle not to carry their preoccupation with the business home into their domestic life. One couple made a rule that the only time they can talk about business at home is from 9:00 to 10:00 P.M.

Spouses who work different hours from each other have additional work-related problems. One couple write to each other extensively in a notebook that they keep on their kitchen table. They find that writing often permits freer disclosures than talking does. Another couple in this situation converse on the phone a lot but find that problems build up during the week, so "we find ourselves badgering each other over the weekend."

Yet some women find staying home all day more stressful than combining a career and a family. A homemaker and mother of three daughters changed her attitudes about how she wanted to live and became a feminist in the process. Her husband responded this way:

I really didn't understand Paula and we had hard times. I was fighting it. We had many arguments over what I thought were *her* changes. We'd go to a party and when someone realized she was a feminist, men at that time seemed to zero in on her and start conversations and they got very heated. I was getting very bored with it.

This same sentiment is echoed by other couples who made the transition from traditional role division to an egalitarian relationship. Once the wife begins her own career, some sources of conflict are resolved, but new ones are fueled. This is especially true if the couple have well-established, old attitudes that view the woman as responsible for a smoothly functioning household.

A woman who is a counselor married to a psychologist finds their workloads very stressful when combined with the care of three teenage children.

> Arn: The last couple of years there has been a breakdown in our direct communication. Part of it is increased stress. Part of it is both of us working and still having kids and not finding time. Frequently things are let go for a long time without really being dealt with in a direct way.

> Rebecca: Our lives, our weekends are overwhelmingly filled with trivial things.

> Arn: We haven't made a lot of time in our relationship and in the family for communication, nonagenda being together. It's usually taken up by activities.

> Rebecca: The weekends are such a nightmare, so draining, there's little pleasure. I'm almost at the point of where separation looks very appealing to me, because I don't want to feel anymore that everything is a mess because I'm not at home seeing that everything isn't a mess. I feel that the message is "If you were around to do it right, it wouldn't be this way," and my life and Arn's wouldn't be so horrible and I wouldn't be in such pain all the time.

Arn: Some of that is Rebecca's internalization of my message. Most of the time, that is not what I'm saying. What I'm expressing is my frustration. Rebecca
seems to take a lot of that and then add the stuff
that comes after the comma, which is that I think she
should be at home. Some place in the past there may
have been more of that. I really am not aware of feeling that now, but feeling a need to share my exas-
peration with another adult. Then that doesn't leave
me free to express any frustration to another adult
because it gets taken as a criticism.

The pressure on Rebecca to be superwoman, accomplishing
all she had done as a homemaker while handling her new job,
is felt by many women. A Wisconsin wife, Deirdre, states:

You want to be successful as a wife and mother and be all
things to all people. Probably more conflict arises when I'm
trying to be all of these things. You can have it all but
there is always an emotional price you're going to pay. So
it's finding a happy medium that is causing pain right now.

In addition to the increased workload, when the wife begins
a career after her husband's is well established, they find themselves in different stages professionally; his career may have
peaked while hers is still advancing. He is ready to give more
time to his family and she is consumed by her work, a problem
experienced by Arn and Rebecca. Arn describes their situation:

I've arrived at where I'm going and my ambition is not to
conquer. I'm a little tired, things are no longer quite as
exciting as they were. My primary ambition at this point
is no longer achievement and career. I'd like to have more
leisure time doing things around the house. Rebecca has
been in her career for only two years; she's at a place where
I was twenty-two years ago. It's new and exciting. She's still
carving out, not sure where her finiteness is. We're really
in different places in that sequence. Sometimes that's good
and sometimes it isn't because I would like to devote most
of my energy to thinking about five years from now, when
I can leave my forty-hour-a-week job and wonder what to

do about leisure recreation. Rebecca is perceiving things more as I would have twenty-two years ago.

As young couples continue the current trend of delaying marriage and childbirth and returning to work soon after their children are born, some of the difficulties of trying to change roles in midstream should be eased.

Personalities

Other sources of conflict within marriages are roommate issues, differences in attitudes and habits. Examples of differences causing arguments are smoking, food preference, tolerance for disorder, how to spend money, how much social activity with colleagues, how much time spent with in-laws, and where to live. Some individuals, used to living alone as only children or as single adults, find it difficult to adapt to another person close at hand. Conflict often revolves around housework issues, such as one person wanting neatness more than the other. A husband says he'll "try and reform" and then "slips back into being sloppy."

Personality differences also cause friction, as one Illinois woman relates:

> We have a constant struggle with the fact that I'm a more serious person than Harlee is in that I always tend to find problems and he always finds the good parts, so sometimes we don't entirely match. He would like me to be more joyful and I would like him to be more serious.

Counselors Tom and Thea Lowry note that people often marry someone who complements their traits. The "engineer's marriage" is a well-known example among marriage counselors: He marries her because she is vivacious, unpredictable, lively, and expressive, and she marries him because he is steady, dependable, and successful. Seven years later she finds him boring and he is disgusted that she cannot balance the checkbook. The danger is that couples often end up disliking the qualities that originally attracted them to each other. Not rushing into marriage seems imperative so one can see beyond one's projections on the other person.

How Do Egalitarian Couples' Conflicts Compare with Others'?

One study of typical couples found their main sources of conflict were, in order: finances, friends and relatives, children, husbands procrastination on tasks, expression of affection, and the woman's autonomy.[12] Eight hundred and fifteen dual-career couples surveyed by Catalyst Foundation reported that the wives' main problem was having too much to do and the husbands' was feeling they did not have enough time with their wives.[13] Their other sources of conflict were money, housework, and poor communication. The women felt more stress than the men.

For a wider perspective, I asked marriage counselor Thea Lowry to describe the major sources of conflict in her clients' marriages. She listed child rearing, money, and sex. As a sex therapist, Lowry defines the impact of sex on marriage:

> Sexual disappointments are the basis for a number of divisions and communication problems. Sex can either be the cause or the effect of relationship difficulties. Visualize, if you will, a two-room place where a couple live when they first start out. Their physical compatibility is wonderful. The things that happen in the bedroom surround it with a golden glow. But through that door and in the next room, there are misunderstandings from the family of origin about who washes the dishes, who cooks the meals or where they store breakfast cereals, or who pays the bills, or how much money goes on the checks, or how much long-distance phone is okay, or what TV channel is okay to watch on Monday. That turmoil leaks through the door and the aura dies in the bedroom, because of the resentments. So, disappointments in the relationship cancel out nice things in the bedroom. That's one scenario.

Another scenario is they both wash the dishes together and they chit-chat, they take turns cooking meals and they both put the Wheaties on the top shelf and they both agree that one of the ways of staying in touch is to make all the long-distance phone calls they want. They both watch Monday night football and everything is fine in that room. It has a golden aura. But over in the bedroom, and every time they make love—premature ejaculation or non-responsive woman or no erection when an erection would be appropriate or a recoiling withdrawal because of vaginismus on the part of the woman. And so the disappointments that happen in this room leak out of the door and start canceling out the golden aura in the other room. When there's a sexual disappointment it begins to be the nonmemory of sharing good times and it loosens the pair-bonding. Masters and Johnson said that those shared good times have something to do with the glue that keeps people together.

Egalitarian couples find talking about sexual needs is vital to satisfying sex; expecting one's partner to intuit likes and dislikes never works. Victor relates, "In the sexual arena our relationship has not been everything that it could be. That has a lot to do with communication in sex. We communicate unusually outstandingly in every area but that one." A wife advises people who have sexual difficulties: "Don't fake it, but talk about it and work it out, even though it's probably one of the hardest areas to talk about." Her husband adds, "And no secrets, no games."

Overall, couples mentioned conflicts caused by work-related issues, division of housework, and personality differences more than money issues, child rearing, or sex. Their shared decision making and responsibility for moneymaking and child care probably prevents major conflicts in those areas. Studies have shown that feminists have more satisfying sex lives, no doubt because they are more assertive about discussing their desires. The pressures caused by combining so many roles in a twenty-four-hour day seem to be their major problem.

Solutions: Working at Communication

All the couples I interviewed agree that maintaining their relationship takes work and time. If attention is diverted from the marriage, the marriage wilts like a plant that lacks water: "It's very precious and if you don't spend time it will dry up," states a Colorado professor. Our cultural mythology does not prepare us for what happens after the honeymoon is over. The skills that make communication possible often need to be consciously learned: from books, from a marriage counselor, or from group counseling such as Marriage Encounter or Re-Evaluation Peer Counseling. Our usual training is to mask unpleasant feelings, to maintain a facade of pleasantness, not to make waves, even though feelings require expression for problems to be resolved.

Men are often taught that expression of any emotion other than anger is feminine, that revealing vulnerability is weak. A male accountant, Mel, relates: "My background has always been to overlook the downs, to pretend they don't exist." As a result he describes himself as a closed, fearful person. Another husband explains, "I was trained in my childhood to hold in my feelings and I'm very good at it. It's taken through the sixties and early seventies working at being able to come out with my feelings."

Women are also taught to suppress feelings, especially anger, as this couple describes:

Geoffrey: Sometimes her feelings would come out with a phone call while I was on a job or a door slam on my way out, but I didn't think of them as the result of building up of tensions and problems. I thought of them more as an unusual feeling at the moment.

Maggie: Somehow I didn't get across because most of the time I swallowed my anger. Part of my nontalking was not wanting him to sacrifice anything. I didn't want to complain. If he preferred a different ac-

tivity, although I wanted his companionship I
would never press that. I wanted him to be happy
and I wanted our marriage to be happy. I really
didn't look at the fact that after a while I was
unhappy.

Couples with successful marriages in which both feel nurtured
realize that communication is the lifeblood of their marriages
and that time must be specifically carved out often to talk about
their feelings. One couple, both psychologists, have a lasting
relationship because

we are both prepared to invest whatever time and energy is
necessary to deal with the problems that come up between
two people. I think what happens in lots of other relationships is that they allow distance to come between them.
When something is bothering them, whether it's from inside the relationship or outside it, they don't talk about it.
There's sort of an emotional separation that happens, a
distance that we've never allowed to happen. Whenever
there's anything that's bothering us we've almost always
dealt with that and talked about it. So whatever problems
we've had have made us get closer together rather than
further apart.

Many traditional couples devote themselves to courtship and
conquest, then when the honeymoon is over they turn to a
career or child rearing. They assume that if they are sexually
monogamous, earn an adequate living or keep a smoothly functioning household, and eat and sleep together the relationship
will take care of itself like a self-cleaning oven. Disaster results
when the two finally realize they are strangers.

The dangers of not communicating are multitudinous. Each
individual is changing with time. If growth is not monitored,
"one day you'll wake up next to a stranger," comments a Cincinnati professor. "If you leave it alone, communication will go,"
reports a North Carolina teacher. The building up of minor
irritations, "gunnysacking" or making a "shopping list" of unspoken displeasure causes resentment toward one's partner. Annie explains:

Communication takes an immense amount of time, but it has to be done because it is the only way to let each other know where you are and where you are going and to keep in constant touch so that there is not misunderstanding. Without a lot of communication, misunderstandings easily come up.

Two lawyers in Maine went to a counselor to get help creating more intimacy. Sharon elaborates:

It's hard sometimes to feel very intimate and I have found that if we are not really focused on each other, closeness starts to go and you start feeling very alone. I think the counselor focused us both on the need for the time together, getting our priorities in order. My everyday concerns were my kids, my job, and my husband—in that order. When I really start thinking about it, if my relationship with Paul is in good shape then the kids are okay. And yet our relationship seems to take the back seat. Lately, we have gone out and had dates together and that has been really good. When we get by ourselves, go out and communicate, we solve conflicts more quickly.

Couples find it easy to see themselves as the cause of the other partner's behavior. If the man is withdrawn, the woman feels she did something to offend him, for example. Instead of withdrawing or becoming angry in response, if she communicates with him she can find out that his withdrawal has nothing to do with her and that she is not responsible for his feelings.

Risking Discomfort: Taking Down Barriers

Facing conflict means that emotions are stirred up, unpleasant feelings surface, and comfortable positions are shaken, but intimacy can exist only when real feelings are expressed. Most of us are reluctant to express our true feelings because we fear rejection or fear being controlled and engulfed, but if small hurts are buried, resentment ensues that inhibits love. Risking disclosure leads to intimacy. A traditional marriage in which bad feelings are repressed is more tranquil in some ways, but the distance necessary to maintain the peace is not conducive to friendship and love.

Egalitarian couples learn to expect ups and downs, alternating periods of closeness and distance. A two-to-three-month cycle is charted by one woman:

> For a week or two, everything he does and says annoys me to the point I think I cannot stand to be around him. Then it usually builds to a peak, something triggers a confrontation, and we sit down and we talk. We always end up discovering or expressing something new that we haven't told each other before and I feel closer to him and everything is cool again. It's never on an even keel.

The false expectation that one should be happy all the time is noted by an Illinois couple:

> Nan: It helps to know that the disillusionment you're in is a natural part of life. You can work through it and it is not the end of the relationship, but it's only one of the constant cycles of the relationship.
>
> Jeff: It seems to me that in the Pepsi generation one of the traps our culture makes for us implies that if you're not happy all the time, you're doing something wrong.

To talk about feelings even if they seem "horrible" appears risky and unpleasant and it may be easier to let sleeping dogs lie. A family counselor believes that 95 percent of a therapist's job is convincing clients that it is safe to express their feelings.[14] A New York writer explains, "You feel really relieved that you've gotten [your feelings] out before they build on other suppressed emotions in the psyche. I always think my husband is going to be furious when I tell him and am amazed when he listens because I was taught by my mother not to get angry and raise my voice."

Communication requires consistent effort to pull down the defenses that we have constructed to hide our feelings, even from ourselves. A North Carolina dentist, Greg, describes the evolution of his awareness:

> I think what I've had to work the hardest with is communication. I have certainly not conquered the barriers yet, but I try. In the early years of our marriage, I wasn't even aware of it; I just thought you had to tell your wife you had a good day at the office; just words, [she] just had to hear something. But, now to try to communicate we spend two hours just talking. When we don't, I miss it. This is something that really is work to me. I've always been a very closed person; I've built up my barriers and it's been hard to take the grips down and let her inside. It's hard work to expose your feelings, to cry in front of your wife; this has been one of the hardest things.

His wife, Robbie, adds,

> People think communication means saying, "Gee, I had a hard day at the office," while what it really means is "I feel awful tonight, I had a hard time dealing with a patient."

She had her own difficulties expressing her feelings, burying anger about being a homemaker and mother of three with no adequate outlets for her own talents. As a result she had a nervous breakdown that forced her to learn about her real feelings. She explains:

> I had to come to grips with the fact that I didn't know how to deal with anger. I think the reason I didn't know how was that women traditionally were not supposed to show it. You were not supposed to say four-letter words. I had gotten to the point that I was so well-controlled, such a wonderful lady, that I didn't even recognize my anger anymore. And the natural anger that would have been perfectly okay I was subverting; it was internalized. I took it out on myself.

The whole family went to a counselor and the parents studied communication skills by reading, talking with friends, and taking Parent Effectiveness Training courses. As a result, Greg felt much closer to Robbie afterward, and she likes herself more although she reports that now when she's angry she could shock a sailor.

A technique used by one woman who finds it difficult to begin talking about uncomfortable issues is to "institute one of our little games or rituals. I'll say 'Knock, knock' and he'll say, 'Who's there?' and then I'm free to blurt it out. It kind of lightens the air and gets me over that awful hump of starting." Another technique used by a couple who are reluctant to talk about angry feelings is to sit down in two chairs back to back, not looking at each other, and take turns unloading without any interruptions from the other person until everything has been said. Writing letters to each other is effective for some couples. Others find it useful to clear the air by yelling at each other, while others need time alone to think about an issue before discussing it.

Some couples abide by the old rule of never going to bed still angry at each other.

> We incessantly talk—all the time. One time there was this painful discussion that I didn't want to deal with so I went to bed. Don came and woke me up. Four hours later as we were ending this intense discussion I remember thinking it was a worthwhile session. I think it's rare to find a man that's willing to talk like that.

But it is naive to think that everything can be resolved in an evening, according to a New York couple. They find some issues take months, as Sarah states:

> We keep dealing with it when there is time: you have to teach a class in the morning and can't stay up. We got to be older and mellower but we never let go of talking things through or noticing when we've gotten a little distant.

The common thread throughout different styles of expressing anger is that anger does not get buried under the guise of niceness.

Talking about Expectations

Egalitarian couples talk about their expectations. They have learned that assuming one person automatically knows what the other expects sets up frustration. Talking over expectations is especially important in the beginning of a relationship. One woman who did not discuss expectations with her future husband was surprised to discover that children were not part of her husband's plans:

> I didn't know that he didn't want kids. It never occurred to me to ask. I always assumed that everybody would want kids. This was from not talking to each other before we got married about anything significant. I thought he would care a lot about how I was, that he would notice that I was happy or unhappy. That was part of the reason that I didn't say anything during the early years. I thought if he didn't ask, he didn't care about me and didn't want to be bothered.

It took much effort for them to make connections about their real needs; they had many years of silence to overcome.

The results of not knowing one's spouse well are described by a remarried woman in Massachusetts:

> Before my first marriage we only spent time together going out and having a good time. We did not share anything as far as living quarters, sex life, or any of the things that create problems, until we were married. And it was a shock when we had to finally share them. We didn't agree on how money should be spent, what time we went to bed, what kind of food we liked. Before that we went out to eat and he ordered what he wanted and I got what I wanted. Illness is another factor. He couldn't stand sick people. If I was sick he wanted me to get up and go about my chores and act like I wasn't sick. He didn't want to deal with it.

She lived with her second husband for five years before their marriage, so the second time there were no unpleasant surprises. Therapist Virginia Satir concurs that many traditional couples marry people they do not really know.[15] A wise woman made a point of telling a man she was contemplating marrying how important it was to her to share parenting. He replied, "Oh, you can't control things like that, you can't plan your life around things like that." She saw the handwriting on the wall and ended the relationship. She now is enjoying shared parenting with a less evasive man.

Communication is necessary to make one aware of different assumptions, based on how one was raised, about how to deal with issues such as anger, money, illness, child discipline, or holiday rituals. Couples face difficulty when they expect their marriages to be like their parents'. One woman's parents did everything together, but she and her husband have very different interests, he in sports and she in ballet. She had to struggle to accept a concept of a good marriage as one in which partners have some separate activities. One older man before he was married would hang his suitcoats on a dining-room chair; his mother brushed them and put them away. When he married, his chairs became covered with suitcoats because his wife had no intention of being his valet as his mother was. A woman expected her husband to carve at the dinner table because her father did so, but in the husband's family his mother carved meat before it was brought to the table. These are minor examples of the major problem of husbands and wives holding different expectations about proper behavior.

Couples advise others to talk explicitly about fundamental choices such as how many children to have, if any, when to have them, and their religious upbringing; sharing child care and housework; having separate or joint banking accounts; and accommodating two careers. Writing a contract or creating their own marriage vows helped some couples clarify their expectations from the marriage. Some couples renew their marriage contract every six months or every year to make sure the relationship is functioning well for both parties. They talk about reasons to stay together and those that would cause them to separate. A New York attorney, Paul, advises couples

> to look upon marriage as an exercise of international relations. Consider each partner to be a separate country with

separate history and goals. Try to identify your mutual interests and common goals. Try to isolate those factors in your
different cultures and histories that may lead to conflict.
Negotiate treaties so that the marriage can continue on the
basis of mutual and common understanding.

Communication Skills

Couples acknowledge that talking about feelings often is not
easy; it is something that has to be worked at all the time. Learning to express feelings as well as thoughts takes effort for some
people. "It isn't just talking intellectually," explains a Texas
pastor. "It's screaming once in a while and expressing the emotions that are tied up with the issue. It's trying to say straight
how we feel about what's happening and running the risk of
tears or anger. And then being around each other to do some
healing."

A necessary step in communicating is to identify one's own
feelings and needs and to be assertive about stating them, such
as "I hate housework" or "I'm feeling jealous of your children,"
to use the examples given by a remarried teacher. A common
theme emphasized by most couples is the importance of honestly stating feelings as soon as they arise rather than keeping
them inside for fear of alienating one's spouse. "We try to bring
things up before they reach the boiling point," states a Saskatchewan man. A couple in their sixties finally learned ten years ago
to confront feelings. The husband explains that "we'd have
some issue, but instead of arguing it out, I'd dodge it and not
wade through it." The impetus to change occurred when his
wife lay down on the floor and had a tantrum. She told him
he had to tell her what was bothering him; he did and he has
continued to do so. Sometimes change occurs only with a dramatic event.

"I" messages, in which each person states his or her needs,
are much more effective than "you" messages that blame the
other person. An Arizona couple who have accumulated nega-

tive feelings are seeing a counselor who encourages them to state, "I need, and you can choose to give me what I need or not," instead of making demands or blaming. They are trying to replace accusations with descriptions of need. Blame breeds defensiveness and counterattack rather than understanding. Instead of saying "You're such a slob, you never do the dishes," couples find that a more effective message is "I really need some order in the kitchen to feel comfortable about working in it." "I" and "you" messages seem simple but they are not easy in practice. One can say "I feel you're a slob" in the guise of delivering an "I" statement, for example. In addition to avoiding "you," psychiatrist Tom Lowry suggests also refraining from beginning sentences with "we," "let's," and "why," as in "We ought to clean my car," "Let's visit my parents," or "Why didn't you do the dishes?"

Communicating also involves "active listening," feeding back to one's partner what he or she said. This may also seem simple, but it is not; one sociologist reacts to a problem of his wife's rationally, trying to provide solutions, not wanting feelings to get in the way, when she is just looking for someone to say "I understand." A woman wanted to express her frustrations about their baby but stopped doing so because her husband always tried to intervene to correct the situation. He was acting out his idea of the good male protector, but what she wanted was the chance to vent her feelings.

Couples are surprised to discover, when they try to repeat a statement that seemed clear, that they actually missed an important part of the message or misunderstood it. Feeling like a parrot saying "You feel . . . because . . ." seems awkward at first until one sees how relieved the other is to be understood and to have his or her feelings acknowledged. A temptation is to try to solve the problem, "Why don't you tell your boss to . . ." but usually the most effective problem solving is done by the person who has the problem, with the help of an active listener. To have our feelings understood and validated is a primary human need. Not interrupting another person to interject one's own experience or opinions is also essential to clear communication, a principle that is frequently violated, but one that egalitarian couples learn.

Communication requires willingness to compromise, negotiate, make trade-offs, seek consensus for the common good, be flexible rather than "taking opposite positions to be right." The goal is not to win by getting one's own desires fulfilled but to satisfy both people. A husband gives an example:

> We have different opinions on how money should be spent, but we have an agreement between us that we'll sit down and we'll discuss this in a way that both of us are satisfied, not one or the other.

The ability to bend one's ego to the greater good is vital, believes one husband; he does not see winning more than his wife from a conflict as a victory. Egalitarian couples' commitment is to solving problems to best suit both persons rather than one person consistently bending to the other. "Friends of ours who have gotten divorces weren't accommodating to each other and didn't have communication skills," remarks a Pittsburgh psychologist. During a deadlock in an argument, one husband appreciates it when his wife reaches over to hold his hand to make positive contact with him. Whoever feels most secure will reach out to the other.

To be defensive and protective of one's own position is ingrained; to imagine one's partner's situation is part of the work involved in communicating. A Colorado attorney, Tanya, appreciates her husband's openness:

> I can talk about things and know that he'll take them okay. If we started reacting defensively, so that I knew if I talked about a certain topic we'd have a fight, I'd quit talking about it. I wouldn't quit having feelings, but we'd quit talking. One of the ways you make sure you stay willing to talk is to keep a positive response going.

Part of negotiating is accepting that the partner is a separate entity with his or her own needs. "One danger that I've seen is getting very symbiotic, thinking you are the other person and they are you. You have to say, 'Wait a minute, they're a separate person,' " advises a New York wife. It is common to view the partner as an extension of oneself and therefore have one's ego invested in the other person in a way that cramps that person's freedom. "I feel what happens with most successful marriages is that by encouraging the spouse to be independent he or she is a more interesting person. That keeps each person growing and as a result the marriage is healthier," says a Pennsylvania husband. In contrast, many of his and his wife's friends are threatened by an independent act of a spouse, such as a wife's returning to school or getting a job.

To find a solution to a disagreement usually requires some compromise. "Successful marriage is really resolvable negotiation," states a Cincinnati business president. Ranking how important an issue is on a scale of one to ten helps some couples by giving the person to whom it is more important more weight in the decision.

"So many people spend so much time harping on the problem and forget to get to the next step of what are we going to do about it," notes a young Oregon husband. A New York pair who fought for years over doing the dishes provide an example of how nonproductive it is to rigidly cling to a position. Larry's job was to wash the dishes and Julia's job was to scrape them first. She often did not get to her tasks and therefore he did not do the dishes. "Instead of throwing it back in his face again, I tried to see what was really going on and came up with a solution that he clears up and I wash. It cracks us up that it took so long to come up with it."

Fighting

Fighting is done in different styles, explosively or rationally, usually determined by how one's parents fought. Difficulties can arise if one person came from a family who expressed their anger by yelling and the other did not. A man who did not yell back at his wife found that she felt ignored and that intensified her anger.

Expression of anger is necessary in a healthy relationship. A University of Utah study in which young couples were asked to fight in a ring with soft padded clubs found that couples who barely tapped each other were unhappier and more distant from each other than couples who were able to hit hard.[16] Some couples find it takes at least two or three sessions to resolve bad feelings. Others know there are times to avoid confrontation, such as late in the evening when one partner is tired. Some are antagonists for weeks and some hardly ever argue. The aim of fighting is to face discord when it occurs, as Spence, a business executive, has learned to do: "We talk more and I don't have the same defense mechanisms I used to of clamming up and escaping from the conflict grounds."

Fighting honorably is defined by a Colorado attorney:

> There's a way of fighting that you can finish the fight and be done with it, and there is a way of fighting that you wound the other person. It requires knowing your partner and where he is vulnerable. And if I get him there and he's wounded, it probably has nothing to do at all with the subject at hand. When you fight you need to stick to the subject matter and not be afraid to really disagree if that's how you feel.

Sticking to the problem at hand is crucial, as a Delaware couple found. Carson recalls:

> For the first few years of our marriage we had a lot of fights about how to fight. The arguments would start on something else and end up on secondary issues overshadowing what had originally rubbed us the wrong way. I would hold on to things for a long time. We'd start an argument about one thing and suddenly all these other things would come pouring out. We learned to talk about things when they happened and not save them up for an argument.

Psychologist George Bach has outlined a fighting system that many couples find effective. His approach consists of five steps:

(1) State the problem specifically. (2) The partner restates it. (3) Outline concrete and reasonable changes that would solve the problem. (4) The partner restates them. (5) The partner agrees or disagrees; compromise is sought. Only one issue is discussed at a time, assumptions are verified by asking one's partner if they are correct, sarcasm is unfair, and the fighters stay in the present.[17]

Couples discovered they can fight angrily and know that love is still present. They attack the issue, not the other person. Blaming the other is easy but ineffective, as one man realized in his first marriage, which began when his future wife pretended she was pregnant. He understandably was angry with her but stayed in the marriage to father two children, because as long as "I was trapped in this marriage with this terrible woman, I could blame her for everything and I didn't have to work."

Instead of blaming, egalitarian couples find it useful to see what wound is touched, what old script or tape is set off that really has nothing to do with the discussion at hand. Often an argument is clouded by the presence of ghosts created by past experiences with parents. The internal voice of a critical parent, for example, can make one feel attacked when that is not the spouse's intent.

Other ineffective but common techniques for conflict solution are distracting the other person from the central issue, being rational to the exclusion of acknowledging feelings, denying the problem exists, withdrawing, and placating. In the fights of her first marriage, Christa, a California teacher, usually gave in to her husband and then "I'd feel resentful because I was always the one to try and make things better." Fighting fair demonstrates that power in an egalitarian relationship shifts back and forth and is made explicit. This is unlike power in many traditional marriages, in which the husband wields power overtly, while the wife is apparently submissive on the surface but manipulatively strikes back with cutting remarks and withholds affection, sex, or his favorite foods.

When a partner or child makes a favorable change as a result of negotiating a conflict, couples find it important to reward and reinforce good behavior with praise and appreciation. One woman realized that it was easier for her to voice criticism than approval and that she needed to give more positive reinforcement to her spouse. Humor is a useful tool to balance irritation; in one marriage, if the wife is being too authoritarian her husband clicks his heels and goose-steps around the kitchen to make her laugh.

Knowing that priorities are shared helps in resolving conflict. A New Hampshire attorney acts on the principle that his family and relationship always come first. He gave up a high-paying private practice to work in a less time-consuming job for the state so he would have time for his two young children. A Cincinnati business manager refused a promotion because it would involve leaving the area where his wife had an established career. He decided to form his own business in the area and now appreciates the freedom he has as the president of his own firm. A professor gave up a position as full professor at a major university because his wife did not get tenure. They moved across the country to a university where they both got hired.

Egalitarian couples compare their relationships to those of others who "don't know how to struggle, who don't have any faith or any models," who are pessimistic about relationships. A California technician explains:

> You work out a serious problem really differently, if you believe deep down that you're going to be together on the other end of it than if you think you might or might not depending on how it works out. And that makes it more possible to do the kind of sharing we do when we're together. It also eliminates a lot of potential resentment.

Getting Help in Learning to Communicate

How to talk about feelings effectively, to negotiate and problem-solve must be learned, because many of us had parents who either hid their disagreements or were poor fighters. Some of the role-sharing couples have learned to communicate, and to fight, from a counselor. An insight gained by a couple who went to a marriage counselor for six months, for example, was that their unstated expectations about how to set up a good life together were based on unrealistic fantasies. With the help of the counselor, they formulated more realistic and conscious goals for their marriage.

Another couple learned from their counselor to really listen to each other, to find out what they could learn from each other. As a result of participation in a group for couples, a Texas couple gained important insights:

Bob: I got in touch with the fact that I was saying things in a teasing way that really were put-downs to Jean.

Jean: I flipped over from being a shy sweet girl to an assertive woman. Since then it kept getting better as we got in touch with awareness. We have our ways of letting each know when one does something that the other one doesn't like. He'll put his middle finger on his nose and I'll say "I got your message." We know how to do it so casually, we'll laugh and no one will notice.

Individual counseling is also useful in order to learn who one is as a separate person, as Philip, a California poet, age thirty-nine, relates:

I didn't think about who I was, so I got counseling for a year and I got a better handle on how to deal with my feelings. I realized that I existed as well as my family and my needs were not only real, but as a human being I should exercise them. Then I felt braver and stronger to communicate who I was and what I wanted because I didn't feel so afraid. Before I didn't know who I was or what I wanted. So for me that set the stage to lose a lot of tension and not feel that I had to run to the top of the career ladder. Also because I was washing dishes and taking care of children— being pretty domestic—didn't make me any less of a person. I realized that if I didn't make my own vision of who I wanted to be, then the one given to me by my culture was going to give me a ruined life.

His wife, Susan, also a poet, describes her growth from counseling:

> The family counseling with all of us together helped. It was a transformative time for me and definitely for our relationship. We were talking about it recently when we had a really bad night. But by the afternoon of the next day, everything was flowing smoothly again. What we learned was how to be responsible for our own feelings, to ask for what we want, how to communicate and how, for me, not to feel responsible for Philip's feelings. To yell if I felt like it and be mad, and not be so nice and caring if I didn't feel it, was another thing I learned. And by the afternoon the pain that before would have lasted for six months was gone in a few hours. That was a major accomplishment.

Philip and Susan are also discovering how their relationships with their parent of the opposite sex interlocks, she being in some ways domineering like his mother and he restrictive like her father. They realize the security in the repetition of deeply rooted behavior but are working to untangle themselves from their family roots. A major task in solving any conflict seems to be freeing one's self from unconsciously repeating parental patterns.

Counseling also reveals that the most simple exchanges are complicated not only by the different rules of behavior learned in one's original family, but also by previous love experiences, stored-up grievances coming out in the present relationship, tendencies to masochism or sadism, and power and control needs. The difficulty is that the habitual behavior fits like a worn pair of slippers and thus seems natural. Giving up part of one's self is frightening, like a child parting with a security blanket. In an insightful book about the unconscious barriers between males and females, Jungian analyst M. Esther Harding concludes that couples rarely are willing to take risks for the sake of awareness.[18] Egalitarian couples have learned that risks are necessary in order to communicate.

A commonly held myth is that a husband and wife will intuit each other's needs and fulfill them. A Texas woman believed that her husband "should meet all my needs for companionship and making life interesting," until she realized her expectations were impossible. Friends are another source of support, a more ongoing source than counseling. Friends augment a relationship and add variety to it. A Minnesota husband, Craig, observes:

> I think when you have trouble is when you put too much of your need into a relationship which in no way can hold it. It cannot bear it; no relationship can. Sometimes I think we appreciate the time we have together more because we are split in so many different directions.

Friends and work provide fresh energy and excitement, and Craig and Jennifer note that consequently their marriage "doesn't need to do that stimulation for us." Friends who are at a similar life stage, such as becoming parents for the first time, are a useful source of information and comparison. A Philadelphia couple organized other couples into a support group that met once a week. The group selected a topic and each person contributed reactions to the topic; all the couples benefited from discovering common perceptions.

Often it is difficult for men to establish male support networks, as psychologist Herb Goldberg states: "Our society is full of success driven men... living in a nightmarish world of not knowing whom to trust, unable to find satisfaction in intimate contact, unaware of what they want and feel, and rigidly resistant to opening up in order to find out." [19] As one spouse puts pressure on the other to provide companionship, dependency results, often accompanied by resentment that the other person is not giving enough to fill up the empty places. Some people attempt to feel full or to ignore feeling unsatisfied by eating, drinking, smoking, taking drugs, watching television, buying, working, playing sports—to excess. Men's groups and books that critically examine sex-typed roles provide men a more positive way to establish friendships deeper than sports and drinking buddies, and some men are learning to have close friendships. Feminism has helped women learn a new respect for other women and for female friendships strikingly different from traditional friendships marred by competition over men.

Resolving conflict requires taking time and effort to work at disclosing feelings and disengaging from ingrained patterns of behavior. Because we bring so many overt and covert habits to a relationship, couples must work hard to erase the old tapes, write a new script, risk lowered defenses, and objectively see and hear what their partners actually say. Egalitarian couples bring as many established habits to a marriage as traditional couples do. The difference is that they confront them, talk about them, and negotiate rather than rely on power or manipulation to resolve conflict.

8
Support systems

"We are so atypical that society does not support us in what we're doing."

—*A Delaware husband*

Married for eleven years, he and his wife have one daughter. He is a planner and part-time college teacher, age thirty-three, and she is a journalist and graduate student, age thirty.

"I'm continually amazed at the lack of social structure in keeping with the needs of the people."

—*A Kansas husband*

He and his wife are both in their second marriage. He is a Ph.D. student and she is a professor with three children from her previous marriage. They have two children together. He is aware that having professional jobs and money gives them the resources to hire good child care and not to punch time clocks.

Unsupportive Institutions

In order to have widespread equality between men and women, social and economic structures need to change. As long as a woman with a college degree earns as much as a man who drops out of school after eighth grade, women will not have the bargaining power to demand that men do their share of family work. As long as the woman earns less, the emphasis in the family will be on the man's job. The woman will stay home from her job with a sick child, work part time, and do more housework to balance her lesser monetary contribution.

The association of money and power makes it harder for a wife to state her needs if her husband is earning much more. Gerrit, a Missouri scientist, comments:

It seems like the money thing can a lot of times get in the way. We try not to let it, but a lot of times it does. It's hard for a woman to get a job and feel equal, where she can go out and earn as much in the same amount of time. How do you equalize it at home? By the dollar or by the hour?

When women do find well-paying jobs, many difficulties remain. Employers often expect employees to give priority to work instead of to family. According to Joyce, a New York public relations director:

If your family comes first, then you don't go anywhere in your job. When my husband's boss wants him to go to work at a certain time and he says first he has to find child care, his boss looks at him like he is crazy. "Why can't your wife worry about that?" I resent that but I'm really proud that Steve feels that way. And I see it on the other side. My boss doesn't offer me a business trip because he thinks I would rather be home with my son. And I resent that. We get it on both sides.

Women still do not have earning power equal to men's, and ancient attitudes about separate domestic and public spheres for women and men still prevail. A book published in 1981 for families of business executives extols the joys of the housewife who supports her husband's career and in return has the leisure to do needlepoint, play tennis, and do volunteer work.[1] The authors dismiss reports of the stress experienced by wives and families of corporate executives and state that one spouse's career requires priority—usually it is the husband's. They are correct that many high-level leadership jobs, such as political office, a college or corporate presidency, often assume the wife will be an unpaid appendage who acts as hostess or, in the case of a clergyman's wife, does social service work or teaches Sunday school in the parish. The wife and children are also expected to be able to move anywhere whenever the man is promoted.

The public division of spheres of men and of women is reinforced by such actions as a resolution passed by the Oklahoma
legislature in 1982 urging that textbooks portray women in their
traditional role as housewife and a Father's Day message by
President Reagan in the same year that praised men for being
breadwinners and protectors of their wives and children. The
rhetoric belongs in the nineteenth century.

Dual-career couples face a major conflict when one finds a
better job in another area. Nell, a California administrator, did
not want to interrupt her job when her husband found a position in Pennsylvania, so she decided to commute until her contract is completed. She spends two weeks a month in California
and two weeks in Pennsylvania with her husband and daughter.
Nell describes the impact of her traveling:

> There is constant adjustment, when I leave and when I
> come back. Certainly one of the major problems for Stan
> and me is the loneliness of not being together for two weeks
> each month. Working at home for two weeks is not as in-
> teresting as having the social stimulation of going into the
> office every day.

Her husband says,

> It's very disruptive, to say the least. It's something that
> you adapt to to a certain degree but it's not very pleasant
> to do, it's a stop-gap type of thing. I can't imagine anyone
> doing it and enjoying it. You would have to be a gypsy. It
> all gets back to trying to run two careers in a single family
> —it's difficult.

Another couple found jobs in Milwaukee and Chicago. They
live in between and use the long train ride to do their professional reading. Other couples worry about future moves. "The
location demands are the biggest problem," states Lorraine, a
physician whose attorney husband is in business graduate school
to begin a new career. They hope Neil will be able to find a job
in their present area. One husband quit his job because "the
company was jerking us around the country and we said enough
of that." They do not want to be in the position of friends who

may make a move to New York City, which means the wife "has to live her life around what her husband is going to do. It's a lopsided value and she doesn't feel like what she's done is important."

The American philosophy of work must be changed in the United States, Benjamin Spock asserted in an interview, as families are expected to sacrifice too much for the father's career. He maintains that it is barbaric to move executives and their families every five years, for example, since establishing roots in a community is important to the family. A four- or six-hour workday could be implemented in an industrial age, Spock advocates, so as to give workers more time with their families.

Lillian Rubin observes that only a few privileged professionals can structure their work time so as to share child care. As more women work outside the home, they still do a double job as long as they have to point out that the sink needs cleaning and the baby's diaper needs changing. "I would bet that we are generations away from true sharing. That is not going to happen in my lifetime or yours either," Rubin predicts. Furthermore, widespread changes are not going to be made by a few individuals; rather they require large-scale collective action, an economic revolution in the way work is organized.

Family life and social institutions are not yet synchronized with an egalitarian ideology. The lag between current ideals and traditional patterns of behavior is not surprising, since we are not far removed from the decade of the fifties and its feminine mystique. School and other institutions still assume that a mother will be home during the day. When one of the mothers I interviewed asked her child's teacher if he had tried to call her at work to make an appointment, he replied he had called her only at home. She felt that the school believed that if she were a really available parent, she would be at home. Schools are also behind the times in preparing both sexes to be parents, to cook, to do household and auto repairs, and to train girls in math and science to prepare them for well-paid careers.

The media is reactionary in its stereotyped portrayal of masculine and feminine behavior. A perfume company advertises its product as "the eight-hour perfume for the twenty-four-hour woman," showing a glamorous wife with a high-paid career, an active social life, and superhuman energy. A Washington, D.C., woman feels the current message from Hollywood is that a woman can make a marriage work, have a career, and breast-feed her baby at lunchtime before flying to California, although actually there are not enough hours in the day or enough human energy for all that. ("Stretch-time mothers" is Betty Friedan's term for working mothers under pressure.) The superwoman myth prevents recognition of the services required by egalitarian couples. This myth is dangerous and is "probably going to kill us all," says Patricia Carbine, an editor of Ms. magazine. She believes that in order for men to begin to share housework, the media need to show men involved in taking care of children and in other domestic scenes.

A Washington, D.C., couple saw a television movie where a man cried, and they realized it was the first time they had viewed an actor crying. Lorraine noted, "Men never, never cry on TV about wanting someone to love or feeling estranged. What is on TV patterns enormously what men will be able to do. Seeing a man on TV doing dishes helps." The fact that American children average more time in front of the television than at school gives credence to egalitarian couples' belief in the impact of television on sex-role development.

One of the rare films that presents a positive example of a couple satisfactorily combining work and career is Adam's Rib, which was made in the 1940s when women were encouraged to do paid work to aid the war effort. Katharine Hepburn and Spencer Tracy play a married couple who are both lawyers who find themselves opponents in a trial. She is victorious; a rare occurrence in American literature and film in any era, she is permitted to be professionally successful and attractive and to have a happy marriage. In most American films the woman has to choose between a man and a career; she cannot have both. In An Unmarried Woman, for example, Jill Clayburgh plays a divorced woman who has an affair with appealing Alan Bates, but she does not follow him when he moves to the country because she wants to establish an identity for herself. Examples of dual-career couples who are married parents are almost nonexistent in film and novels.[2]

Counseling and psychology still perpetrate Freudian views about "normal" feminine and masculine behavior. A Texas couple, for example, went to a counselor for help with their adolescent son who was not doing well in school. The wife reports they were told that

> a male needs to contrast his maleness with what it means to be a female. I didn't provide a very good model to contrast against. I was doing all the sorts of things a male is supposed to do—going out and working and having interests. But I think that's the way the world is becoming.

The definition of masculinity as reactive, with a need to repress attributes associated with femininity, is still pervasive. Family counselors also have very little information available to them about how to work with dual-career couples.

Reform Efforts

Efforts to build supports for role-sharing have a long history in North American society, but no reform movement has succeeded in injecting it into the mainstream. The marriages of reformers John Stuart Mill and Harriet Taylor and of Lucy Stone and Henry Blackwell are nineteenth-century examples of equality in domestic relations. Stone and Blackwell deleted the word *obey* from their marriage ceremony in 1855 and she retained her own name.[3] These predecessors of egalitarian couples faced some of the same pressures as today's pioneers face. The men were called "henpecked husbands" who "ought to wear petticoats," but they too were secure in their masculinity. Suffrage leader Elizabeth Cady Stanton noted in 1853 that women's rights "turn on the pivot of the marriage relations." The struggle for women's suffrage, however, overshadowed the effort for changes in family life until the second wave of feminism in the 1960s.

Surprisingly, the nineteenth century provides more experimental alternatives to the isolation of nuclear families than does the twentieth century. In 1895 Charlotte Perkins Gilman observed that nuclear families were an "outgrown way of living [that] keeps us apart." [4] She proposed apartment complexes with dining rooms, paid workers to do cleaning, nurses, kindergartens, roof gardens, libraries, and gymnasiums. She believed that "when parents are less occupied in getting food and cooking it, in getting furniture and dusting it, they may find time to give new thought and new effort to the care of their children." In a novel by Gilman, *What Diantha Did*, the heroine establishes a successful business delivering cooked dinners to families in a fleet of wagons. After her baby's birth she brings the child and its nurse along with her to work. [5]

In *The Grand Domestic Revolution: A History of Feminist Designs for American Homes, Neighborhoods and Cities*, Dolores Hayden describes many nineteenth-century plans for easing domestic workloads. Family dining clubs, for example, hired cooks who delivered food to homes or served it in a dining club at a cost of about $2.70 per week per person. Groups—usually the wives—took turns planning the menu and budget for the week. One such club in Warren, Ohio, maintained a cook, two waitresses, and a dishwasher for more than twenty years. [6]

Communal societies such as New Harmony in Indiana or Charles Fourier's New Jersey Phalanx built community kitchens, laundries, and child-care centers, with kitchenless apartments. The Oneida community organized in New York by John Humphrey Noyes in the 1840s is an example of communal living in which men and women shared nontraditional tasks. Cooperative housing complexes with restaurants and clubhouses were built by trade union groups in New York City in the 1920s; one had a nursery, kindergarten, supervised playground, baby carriage garage, and nearby stores. Unfortunately, business interests, such as those selling appliances, defeated the collective-service movement, since more appliances can be sold to single-family housing occupants than to dwellers in collective housing. Betty Friedan, a major voice in the 1960s resurgence of the women's movement, in 1980 called for the second phase of the movement to work for equality in family life. She advocates adapting the organization of work to suit the needs of parents and to actively involve men in the family. Friedan's controversial book *The Second Stage* provides rhetoric for wide-scale reorganization of society to enable both men and women to live more human lives.

What Families Can Do

Individuals can join forces to share work. Some contemporary families live together in order to provide one another with child care, cooking services, and companionship. A Colorado group of nine, for example, have lived together in two large neighboring houses for eight years. A husband, wife, their two children, and a single male live in one house and a married couple, their child, and another single male live next door. The two married men are brothers.

The group eat together six nights a week and have a common bank account for house-related purchases. Each adult cooks and cleans up once a week. An additional food-related job is done once a month—shopping, bulk food buying, or keeping accounts of expenditures. Both households divide up their cleaning chores: Each person has a weekly job and the group also pay outside workers to do some of the cleaning.

The advantages for the three children and their parents are many. When the children were younger the adult who was doing the cooking came home at 3:00 P.M. and was also responsible for child care. A student was paid by the two sets of parents to baby-sit on the weekdays when an adult could not be home. The "only" child has the opportunity to be close to two other children and all the children have close contact with more than one adult woman and man. The result is that the children "are much more comfortable in dealing with adults, more relaxed and able to hold their own and, therefore, engage much less in the passive-aggressive syndrome" of acting out negative feelings indirectly.

Weekly house meetings for the adults last about two hours. Topics might include conflict with someone in the group, the children's behavior, couple relationships, aging parents, or house problems, more specifically the hectic dinner hour especially when the children were younger; the teenager trying to monopolize dinner conversation; needs for privacy ("If you go out on the deck people will follow you out unless you make it explicit you want to be by yourself"); and the amount of work to expend on a vegetable garden.

Two families share a home in West Virginia. Each family is responsible for cooking three days a week. The adults find discussing the day's events at dinner "peps each other up." Child care for the five children is shared, so none of the four adults feels overwhelmed by child-care responsibility. At dinner a couple can decide on the spur of the moment that they want to go to a movie and do not have to search for a baby sitter.

Regarding problems that arise the couples comment, "You don't know how you're supposed to act," because models do not exist for nonrelated adults sharing family life. "You have to work it out until it is comfortable." Being structured also requires that one person gets dinner on the table at 6:00 or 7:00 P.M., even if he or she does not find it convenient that day. As the children grew older, the families found their house with one bathroom too cramped, and one family is moving to the country.

A San Francisco group jointly bought a small apartment building and converted the nine units into six by knocking out walls. Two families with children have the larger five-room apartments and two single men live in the intact single apartments. They work together on the building and yard half a day a month, borrow cooking implements and use each others ovens when entertaining, give the children freedom to visit the other families in the building, have pot-luck brunches and dinners, celebrate holidays together, share reading material, and provide partners for sports such as racquetball. Meetings, in conjunction with pot-luck dinners, are held every two weeks to discuss house business, with a rotating chairperson. A bulletin board in the hall gets a lot of use, with queries such as "Has anyone been to the new

Chinese restaurant?" or "Should we buy flowers for the yard?"

Another couple with an infant bought a duplex together with a single parent. They each cook once a week, and a neighbor cooks the fourth night. An intercom system permits easy child care when one of the parents goes out. They also do errands for each other, share some baby equipment and a laundry room, and take care of each other's pets. Areas of friction arise over scheduling dinner preparation, different attitudes toward child care, and the ability to say no to a request to baby-sit. A safety valve is knowing that the door between the two units can be closed, with the other family's pet and baby behind it, and privacy reclaimed.

Three families built homes near each other in rural Washington state. Each family cooks for the others at least once a week. One night a week the older children cook a dinner for all the children to eat together. They have a cooperative child-care system paid for with play money (a dollar an hour for one child and $1.50 for two) and they share leisure activities.

Some families live in groups bonded by a political and spiritual crusade, such as the Catholic Workers' peace movement. Eight people sharing that ideology lived together in New York City. The couple I interviewed later moved to Connecticut where they share a house with two women. The husband explains, "I don't think I could handle a nuclear family situation. In this society there are so many pressures from so many directions. The more heads there are together the easier it is for people to deal with their problems." The kinds of conflicts they face are mainly small ones, such as whether to buy margarine or butter, whole milk or powdered.

Some couples do not live in the same location but have a friendship network. For example, six members of a women's group act as an extended family for each other by celebrating holidays together or helping one another in times of sickness. A Montana couple are thinking of bringing a retired person into their home to do child care in exchange for room and board and a family environment; the wife believes that "people are isolated into little units. I would like to see more support of each other by sharing child care and other tasks." A Michigan family shares meals with other couples two nights a week and would like to do it more often.

Families can also form cooperatives to share child care, marketing, and transportation. One family joined with others to pay a teenager four dollars an hour to take care of four children after school. Families can provide back-up telephone numbers for school-age children during work hours, hire a teacher for after-school child care in a local church or synagogue, or hire a college student to drive children, do errands, and cook dinner. Parents in San Francisco organized a Child Care Switchboard, providing referral information, a resource center, toy lending, and a newsletter.

Contemporary architects and planners are reviving Charlotte Perkins Gilman's criticism of the nuclear family isolated in a single frame house or apartment as unnecessarily burdening women with housework. A remodeled city block, consisting of forty households, envisioned by architect Dolores Hayden, would provide the following services: a day-care facility including after-school care; a laundromat; a kitchen providing meals for children in day care, for the elderly, and take-out dinners; a cooperative grocery store; a garage with a "dial-a-ride" service; a garden; and an office providing home help for the elderly and the sick.[7]

Some of Hayden's vision already exists in the planned community of Reston, in northern Virginia, where one of the couples I interviewed lives. In 1967 they left their jobs in New York City to live in Reston because of the services and sense of community it offers. Reston is an example of how much help an intelligently planned town can provide to families. The original developer was Robert E. Simon, who conceived of an alternative to the haphazard suburban sprawl. Forty thousand individuals lived there in 1982, with plans for further growth by the profit-making corporations that own it.

For recreation and beauty, Reston has four lakes with boating facilities, two ponds (used for ice skating in the winter), golf courses, walkways through woods, horse-riding paths and stables, and swimming pools, tennis courts, playgrounds, and numerous sports fields. Outdoor sculptures and wall murals add to the enjoyment of walking through the community. The maintenance is paid for through a yearly homeowner's fee of $115 and users' fees for the swimming pool ($60 a summer per family) and tennis courts ($12 a year).

Housing clusters around four village centers containing stores, offices, and community meeting centers. Walkways make the center accessible to all residents. The meeting space is frequently used by community groups. For example, when the wife I interviewed became interested in feminism she put a notice in one of the two local newspapers and held weekly seminars of sixty to seventy people in the meeting space. No one had far to travel and the space was easy to obtain.

Services for child care are abundant. Two centers for infants provide a one-to-four staff-to-children ratio. Twenty-two day-care centers are available. The one attended by the children in the family I interviewed became parent operated after the original nonprofit Reston foundation established child-care centers and then withdrew. One hundred families currently participate in that facility. A walkway connects the center to the elementary school for after-school care, and a bus is also available to transport schoolchildren to the center in poor weather. Three of the elementary schools provide extended days, in which teachers supervise crafts and sports after school hours.

To meet the needs of many families, some of the housing was federally subsidized for low-income families. To integrate the community, Reston residents also recruited black families from Washington, D.C.; consequently, about 14 percent of the community is black. The federal government built a geological survey center in Reston, which provides nearby employment. Almost half the adult population could work in Reston if they chose, although many commute to jobs in Washington, D.C. Residents find the community beautiful, convenient, and friendly.

In Berkeley, California, residents of Derby Street join their backyards to create a shared play area. The parklike space, called

The Meadow, gives children a large and safe playground with jungle gyms and other equipment. Residents fence in their front yards to keep children from the streets. A child-care center provided care for neighborhood children, with indoor space donated by one of the families and with a staff of paid child-care professionals and parents. The center closed in 1982 when many of the children went on to elementary school, including those whose parents had lent the use of their home. Closeness results between the children of The Meadow as they play in their common space, and parents can share supervision of their children.

What Employers Can Do

Kathy, an attorney with two young children, tells herself to "slow down, the world is going to be there for a long time." But it is hard for her "not to run when someone else is trotting next to me" at work. If employers recognized that many of their employees are parents of young children and wish to participate in their development, employers could relax expectations for rapid career advancement for parents of young children and could provide parental leave, flexible work hours, and permanent part-time jobs, and they could stop routinely transferring professional employees.

Flexible working hours are crucial to permit both parents to spend time with their children, to stay home with a sick child, to attend school functions or children's medical appointments, and so on. Only about 12 percent of U.S. workers (7.6 million in 1980) have the opportunity for flex-time or other flexible work hours. About 1.9 million workers have compressed work weeks of three, four, or four and one-half days. Companies that offer flex-time tend to cluster in the fields of insurance, finance, and real estate and the federal government also provides alternative scheduling. European firms are ahead of American companies. Flex-time began in West Germany in the 1960s; currently 50 percent of white-collar workers in Germany have flexible work hours, as do 40 percent of Swiss workers and 30 percent of

French workers. By 1975 about 6,000 European companies provided flex-time. Firms find that flex-time results in greater productivity that makes up for higher utility costs.

Certain jobs currently permit workers' control over their working hours. Some salespeople can schedule their own hours and can have offices at home. An Ohio salesman explains, "If I needed to be home I stayed home. I worked my business around our daughter, using the telephone at home." People who are self-employed often enjoy control over their hours, as did an optometrist whose office hours could be altered to suit his children's needs.

Two New York attorneys set up their own office on the ground floor of their home because they got tired of not seeing each other enough. Previously, when they worked for large corporations, they left for work at 7:00 A.M. and got home at 8:00 P.M. to see each other for two or three hours. They were "rolling in money" but they felt it was impossible to raise their son and to enjoy each other as well. Now they often close their office in the afternoon when their son comes home from day care. Combining office and home has its own drawbacks: Their son is prohibited from playing with phones and files and is supposed to be quiet when he comes back from day care, for example. (They do permit him to answer the phones after working hours to discourage clients from calling.) Some of their clients feel it is unprofessional to have a home office, with cats walking in and out or the little boy yelling from upstairs.

Some skilled workers in technical areas also can determine their own working hours. After his second son was born, a computer programmer went to work after 11:30 A.M. so he could share in child care. An aerospace scientist sometimes stays home until his children leave for school.

An attorney for a large corporation decided to work from 6:30 A.M. to 3:30 P.M. in order to have afternoons at home. A director of a counseling center arranged for her secretary to work from 7:00 A.M. to 2:30 P.M. so the secretary can be home when her daughter arrives from school. Shift work can also allow parents more time with their children. A nurse, for example, goes to work at 2:00 P.M.; her children are at a day-care center from 2:00 until 4:30 when their father gets home from work. To avoid being consumed by their jobs, some couples find companies that offer work three or four days a week or a compressed work week of four days.

Smaller companies often have sympathetic employers: A marketing director who gave birth to her second child worked for a small consulting firm that was understanding of her desire to combine motherhood and career. The firm arranged for her to work twenty-five hours a week for four months. She appreciated the time to become accustomed to her son and to mother him. Another new mother, one of four partners in a law firm, could not find a competent baby sitter. When she explained why she needed to work part time, her partners agreed.

Part-time work for both parents of small children seems ideal to those who do it.[8] An Iowa couple arranged that one parent would work in the morning and the other in the afternoon. They exchange their infant at the mother's work place: "The baby is usually there only fifteen minutes, but all the other secretaries are trying to convince her to stay longer. They told me I could have my baby at work any time I want." That couple think that having flexible jobs in a university setting contributes significantly to their ability to share child care so easily and naturally. A Michigan husband and wife, Marlene and Syd, work twenty hours a week each; he works Monday to Wednesday as a carpenter and she works Wednesday evening, Thursday, and Friday as a therapist. They agree that part-time work is the key that enables them to be truly egalitarian. "Marlene and I have a perspective on career. Being away from it five to eight years out of a whole lifetime isn't a long time," Syd explains. A Pennsylvania couple alternate days at work in order to be able to have close contact with their toddler. They cope with their reduced income by finding enjoyment in watching TV, taking a bath together, or going for a walk rather than going out to a film or to dinner. Another couple, in California, like the hours of part-time work but are giving it up because the pay is not enough: "It often seems like we continually run as fast as we can, to just stay in one place."

One way to find part-time work is to share a job, as did a French teacher married to a music teacher. They were each home with their daughter half the day and teaching the other half. Another couple decided to split a bus-driving job. Joann explains:

> Both of us have college educations and could have pursued professional careers but instead we are working as bus drivers for $4.36 an hour because we want to share child care, have time together, and do the garden. You have to decide what is really important in life. You can't have large incomes and both be around a whole lot to take care of the kid. I think it is really unfair to expect either person to work all day and then come home and do child care with no time for himself.

Her husband, Rich, adds:

> Now that we are in the industrial age there is no reason for people to work eight hours a day for their daily bread. To have a worthwhile income with all the technology shouldn't take more than four or five hours' labor five days a week. That kind of a change in our social and economic system would enable people to take more of a hand in child raising. Actually, the intensive part of child raising is that first five to six years. I'm not going to be needed around here as much after the first six years and I'll have time to go and do some other things. I think a lot of people feel resentment toward the amount of time a small child takes because it is interfering with their career plans because of the way things are set up. It would be very helpful if things weren't set up this way.

One West Virginia couple shared an administrative job. They experimented with alternating by day and by week: "After a week on the job you thought how good it would be to stay home and read a book. At the end of that week you'd be saying 'I want to get out of here, these kids are driving me crazy.' I don't think we ever had a more pleasurable work situation."

Two pastors in Minnesota successfully share a ministry. Another couple shared a church job in Ohio as director of Christian education, but the church members had difficulty adjusting to a nontraditional pattern. They expected the husband to work full time and did not count the wife's work as important. When members telephoned for him, for example, the secretary would say, "He's at home this afternoon taking care of the baby," not mentioning that his wife was available in the office.

But most couples do not have access to job sharing or part-time jobs. To discover corporate attitudes toward two-career family issues, the Catalyst Career and Family Center surveyed 374 of the top Fortune companies.[9] The survey found that only 9 percent of the respondents thought companies should not be involved in dual-career family problems and 51 percent thought their companies had the resources to assist in solving them. The results are given in the following table.

	Percent Companies That Offer Benefit (N = 374)	Percent Respondents Who Favor Benefit (N = 374)
Flexible working hours	37	73
Maternity benefits	96	94
Paternity benefits	9	26
Flexible work places	8	35
Sick leave for children's illness	29	44
Leave without pay, position assured	65	69
On-site child care	1	20
Subsidies for child care	1	9
Monetary support for child-care facilities	19	54
Cafeteria approach to benefits (workers can select from among various benefits)	8	62

Forty-two percent of the 374 corporations surveyed thought they were not yet affected by dual-career family issues. Traditional attitudes are reflected by the president of General Motors, Thomas Murphy, in a 1980 speech made before his retirement. He stated:

> I have a gnawing feeling that American society today is coming unglued simply because the essential mucilage of the family is evaporating. It appears to me that the traditional values of this most elemental foundation of our society are disappearing . . .
>
> Today the role of the homemaker—the role that most of our mothers and our wives filled to perfection—is classified as lacking fulfillment. And the working partnership of breadwinner and homemaker . . . has been relegated to the scrap heap . . .[10]

Murphy reiterates the nineteenth-century idealization of the woman's place in the home. He is preoccupied with fears of changes in the family caused by the entry of women into the work force, rather than examining the benefits of men sharing more in family life. Murphy blames the "me decade" of the 1970s. If his attitude is representative of the attitudes of the heads of large American corporations, rapid progress will not occur. When I asked about General Motors' personnel policies, such as parental leave, in 1981, the public affairs manager replied, "We're not sure what you mean by 'parental leave.' Perhaps it applies also to flexible working hours."

In addition to learning about parental leave, employers can adopt these policies for working parents:

1. Paid parental leave and an option for extended unpaid leave (for adopting parents as well).
2. Sick leave may be used to care for sick children.
3. Personal leave days, as for use in attending a child's important school function.
4. Reimbursement of child-care expenses incurred by business-related travel and overtime.

5. Child care: Provide centers at work, support existing centers, or purchase corporate slots in existing centers. Provide referral information, establish an after-school care center and programs for school holiday care.

6. Permit personal phone calls to and from children during work hours. Have family days when children can visit and learn about their parents' work place.

7. "Cafeteria" benefit plans, in which employees select the benefits that best meet their family's needs. Only one spouse needs to sign up for family health insurance, for example. Credits for child care could be substituted.

8. Flexible work hours: flex-time; matching working hours with school hours; four-day weeks of ten-hour days, and so on.

9. Part-time jobs that are permanent and have fringe benefits, job sharing, or split-level jobs shared by a professional and a clerical worker.

10. Flexible work places; permit some work done at home or a task system without a set number of hours at work.

11. Spouse job placement programs for transferred employees and assistance in buying and selling homes. Permit hiring family members.[11]

Some U.S. employers have progressive policies. The Ford Foundation was perhaps the first employer to provide twenty-six weeks of parental leave (for adoption as well). The first eight weeks are with full pay and the remaining eighteen weeks without. Parents are also reimbursed 50 percent for child-care costs incurred during working hours if both parents work full time, if one is a full-time student, or if the worker is the sole support of the family and the total family income does not exceed $25,000. Parents can also receive $100 a year for four consultations with a child-care specialist. A bill to require all companies to give men up to four months' unpaid paternity leave was introduced into the California legislature in 1982. CBS permits unpaid paternity leave, as does Procter and

Gamble, American Telephone and Telegraph, Security Pacific
Bank, and the New York City school system. *Atlantic Monthly*
magazine staff get parental leave; at *Atlantic* and *Ms.* magazine,
parents are not prohibited from having children at work. Good-
measure, a Boston firm, permits children at work: the father of
a six-month-old feels she "benefits from a lot of stimulation."
Child care is provided at work by Control Data in Minnesota:
The company pools resources with two other firms and shares
costs with parents. Connecticut Savings Bank in New Haven
provides flexible work hours that match school hours. Levi-
Strauss in San Francisco offers flex-time, as does the city of
Berkeley.

The U.S. government provides permanent part-time jobs for
federal employees and experimented with flexible and compressed working hours in a three-year program funded by a 1978
law. More than 325,000 employees participated in the experimental program. A survey of the employees found that 90 percent wished to continue their flexible work hours permanently
and Congress complied. Working mothers with flex-time schedules experience no less stress than before, although other workers
feel less pressured.[12] Federal employees also have access to nine
child-care centers in Washington, D.C., where employees ad-
minister the programs while the agency provides the space without charge.

Organizations are at work collecting information about alternative work patterns. New Ways to Work, a San Francisco
group, promotes work options for individuals and organizations
and provides information such as a bibliography about job sharing and permanent part-time employment. It maintains a resource file for potential job-sharing partners and provides staff
training for companies interested in job sharing. In Seattle, Focus on Part-Time Careers helped place over 5,000 job seekers.
The National Council for Alternative Work Patterns in Washington, D.C., provides information to employers about flexible
work scheduling and produces a newsletter and a directory of
organizations that have flex-time, compressed work week, permanent part-time, and job-sharing programs. Catalyst, in New

York City, provides up-to-date information in its newsletters and books about progressive corporate policies for dual-career parents. The American Association of University Women has published *Families and Work Guide*, which is based on its multifaceted study project. The Fatherhood Project at Bank Street College of Education in New York City is researching paternity leaves and on-site child care, among other issues affecting fathers.

Employers can also aid employees by providing services such as those developed in socialist countries. In Cuba, factories have dining rooms, some have laundry services, and stores fill workers' shopping bags with requested items during the working day. In China, factories provide canteens that offer inexpensive meals, child-care facilities for infants, and breaks for nursing mothers. U.S. employers need to catch up with the movement of women into the work force, which necessitates a rethinking of a work environment structured for a working man with a wife at home.

What Governments Can Do

Equal Rights
A couple who shared equally in a progressive Iowa university town found their lives much changed when they moved to a rural Colorado town. They feel "frustration in our ability to make things more equal because of the social fabric and the way things are organized in this community." They visited twenty day-care centers, for example, and could not find one that gave their daughters adequate stimuli, so the wife quit her job to care for them. In contrast, an American couple who lived in Saskatchewan noted the importance of the political climate in attitudes toward role-sharing. "Living in that social environment with our friends who acted on Chinese Marxist thought about women holding up half the sky was very dramatic in terms of splitting responsibility," Rex stated. The province's governing Social Democratic party (until 1982) had socialist roots and imple-

mented legislation providing public health care, regulation of utilities, and hiring quotas for affirmative action groups, as well as paid maternity leave. (Canadian provinces have more autonomy than U.S. states.)

For the past six decades the White House Conference on Children and Youth passed almost identical proposals: a guaranteed basic income, maternal and child health care, maternity leave, sick leave for parents of ill children, provision for more day care, after-school programs, job programs for teenagers, and visiting housekeeper services for the sick and elderly. Its emphasis in 1980 was on personnel policies that consider the needs of families, including flexible working hours, part-time jobs, and reasonable leave and transfer programs. None has been implemented. The United States is the only major industrial nation without prenatal, maternity, child, and family health and day-care policies.

An Equal Rights Amendment in the United States would help create a climate of commitment to equality. Some states make egalitarian marriage difficult when they designate the husband as head of the household, with legal charge of financial matters and of where the family lives and with a right to his wife's domestic and sexual services. In Ontario, Canada, a married man can claim credit for child-care expenses only if his wife is disabled, one of the reasons a couple who live together in that province view marriage "as a status which diminishes and jeopardizes personal rights." Cuba, in contrast, has legislation that requires each spouse to "participate in governing the home and cooperate toward its best possible care." [13] If only one spouse works outside the home, the wage earner is not "relieved of the obligation of cooperating with the housework and child care." A spouse who feels his or her rights are being violated can seek redress in court or request help from a union or neighborhood committee.

The Cuban constitution of 1976 states that marriage rests on the "equal rights and obligations of both spouses, both of whom must attend to the home..." The constitution also mandates paid maternity leave, health care, birth control counseling, early-

term abortions on demand, and day care. Employers are required by law to provide women eighteen weeks of paid maternity leave and extended leave without pay.

Equal rights legislation does not ensure equal work at home, however. While in socialist countries women have legal rights and almost all women do paid work, men still do not assume their fair share of family work. In the Soviet Union, for example, studies of family roles from the 1920s to the 1960s showed no tendency for men to assume a greater share of domestic labor.[14] Socialist theory teaches that women are liberated by doing paid productive work and by the socialization of housework to prevent them from bearing two jobs. In China, for example, urban service centers, usually staffed by retired people, look after old people and children, providing the latter with help with homework and after-school supervision, counsel married couples, provide practical information, and do laundry, housework and other chores. Socialist countries have fallen short, however, by not allocating enough resources for professional child care, food preparation, and other paid household services. If women bear a double load, they are not liberated, their marriages are not equal, and they do not have time to assume political power.

Child Care

All other industrial nations provide more support for working parents than the United States does. The U.S. government is also unique among other industrial nations in its neglect of child-care facilities. Since President Nixon's veto of child-care legislation in 1971, on the grounds that it would cause the demise of the family and "collectivization" of child rearing, no federal action has been taken despite projections that by 1990 ten million children under the age of six will need day care. Only 10 to 15 percent of American families have access to day-care centers (900,000 children in 1978). One in five nonworking mothers of preschool children would like to be employed but cannot find adequate child care.[15]

The U.S. has such a poor record of day care for the children

of working parents that many children are "latchkey kids" who
have no supervision after school. In San Francisco, for example,
there are only 2,367 slots in licensed child-care programs for after-
school care, while approximately 35,750 children age four to fourteen have working mothers.[16]

A couple in Ontario, in contrast, feel their work as parents is
lightened by public services such as a good public transit system.
Their children come and go on their own without any need for
chauffeuring. A professor in Quebec gets twenty weeks of maternity leave at 93 percent of her usual salary, as do other teachers
in Quebec schools and colleges. Her husband gets five days' paid
leave after the birth of their child. Since 1971 the Canadian
federal and provincial governments have been providing seventeen weeks' maternity leave, through unemployment insurance.
In a 1981 strike, postal workers won an increase to 93 percent of
their pay during maternity leave. Provinces may add to the federal benefit (60 percent of average earnings, with a maximum
of $189 a week).

The Canadian government, like European countries, grants
families a child benefit payment; the amount varies in different
provinces but averages around $20 a month. The Saskatchewan
government subsidizes day-care homes for children older than
eighteen months but the waiting lists are so long that parents
sign up their children the day they are born. Day-care workers
are obliged to take a forty-hour training course and are paid mini-
mum wages by the province. Unfortunately, the low wages do
not attract highly educated workers.

Most European countries provide numerous benefits for parents: cash payments for each child, paid maternity leave ranging
from three months (Denmark) to three years (Hungary), but
averaging six months, paid leave to take care of a sick child, and
free public preschool.[17] France provides the most comprehensive
day care among Western countries. Ninety-five percent of children over age three are in free public preschool programs. Centers
are open from 7:00 A.M. to 7:30 P.M. for working parents. Thirty-
two percent of two-year-olds attend programs, which are available

from age three months (with long waiting lists). Some centers are in public buildings and some in subsidized licensed homes. Few programs are at work sites because parents prefer to have the centers close to home. Low-income families with children under age three receive a supplementary family allowance, working mothers receive a sixteen-week paid maternity leave, and either parent may take up to two years leave without pay to care for a new baby.

West Germany provides twenty-four weeks' maternity leave, paid by national health insurance and employers, and paid leave to care for sick children. In East Germany, 90 percent of three- to six-year-olds are in full-day preschools and 60 percent of children under age three are in child-care programs. Builders of new housing are required to include day-care and school facilities. The support for working mothers does not, however, extend to fathers but instead perpetuates a double standard for men's and women's work. A cash grant is given to a mother at the birth of her child; maternity leave is twenty-six weeks with full pay and can be extended with no pay until the child is one year old. If a mother cannot find child care she receives about 40 percent of her average wage until a space opens up. Working mothers are also granted three personal leave days a month to catch up with family work.

In the United States, communities could be built with the needs of families with children in mind, such as is done in new French towns that include play areas, schools, health care, eating facilities run by the management or as a concession, laundries, and libraries. City governments can encourage building contractors to include community services in suburban developments. In Atlanta, Georgia, for example, tennis courts, swimming pools, and community recreation centers are owned and operated by homeowners' associations in developments built in the last five years.

Schools can extend their support for children of working parents by establishing programs for summer, school holidays, and after school. They can extend kindergarten hours and provide schooling for three-year-olds. Parents in Brookline, Massachusetts, designed an after-school program for eight elementary schools. A board of parents shares administration, including fund raising and staff hiring, with school principals. Elementary school children can be taught domestic survival skills such as simple cooking and comparison shopping. Kindergarten pupils in Cranston, Rhode Island, learn how to do laundry, mending, setting the table, starting dinner, vacuuming, and building a bookcase. The boys are just as involved as girls in the HELP program (Homemaking Elementary Learning Procedure). Programs similar to HELP are becoming popular in eastern coast schools. A course on infant care for boys is part of a $500,000 Fatherhood Project funded by private foundations and headed by James Levine at the Bank Street College of Education, New York City. Such educational programs are needed to counteract the effect of resistant public officials like California's commissioner of fair employment practices, who stated in 1974, "I think this women's lib stuff is fine . . . but for a father to get leave is completely ridiculous." [18]

Taxation

The "marriage tax" in the United States penalizes dual-earner families. Until 1982, if each spouse earned $20,000 they jointly paid $1,872 more in taxes than a single person earning $40,000. They also paid more in Social Security taxes: If they each earned $30,000 they paid $3,950 while a single person who earned $60,000 paid $1,975 in Social Security taxes. [19] For 1982 earnings, married taxpayers could take a 5 percent deduction, up to a maximum of $1,500. For 1982 and thereafter, they can take a 10 percent deduction, up to $3,000.

The Economic Recovery Tax Act of 1981 eased the child-care burden. The law allows taxpayers a maximum tax credit of $2,400 for one child and $4,800 for two or more, depending on income. It also permits employers to deduct child care as a business expense either by establishing a center for workers, paying a community center, or paying employees directly for baby-sitting costs. The employee does not have to pay taxes on the reimbursement.

The Swedish Model

Sweden is perhaps the most advanced country in the world in its support for working parents. In July 1980 I traveled to Stockholm, with my baby in a back carrier, to find out if the programs looked as good in practice as they do on paper. They did: As I (and Renee Kogel) interviewed leaders in unions, government agencies, women's organizations, journalism, and architecture, I discovered that the government is committed to working for equality between women and men. Its goal is to change attitudes that result in a sex-segregated work force, a double job for women, and the resultant lack of time for women to assume leadership positions. The Swedish equality programs are an impressive model for concrete steps toward a more equitable society.

Sweden gave official commitment to shared roles in the late 1960s, partly as a result of the groundwork laid earlier in the decade by thinkers such as Eva Moberg. Swedish experimentation with social programs was led by the socialist Social Democratic party, in power from the 1930s to 1976 and again in 1982. (Sweden is a mixed economy with 80 percent private ownership of industry.) Although its leadership is predominantly male, the leaders are sincere about the need for sex-role equality, perhaps because the discussion since the 1950s has been couched in terms of freeing men to participate in family life and to share the burden of breadwinning, as well as the need to relieve women of their double job.

Prosperity is another major ingredient in Sweden's progressiveness, and the current recession is indeed slowing social programs. Sweden stayed out of this century's wars, it has abundant resources and a small, homogeneous, well-educated population—about one third of the adults participate in continuing education classes. The sparse population and seafaring tradition, with men away from home for long periods, have meant that women's work has long been valued. Furthermore, Christianity came late to Sweden, and when it did it was unaccompanied by the Catholic cult of the Virgin that puts women on a confining pedestal. These conditions are difficult to match.

In terms of actual practice, the Swedish job market is highly gender-segregated, with women's work earning 90 percent of what men earn. Since women earn less, their jobs are more expendable and they are the ones who take parental leave and who work part time. Part-time workers do get full benefits, such as a five-week paid vacation. Women take responsibility for most of the child care and housework. One study of Swedish working couples found that 51 percent of the women worked twenty hours or more a week in their homes while only 18 percent of the men did, and studies do not show much difference in the participation of younger men.[20]

A difference between the United States and Sweden is that even the most conservative Swedish political party is dedicated to working for equality and would not dream of advocating that women's place is in the home. The nonsocialist coalition government, which replaced the Social Democrats in 1976, took steps to integrate the labor market by continuing to give grants to companies that start new branches that attempt to hire 40 percent of the nontraditional workers and by funding experimental programs to train women workers in technical work. A 1980 law prohibits discrimination in employment and requires employers to actively promote equality. A female ombudsman currently oversees the implementation of the law. Secondary school students are required to visit nontraditional work places, technical areas for girls and helping professions for boys.

An equality committee oversees all the programs, suggesting legislation and acting as a pressure group. In addition to promoting equity in the job market and in the schools, the committee works on pilot programs such as one encouraging female involvement in sports and another campaigning against sexist advertising. In existence since 1972, the equality committee is housed under the ministry of labor and has a secretariat of ten persons and several advisory groups.

In Sweden the community shares the responsibility for children beginning in infancy. Parents may attend free classes in the care of infants for ten meetings before the birth and 10 meetings afterward. Prenatal care and birthing are paid for by national health insurance. District nurses visit new parents to answer their questions and examine the newborn. Young children also receive instruction in child care in elementary schools. Parental leave from work is provided at about 90 percent of the normal salary (with a ceiling) for nine months after the birth of an infant, and in addition parents may spread out the equivalent of three more months of reduced work hours until the child is eight. A father receives ten days' leave even if the mother is using their parental leave. The employer pays for 85 percent and the state pays the balance. (If a parent was not working outside the home, he or she receives about $8.50 a day.)

Because only 12 percent of the fathers take advantage of the parental leave, the national insurance agency marshaled a poster campaign to encourage men to stay home with their infants by portraying a well-known wrestler taking care of a baby. Teachers of the prenatal classes encourage fathers to take leaves. Proposals have been made to require the mother and father to share the last six months (unless the mother is a single parent). Parents may also take up to sixty days off work per year, with pay, to stay home with a sick or needy child under age twelve.

Parents have the option to work a six-hour workday until their child's eighth birthday. Wages are reduced, however, so many single and low-income parents cannot take advantage of this law. Also, it is usually women who reduce their work hours, which hinders their career advancement. The Social Democratic party advocates a six-hour workday at regular pay to truly equalize sex roles, but no one sees this as economically feasible in the near future.

Although Sweden is committed to parental leave shared by both parents and to day care for all children who need it, the burden of parenting still falls on the mother. Almost half of the working women in Sweden work part time because of their double role, but at least they have the option to work part time.

Child care is provided by local municipalities, supplemented by state subsidies, with a sliding scale for parents' payment. The adult-child ratio averages one to four. Since there are not enough places in these centers, government funds also subsidize child care provided by private individuals in their homes. "Free-time centers" provide supervision for some children after school. The government voted in 1976 to establish 100,000 new places in pre-school care and 50,000 in after-school care, but economic recession has slowed the planned expansion of day-care centers.

Socialization of responsibility for children can also be seen in the 1979 government ban on the sale of war toys and its ban on corporal and mental punishment of children, including humiliating treatment and ridicule (no specific penalty was established; the intent was to express public opinion against archaic means of disciplining children). A government commission on children's rights proposed further legislation establishing a children's ombudsman in every community, the right for children to have legal assistance in divorce and custody hearings, and the duty of each municipality to provide counseling in divorce proceedings, with joint custody the preferred disposition.

To prevent unwanted pregnancy, free contraceptive counseling is available at clinics and hospitals, which also dispense free or low-cost contraceptives. Midwives are trained to give advice about birth control and can prescribe birth control pills. Some school doctors and nurses also provide information about contraceptives.

Living conditions are an important factor in shared parenting. Swedes recognize that isolated suburban dwellings make it more difficult to combine work and child rearing and that families need access to services and recreation. Proposals to solve this problem include decentralizing work places by bringing light industry and public jobs to the suburbs, developing even better mass transit, and building common rooms in apartment buildings for recreation and meeting space.

"Family hotels" have existed in Sweden since the 1930s. Interest in them recently revived, and new units are being built by various municipal governments, combining the needs of the elderly and of families with young children. In Stockholm, I visited the Hässelby family hotel, which has numerous common facilities and services. The apartments are built around several courtyards where children can play. One wing of the complex contains the communal services: kitchen, dining room, laundry, lounge, church, beauty parlor, grocery shop, sauna, weaving room, carpentry room, photography darkroom, and a meeting place for interest groups such as a bridge club, a book group, a film club, a theater group, and other activities such as fairy-tale readings for children every Friday afternoon.

A new landlord stopped providing services, and residents' struggle with him became publicized in 1979 when they took control of the common rooms in spite of the landlord's calling in police to try to stop them. A dozen tenant teams are responsible for ordering food, cooking, serving dinner buffet style, and doing the dishes. Coupon books for fifteen dinners cost 200 Swedish crowns (forty dollars). One team cooks for one hundred people once every other week: The food team enjoys using the time together to talk. Dinners can be festive occasions, as when birthdays are celebrated and the celebrant invites friends from outside the apartment complex to join the group at dinner.

A day-care center and after-school center for children age seven to ten are on the premises, run by the municipal government with the agreement that the family hotel pays the housing costs in return for its children being given priority admission to the center. Parents are especially grateful for the community support that permits them to be late getting home from work because they know the children can go to the after-school center, then to the community dining room for dinner and eat with familiar people. Teenage baby sitters are easy to find, and parents trade child care with each other. Old people act as grandparents, and children play with each other in the corridors because families know each other well.

The advantage in terms of sex roles, according to journalist Ami Lönnroth who lives in the Hässelby collective house, is that patriarchal patterns of behavior dissolve because all adults are involved in cooking and cleaning up. Men with chauvinist attitudes are teased by others. Several men at Hässelby who used to think they were above such mundane work have changed their attitudes. Getting adolescents to do their fair share of the work is more of a problem. The only disadvantage of living in a group that Lönnroth could think of is the social pressure: like a small village that views leaving the group in the evenings as disloyal, or a couple having marital problems feel in the spotlight as they walk into dinner.

More collective houses are being built in Stockholm and in Linköping and Göteborg. In 1977 planning for construction in Linköping was shared by a tenants' group that grew out of a women's discussion group and by municipal authorities in charge of housing and social welfare. The 180 apartments integrate facilities for the elderly (about thirty-five apartments), the physically and mentally handicapped (nine apartments), and the rest for other families. Children adopt older people as their local grandparents. Within the complex are a cafeteria, a library and game room, a carpentry shop, a weaving room, and child-care facilities, although it is sufficient for only half the children who need it. A staff of thirty-five takes care of the children and the elderly. Neighbors also use the child-care facilities and home helpers bring in the elderly. The rental cost is similar to any modern apartment and rent subsidies are given to low-income people such as single parents.

In Göteborg, an unused apartment house was converted to a family hotel by remodeling one floor and adding a community kitchen and dining room. Tenants—fifty-three adults and thirty-three children—meet together once a month and organize into work groups.

Sweden provides a model of steps toward equity between men and women that are possible now. A country whose official policy is equality, it provides the support systems necessary to be a parent, to have a career, and to hold positions of leadership. The structure is built but attitudes still need changing.

Other Models

To create a rational society that benefits those who live in it, a vision for the future is necessary. Authors of science fiction novels provide some possible goals: shared child care, alternatives to the isolated family, and freedom from sex-role stereotyping. Aldous Huxley's novel *Island* (1962) is a male vision of a society that provides more supports for individuals than our own society presently provides.

In *Island* and in feminist future fantasies, a common theme is communal responsibility for child care rather than placing almost total responsibility on the biological mother. A radical feminist goal for the future, as explained by Shulamith Firestone in *The Dialectic of Sex* (1970), is a contractual agreement between various adults and children living in a household. No roles are determined by gender—not even birthing. Marge Piercy's *Woman on the Edge of Time* (1976) illustrates some of Firestone's goals. Piercy describes a Massachusetts town in the year 2037 in which there are no stereotyped sex roles. Three adults join together to mother a baby. All three of the mothers, regardless of their gender, take hormones so that they can nurse their baby. Children live in their own communal house, cared for by adults who are especially skilled with children, while each adult has her or his own living space. Children are not segregated into schools but learn by interacting with adults. Meals are provided in common dining rooms where villagers take turns working.

Older children also live in their own centers, maintaining close contact with their parents, in Ursula LeGuin's *The Dispossessed* (1974), and the children are cared for by the whole community in Dorothy Bryant's *The Kin of Ata Are Waiting for You* (1971). These novels are not blueprints for altering society and would seem far-fetched to most readers, yet they are useful for sparking discussion and reexamining our inherited assumptions about family life. Science fiction, histories of nineteenth-century experiments with collective services, accounts of other countries' supports for families, reports of recent experiments in U.S. industry with flexible work hours, and the struggles of the 150 egalitarian couples whose stories compose this book can all provide gleanings of ways to lighten the burden of dual-job couples.

Conclusion

What is most striking to me after talking with egalitarian couples is the realization that for the first time in human history the worlds of men and women are beginning to merge. While many couples still live in different gender spheres, the 150 role-sharing couples who compose this book are a glimmering of the future. As we approach the year 2000 their experiences are timely. Both sexes will have the freedom to engage in a full range of activity without fear of loss of masculinity or femininity. The majority of women and men still have separate professional, economic, and political positions that are reflected in attitudes toward power, in differences in self-esteem, and in amounts of time spent in family work. Misconceptions about falling in love and effortlessly living happily ever after in wedded bliss with doll-like children are still powerful, as the divorce rate indicates.

In the evolution away from polarized family roles, men may stand to gain the most. By shifting the burdens of sole responsibility for their families' support and for major decision making to shared responsibility with an equal partner, stress is relieved. Men's life expectancies may then become as long as women's. Becoming closer to their children is another benefit. It is a hopeful sign that men exist now who are so unthreatened that they can successfully switch from business suits to aprons, from managing a career to bathing children and cooking a soufflé.

Families also gain when women are fulfilled in their adult potential. We have seen that the happiest marriages are those in which both spouses feel equally benefited and in which their daily experiences are most similar. Rigid stereotyped roles are by definition limiting, restricting, and arbitrary. Growth is more possible without fear of trespassing beyond limits we inherited from past centuries. These limits are outdated and artificial.

Girls especially gain from having mothers who exercise their options and talents, but in the long run boys with respect for their mothers' achievements can also change the tone of society.

The implications of role-sharing are not only to permit men to live less hazardous lives and women to live with more freedom of choice and thus to enhance marriage and child rearing, but also to carry over egalitarianism from the microcosm of the family to the macrocosm of the culture. If family structure is autocratic and patriarchal, children learn that males are authority figures to be obeyed and that women are servants. Those attitudes color the structure of work and politics. Social support systems will be reshaped to accommodate dual-earner families. Releasing the abilities of women to achieve and men to be emotionally expressive provides a larger reservoir of talent, energy, and awareness. Practice in shared decision making sets ripples moving that may never cease. Women and men will understand each other better and love each other more and so put an end to the war between the sexes.

Notes
Selected Bibliography
Appendices

Notes

Introduction

1. Joseph R. Hochstim, "A Critical Comparison of Three Strategies of Collecting Data from Households," *Journal of American Statistical Association*, vol. 62, no. 319, September 1967, pp. 976–989.
2. Linda Haas, "Determinants of Role-Sharing Behavior: A Study of Egalitarian Couples," *Sex Roles*, 1982, forthcoming. Haas's study of thirty-one role-sharing couples in Madison, Wisconsin (1976), found similar characteristics to those cited in the text. The couples were highly educated professionals; 86 percent had done postgraduate course work, mainly in the liberal arts (one third were still students). Two thirds of the husbands and one third of the wives had job flexibility. The Wisconsin couples were younger, mostly twenty-six to thirty, and a little more than half did not yet have children.

   John DeFrain, "Androgynous Parents Tell Who They Are and What They Need," *Family Coordinator*, vol. 28, no. 2, April 1979, p. 238. DeFrain's 1977 study of Nebraska parents who shared child care also found them to be highly educated. One third had graduate degrees and 57 percent had professional careers. Sixty-seven percent had more job flexibility than the average couple. Their mean age was in the early thirties and the mean number of children was 1.68.

Chapter 1: The setting

1. Michael Young and Peter Willmott, *The Symmetrical Family* (New York: Pantheon, 1973), p. 275.
2. Terri Schultz, "Does Marriage Give Today's Women What They Really Want?," *Ladies Home Journal*, vol. 97, no. 4, May 1980, pp. 89–155.
3. Susan Seliger, "Why Big Boys and Girls Should Cry," *San Francisco Chronicle*, 20 November 1981, p. 17. Reprinted from *The Washington Magazine*.
4. *Catalyst Career and Family Bulletin*, no. 3, Fall 1981, p. 8.
5. Norma Heckman, Rebecca Bryson, and Jeff Bryson, "Problem of Professional Couples," *Journal of Marriage and Family*, vol. 39, no. 2, May 1977, p. 328.

6. *Families at Work: American Family Report, 1980–81*, a Louis Harris poll for General Mills (Minneapolis, Minn.: General Mills, 1981), pp. 26, 28.
7. Jessie Bernard, "One Role, Two Roles, Shared Roles," in Louise Howe, *The Future of the Family* (New York: Simon & Schuster, 1972), p. 239. A recent study also found that more "role-differentiated" couples were less satisfied: Mona Carell, Stephen Finn, and Jeanne Marecek, "Sex-Role Identity, Sex-Role Behavior, and Satisfaction in Heterosexual, Lesbian, and Gay Male Couples," *Psychology of Women Quarterly*, vol. 5, no. 3, Spring 1981, p. 493.
8. Elaine Walster and G. William Walster, *Equity Theory and Research* (Boston: Allyn and Bacon, 1978), p. 178. A study of friendship found that traditional couples have the least closeness and that working wives more often considered their husbands friends than did homemakers. Joel Block, *Friendship* (New York: Macmillan, 1980), pp. 122, 123.
9. A study by American Demographics, cited in *California Women*, published by California Women in Higher Education, Sacramento, Calif., January 1981, p. 2.
10. Caroline Bird, *The Two-Paycheck Marriage* (New York: Rawson, Wade, 1979), p. xii. Robert Lewis and Joseph Pleck, eds., "Men's Roles in the Family," *Family Coordinator*, vol. 28, no. 4, October 1979, p. 405.
11. Paige Smith, *Daughters of the Promised Land* (Boston: Little, Brown, 1970), p. 71.
12. "Who's Boss in American Marriages," *San Francisco Chronicle*, 12 February 1981. Cited a study by David Olson, University of Minnesota.
13. Carl Degler, *At Odds: Women and the Family in America* (New York: Oxford University Press, 1980), p. 47; see also pp. 436, 466, and 471. "The family historically has denied or repudiated equality . . . The tension between it and the individual interests of women was inevitable." Jessie Bernard, *The Future of Marriage* (New York: World, 1972), p. 56.

Chapter 2: Egalitarian wives

1. Denise Skinner, "Dual-Career Family Stress and Coping: A Literature Review," *Journal of Family Relations*, vol. 29, no. 4, October 1980, p. 477.
2. Diane Sundby, "The Career Quad, a Psychological Look at Some Divergent Dual-Career Families," in C. Brooklyn Derr,

ed., *Work, Family and the Career* (New York: Praeger, 1980), p. 330.

3. Donald St. Johns-Parsons, "Continuous Dual-Career Families," in Jeff Bryson and Rebecca Bryson, *Dual-Career Couples* (New York: Human Sciences Press, 1978), p. 37.

4. Sundby, p. 330.

5. John Scanzoni, *Sex Roles, Women's Work and Marital Conflict* (Lexington, Mass.: Lexington Books, 1978), p. 154.

6. Julia Ericksen, William Yancey, and Eugene Ericksen, "The Division of Family Roles," *Journal of Marriage and Family*, vol. 41, no. 2, May 1979, p. 303.

7. Scanzoni, p. 9.

8. Dennis Orthner and Leland Axelson, "The Effects of Wife Employment on Marital Sociability," *Journal of Comparative Family Studies*, vol. 11, no. 4, Autumn 1980, p. 542.

9. Jane Hopkins and Priscilla White, "The Dual-Career Couples: Constraints and Supports," *Family Coordinator*, vol. 27, no. 3, July 1978, p. 254.

10. Linda Beckman and Betsy Houser, "The More You Have, the More You Do," *Psychology of Women Quarterly*, vol. 4, no. 2, Winter 1979, pp. 162, 169.

11. Beckman and Houser, p. 170.

12. Suzanne Model, "Housework by Husbands," in Joan Aldous, ed., "Dual-Earner Families," *Journal of Family Issues*, vol. 2, no. 1, June 1981, pp. 226, 227, 234.

13. Ericksen, p. 301. Rhona and Robert Rapoport, "Three Generations of Dual-Career Family Research," in Fran Pepitone-Rockwell, ed., *Dual-Career Couples* (Beverly Hills, Calif.: Sage, 1980), pp 83, 89.

14. Scanzoni, pp. 78, 79.

15. Lois Hoffman and F. Ivan Nye, eds., *Working Mothers* (San Francisco: Jossey-Bass, 1974), p. 173. Ida Simpson and Paula England, in "Conjugal Work Roles and Marital Solidarity," Aldous, p. 193. Eriksen, p. 308.

16. Laurel Richardson, *The Dynamics of Sex and Gender* (Boston: Houghton Mifflin, 1980), pp. 280, 222 (she points out that men with no children do more family work). Kathy Weingarten, "The Employment Pattern of Professional Couples," in Bryson and Bryson, p. 44.

17. Linda Haas, "Determinants of Role-Sharing Behavior: A Study of Egalitarian Couples," *Sex Roles*, 1982, forthcoming.

18. Sandra Bem, "On the Validity of Alternating Procedures for Accessing Psychological Androgyny," *Journal of Consulting Psychology*, vol. 45, no. 2, 1977, p. 196. Bem, "Androgyny vs. the Tight Little Lives of Fluffy Women and Chesty Men," *Psychology Today*, vol. 15, no. 4, September 1975, pp. 60–62.
19. Janet Spence and Robert Helmreich, *Masculinity and Femininity* (Austin, Tex.: University of Texas Press, 1978), p. 218.
20. Diana Baumrind, "Are Androgynous Individuals Effective Persons and Parents?," *Child Development*, vol. 53, no. 1, February 1982, pp. 44–69.
21. Baumrind, pp. 48, 61.
22. Elizabeth Allgeier, "The Influence of Androgynous Identification on Heterosexual Relations," *Sex Roles*, vol. 7, no. 3, 1981, p. 329 (she found androgynous female students were most favorable to a wife's assuming primary responsibility for child care).
23. Donna Hoffman and Linda Fidell, "Characteristics of Androgynous, Undifferentiated, Masculine and Feminine Middle-Class Women," *Journal of Sex Roles*, vol. 5, no. 6, 1979, pp. 777–779.
24. Jessie Bernard, *The Female World* (New York: Free Press, 1980), p. 502.

Chapter 3: Egalitarian husbands

1. Jeff Bryson and Rebecca Bryson, *Dual-Career Couples* (New York: Human Sciences Press, 1978), pp. 37, 64. Linda Holmstrom, *The Two-Career Family* (Cambridge, Mass.: Schenkman, 1972), p. 111. Ronald Burke and Tamara Weir, "Some Personality Differences between Members of One-Career and Two-Career Families," *Journal of Marriage and Family*, vol. 38, no. 3, August 1976, p. 457.
2. Rhona and Robert Rapoport, "Three Generations of Dual-Career Family Research," in Fran Pepitone-Rockwell, ed., *Dual-Career Couples* (Beverly Hills, Calif.: Sage, 1980), p. 30.
3. Aida Tomeh and Catherine Vasko, "Analysis of Reversed Sex Roles," *Journal of Comparative Family Studies*, vol. 11, no. 2, Spring 1980, p. 167.
4. John Moreland, "Age and Change in Adult Sex Role," *Journal of Sex Roles*, vol. 6, no. 6, 1980, p. 815.
5. Jeffrey Jacques and Karen Chason, "Cohabitation: Its Impact on Marital Success," *Family Coordinator*, vol. 28, no. 1, Janu-

ary 1979, p. 35. Rebecca Stafford, Elaine Backman, and Pamela Dibona, "The Division of Labor among Cohabiting and Married Couples," *Journal of Marriage and Family*, vol. 39, no. 1, January 1977, p. 54.

6. Michael Lamb, ed., *The Role of the Father in Child Development* (New York:Wiley, 1981), p. 303.

7. Donald St. Johns-Parsons, "Continuous Dual-Career Families," in Bryson and Bryson, p. 37.

8. George Farkas, "Education, Wage Rates and the Division of Labor between Husband and Wife," *Journal of Marriage and Family*, vol. 38, no. 3, August 1976, p. 452.

9. Herb Goldberg, *The Hazards of Being Male* (New York: Signet, 1976), and *The New Male* (New York: Signet, 1979).

10. Diana Baumrind, "Are Androgynous Individuals Effective Persons and Parents?," *Child Development*, vol. 53, no. 1, February 1982, p. 68. Judith Fischer and Leonard Narcus, "Sex Roles and Intimacy in Same Sex and Other Sex Relationships," *Psychology of Women Quarterly*, vol. 5, no. 3, Spring 1981, p. 452.

11. Baumrind, pp. 58, 61.

12. Robert Bell, "Friendships of Women and Men," *Psychology of Women Quarterly*, vol. 5, no. 3, Spring 1981, p. 42.

13. Baumrind, pp. 57, 63. Graeme Russell, "The Father Role and Its Relation to Masculinity, Femininity and Androgyny," *Child Development*, vol. 49, no. 4, December 1978, p. 1175 (he found that androgynous fathers were more nurturing).

14. Robert Arkin and Karen Johnson, "Effects of Increased Occupational Participation by Women on Androgynous and Non-Androgynous Individuals' Rating of Occupational Attractiveness," *Sex Roles*, vol. 6, no. 4, 1980, p. 594.

15. Elizabeth Allgeier, "The Influence of Androgynous Identification on Heterosexual Relations," *Sex Roles*, vol. 7, no. 3, 1981, p. 328.

Chapter 4: Staying together

1. Elaine Walster and G. William Walster, *A New Look at Love* (Reading, Mass.: Addison-Wesley, 1978), p. 159.

2. Stan Albrecht, "Correlates of Marital Happiness among the Re-Married," *Journal of Marriage and Family*, vol. 41, no. 4, November 1979, p. 862.

3. "Sexuality: It Says Here Wives Prefer Reading to Sex," *Psychology Today*, vol. 12, no. 10, March 1979, p. 17.

4. Leslie Fiedler, *Love and Death in the American Novel* (New York: Criterion, 1960).

5. *San Francisco Chronicle*, 20 September 1978, citing a study by Fredrich Neeker of California Polytechnic at Pamona. Francine and Douglas Hall, *The Two-Career Couple* (Reading, Mass.: Addison-Wesley, 1979), p. 154.

6. Shulamith Firestone, *The Dialectics of Sex* (New York: Bantam, 1970), Chapter 7.

7. George Bach and Ronald Deutsch, *Pairing* (New York: Avon, 1970), p. 216.

8. Erich Fromm, *The Art of Loving* (New York: Harper and Row, 1956), pp. 86, 87.

9. Robert Weiss, *Marital Separation* (New York: Basic Books, 1975), p. 38. Joel D. Block, *Friendship* (New York: Macmillan, 1980).

10. Jean Stapleton and Richard Bright, *Equal Marriage* (Nashville, Tenn.: Abingdon, 1976), p. 127.

11. Robert L. Borgess and Ted L. Huston, eds., *Social Exchange in Developing Relationships* (New York: Academic Press, 1979), pp. 115, 116, 130.

12. Rhona Rapoport, Robert Rapoport, and Victor Thiessen, "Couple Symmetry and Enjoyment," *Journal of Marriage and Family*, vol. 36, no. 3, August 1974, p. 590.

13. Arlene Skolnick, *The Intimate Environment* (Boston: Little, Brown, 1978). Albrecht, p. 863.

14. Graeme Russell, "The Father Role and Its Relation to Masculinity, Femininity and Androgyny," *Child Development*, vol. 49, no. 4, December 1978, p. 118.

15. Ronald Burke and Tamara Weir, "Some Personality Differences between Members of One-Career and Two-Career Families," *Journal of Marriage and Family*, vol. 38, no. 3, August 1976, p. 457.

16. Virginia Satir, *People Making* (Palo Alto, Calif.: Science and Behavior Books, 1972), p. 128. Carl Rogers, *Becoming Partners: Marriage and Its Alternatives* (New York: Dell, 1972), p. 205.

17. Constantina Safilios-Rothschild, *Love, Sex and Sex Roles* (Englewood Cliffs, N.J.: Prentice-Hall, 1977). Joan Aldous, ed., "Dual-Earner Families," *Journal of Family Issues*, vol. 2, no. 6, June 1981, pp. 185, 186, 230. Barbara Lusk Forisha, *Sex Roles and Personal Awareness* (Morristown, N.J.: General Learning Press, 1978), p. 205.

18. William Masters and Virginia Johnson, *The Pleasure Bond* (Boston: Little, Brown, 1974).

19. Carole Kirkpatrick, "Sex Roles and Sexual Satisfaction in Women," *Psychology of Women Quarterly*, vol. 4, no. 4, Summer 1980, pp. 449, 457.

20. Forisha, p. 295.

Chapter 5: Housework

1. Jessie Bernard, *The Future of Marriage* (New York: World, 1972), pp. 53, 56.

2. Charles and Barbara Lawe, "The Balancing Act," in Fran Pepitone-Rockwell, ed., *Dual-Career Couples* (Beverly Hills, Calif.: Sage, 1980), p. 192. Sara Yogev, "Do Professional Women Have Egalitarian Marital Relationships?," *Journal of Marriage and Family*, vol. 43, no. 4, p. 867.

3. Joseph Pleck and Michael Rustad, "Husbands' and Wives' Time in Family Work and Paid Work in the 1975–76 Study of Time Use," Wellesley, Mass., Wellesley College Center for Research on Women, Working Paper No. 63.

4. John Robinson, "Housework Technology and Household Work," in Sarah Fenstermaker Berk, ed., *Women and Household Labor* (Beverly Hills, Calif.: Sage, 1980), p. 55.

5. Linda Haas, Indiana University, conducted a phone survey of 319 dual-earner couples in the Indianapolis area in 1980. She used random-digit dialing techniques, with a 70 percent response rate. Her study was unpublished at the time of this writing. Other studies concur with her findings. See Appendix 4.

6. Jerome Tognoli, "The Flight from Domestic Space: Men's Role in the Household," *Family Coordinator*, vol. 28, no. 4, October 1979, pp. 604–605.

7. Jessie Bernard, "Family Life Cycles and Work: Myth and Realities," paper published by the American Association of University Women, Washington, D.C., 1981, p. 36.

8. Yogev, pp. 867, 868.

9. Pat Mainardi, "The Politics of Housework," in Robin Morgan, ed., *Sisterhood Is Powerful* (New York: Vintage, 1970), p. 447.

10. Stephanie Winston, *Getting Organized* (New York: Warner, 1980). Francine and Douglas Hall, *The Two-Career Couple* (Reading, Mass.: Addison-Wesley, 1979), pp. 101–102, 122–123. Marjorie and Morton Schaefitz, *Making It Together* (Boston: Houghton Mifflin, 1980), p. 39.

11. Robinson, p. 65.

Chapter 6: Child care

1. Sharon Housenecht and Anne Macke, "Combining Marriage and Career," *Journal of Marriage and Family*, vol. 43, no. 3, August 1981, p. 658.

2. Adele Faber and Elaine Mazhish, *How to Talk So Kids Will Listen and Listen So Kids Will Talk* (New York: Rawson, Wade, 1980); *Liberated Parents—Liberated Children* (New York: Avon, 1975). Ronnie Friedland and Carol Kort, *The Mothers' Book: Shared Experiences* (Boston: Houghton Mifflin, 1981). Murray Kappelman and Paul Ackerman, *Parents after Thirty* (New York: Rawson, Wade, 1980). Sydelle Kramer, ed., *The Balancing Act: A Career and Baby* (Chicago: Chicago Review/Swallow) (some accounts are very traditional). Kay Kuzma, *Prime-Time Parenting* (New York: Rawson, Wade, 1980). Gloria Norris and JoAnn Miller, *The Working Mother's Complete Handbook* (New York: Dutton, 1979) (contains useful resource lists). Letty Cottin Pogrebin, *Growing Up Free: Raising Your Child in the 80's* (New York: McGraw-Hill, 1980). Randy Meyers Wolfson and Virginia DeLuca, *Couples with Children* (New York: Dembner, 1981) (deals mostly with infants). Look for a book combining dual-careers and parenting, probably in 1984, *New Directions in Parenting*, being prepared by Betsy Niles for Catalyst, 14 E. 60th St., New York, NY 10022. The book focuses on alternative child-care arrangements based on interviews with dual-career couples. Two books on men's role in parenting are planned by the Fatherhood Project: *Fatherhood, USA*, a description of innovative U.S. programs, and *The Future of Fatherhood*, giving research results. For more information contact James Levine, Bank Street College of Education, 610 W. 112th St., New York, NY 10025.

3. Laurel Richardson, *The Dynamics of Sex and Gender* (Boston: Houghton, Mifflin, 1981), p. 280. Carolyn Perrucci, "Determinants of Male Family-Role Performance," in Jeff Bryson and Rebecca Bryson, *Dual-Career Couples* (New York: Human Sciences Press, 1978), p. 64. Henry Grunebaum and Jacob Christ, eds., *Contemporary Marriage* (Boston: Little, Brown, 1976), p. 322.

4. John DeFrain, "Androgynous Parents Tell Who They Are and What They Need," *The Family Coordinator*, vol. 28, no. 2, April 1979, p. 240.

5. Rosalind Barnett and Grace Baruch, "Multiple Role Strain, Number of Roles and Psychological Well-Being," Wellesley,

Mass., Wellesley College Center for Research on Women, Working Paper No. 73, 1981, p. 10.

6. Colleen Johnson and Frank Johnson, "Attitudes toward Parenting in Dual-Career Couples," *American Journal of Psychiatry*, vol. 134, no. 4, April 1971, pp. 393, 394.

7. Alice Yohalem, *The Careers of Professional Women* (Montclair, N.J.: Allanheld Osmun, 1979), p. 41.

8. George Masnick and Mary Jo Bane, *The Nation's Families: 1960–1990* (Boston: Auburn House, 1980), p. 40.

9. *Catalyst Career and Family Bulletin*, vol. 1, no. 3, Fall 1981, p. 8. Sharon Araji, "Husbands' and Wives' Attitude-Behavior Congruence on Family Roles," *Journal of Marriage and Family*, vol. 39, no. 2, May 1977, p. 318.

10. Carol Tavris, *The Longest War* (New York: Harcourt Brace Jovanovich, 1977), p. 232. Letty Cottin Pogrebin, "Are Men Discovering the Joys of Fatherhood?," *Ms.*, vol. 10, no. 8, February 1982, p. 46. Joseph Pleck, "Changing Patterns of Work and Family Roles," Wellesley, Mass., Wellesley College Center for Research on Women, Working Paper No. 81, 1981, p. 8.

11. Charlotte Perkins Gilman, *Women and Economics* (Boston: Small, Maynard, 1898), p. 281.

12. Carol and Theodore Nadelson, "Dual-Career Marriages," in Fran Pepitone-Rockwell, ed., *Dual-Career Couples* (Beverly Hills, Calif.: Sage, 1980), p. 107.

13. Sheila Kamerman, *Parenting in an Unresponsive Society* (New York: Free Press, 1980), p. 114.

14. Lois Hoffman and F. Ivan Nye, eds., *Working Mothers* (San Francisco: Jossey-Bass, 1974), p. 120.

15. Carol Nadelson and Theodore Nadelson, "Dual-Career Marriages," in Pepitone-Rockwell, p. 107. Colleen Johnson and Frank Johnson, "Parenthood, Marriage and Careers," in Pepitone-Rockwell, pp. 154, 157. David Rice, *Dual-Career Marriage* (New York: Free Press, 1979), p. 50.

16. Dorothy Dinnerstein, *The Mermaid and the Minotaur* (New York: Harper and Row, 1976). Wolfgang Lederer, *The Fear of Women* (New York: Grune and Stratton, 1968). Hoffman R. Hays, *The Dangerous Sex: The Myth of Feminine Evil* (New York: Putnam, 1964). Karen Horney, *Feminine Psychology* (New York: Norton, 1967).

17. *Catalyst Career and Family Bulletin*, vol. 1, no. 3, Fall 1981, p. 8.

18. DeFrain, p. 241.
19. Jessie Bernard, *The Future of Marriage* (New York: World, 1972), p. 69.
20. Hoffman and Nye, p. 184. Robert Schafter and Patricia Keith, "Equity in Marital Roles Across the Family Life Cycle," *Journal of Marriage and Family*, vol. 43, no. 2, May 1981, p. 363 (found an increase in equality when children leave home).

Chapter 7: Resolving conflict

1. Rhona and Robert Rapaport, with Janice Bumstead, eds., *Working Couples* (New York: Harper & Row, 1978), p. 162. David Rice, *Dual-Career Marriage* (New York: Free Press, 1979), pp. 2, 9. *Catalyst Career and Family Bulletin*, vol. 1, no. 3, p. 8.
2. *Families at Work: American Family Report, 1980–81*, a Lou Harris poll for General Mills (Minneapolis, Minn.: General Mills, 1981), p. 14.
3. Jessie Bernard, *The Female World* (New York: Free Press, 1981).
4. Matina Horner, "Fail: Bright Women," *Psychology Today*, vol. 3, no. 6, November 1969, pp. 36–38, 62.
5. Elizabeth Pleck and Joseph Pleck, eds., *The American Man* (Englewood Cliffs, N.J.: Prentice-Hall, 1980), pp. 420–426.
6. Pierre Mornell, *Passive Men, Wild Women*. (New York: Simon & Schuster, 1979), pp. 79, 31. The following are some comments of male writers or interviewers of men who view men as unskilled in relationships. Man has "exaggerated either [woman's] faults or his virtues": Myron Brenton, *The American Male* (New York: Fawcett, 1966), p. 67. Sex roles set up male hostility toward women and men desire to control women: Warren Farrell, *The Liberated Man* (New York: Bantam, 1974), p. 54. "Men tend not to be good companions to their wives," they fear "spontaneous talk will reveal unacceptable feelings": Marc Feigen Fasteau, *The Male Machine* (New York: Dell, 1975), pp. 82, 84. "The need we feel to keep our emotions under control impedes our experiencing closeness with others": Joseph Pleck and Jack Sawyer, eds., *Men and Masculinity* (Englewood Cliffs, N.J.: Prentice-Hall, 1974), p. 31. "Man resists closeness and dependency on the woman," sex is associated with "challenge, variety, conquest," men are "anesthetized and robotized," "boring"; "early male conditioning almost makes real satisfaction in marriage impossible": Herb Goldberg, *The Hazard of Being Male* (New York: Signet,

1976), pp. 12, 30, 44, 55, 143. "Men grow up with a basic distrust of women"; they want "a woman's interest in a man and her willingness to gratify him as a good mother would"; "women are often viewed as madonnas or whores": Anthony Pietropinto and Jacqueline Simenauer, *Beyond the Male Myth* (New York: Times Books, 1977), pp. 222, 187, 22. "Men sense the forbidding shadow of the primitive, pre-oedipal mother behind every woman to whom they are attracted": Nancy Friday, *Men in Love* (New York: Dell, 1980), p. 7.

7. Cannie Stark Adamec, J. Martin Graham, and Sandra Pyke, "Androgyny and Mental Health," *International Journal of Women's Studies*, vol. 3, no. 5, September–October 1980, p. 490.

8. Judith Bardwick, et al., *Feminine Personality and Conflict* (Belmont, Calif.: Brooks/Cole, 1970), p. 16.

9. Mornell.

10. Rice, p. 75.

11. Alice Yohalem, *The Careers of Professional Women* (Montclair, N.J.: Allanheld Osmun, 1979), pp. 3, 35, 75.

12. John Scanzoni, *Sex Roles, Women's Work, and Marital Conflict* (Lexington, Mass.: Lexington Books, 1978), p. 95.

13. *Catalyst Career and Family Bulletin*, vol. 1, no. 3, Fall 1981, p. 8.

14. Virginia Satir, *People Making* (Palo Alto, Calif.: Science and Behavior Books, 1972), p. 93.

15. Satir, p. 126.

16. *San Francisco Chronicle*, 16 July 1978, quoted from *Human Behavior Magazine*. The study was by Gill, Young, Beier, and Korner.

17. George Bach and Ronald Deutsch, *Pairing* (New York: Avon, 1970), pp. 202–205.

18. M. Esther Harding, *The Way of All Women* (New York: Jung Foundation, 1970), p. 298.

19. Herb Goldberg, *The New Male* (New York: Signet, 1979), p. 45.

Chapter 8: Support systems

1. Ronya and George Kozmetsky, *Making It Together: A Survival Manual for the Executive Family* (New York: Free Press, 1981), pp. 47, 101, 103, 104.

2. I asked a film instructor, Tom Reck, to name some American films in which a couple have an equal relationship. His choices were the following. *Pat and Mike* (1952): Katharine Hepburn is an athlete and Spencer Tracy is a sports promoter. *Bonnie and Clyde* (1968): equal partners in crime but she has sexual superiority since he is impotent. *McCabe and Mrs. Miller* (1972): Warren Beatty and Julie Christie own a business together, but it is a house of ill repute and he dies. *Loving Couples* (1980): Shirley MacLaine and James Coburn are both physicians, married to each other. She becomes bored with the marriage and has an affair with a younger man. He retaliates and they establish their "equality" once again. *Change of Seasons* (1980): a professor, Anthony Hopkins, has an affair with a student. His wife, Shirley MacLaine, takes a younger man as a lover, which gives her the upper hand even when he wants the marriage to return to normal.

3. Leslie Wheeler, ed., *Loving Warriors: Selected Letters of Lucy Stone and Henry Blackwell* (New York: Dial Press, 1981).

4. Charlotte Perkins Gilman, *Women and Economics* (Boston: Small, Maynard, 1898), p. 312.

5. Charlotte Perkins Gilman, *What Diantha Did*, in Ann Lane, ed., *The Charlotte Perkins Gilman Reader* (New York: Pantheon, 1980).

6. Dolores Hayden, *The Grand Domestic Revolution* (Cambridge, Mass.: MIT Press, 1981), pp. 121, 212.

7. Dolores Hayden, "What Would a Non-Sexist City Be Like?," in Catherine Stimpson, ed., *Women and the American City* (Chicago: University of Chicago Press, 1981), pp. 167–184.

8. A study of sixteen job-sharing couples in Norway found that nine of them shared family work equally, they appreciated being more aware of what occurred in each other's lives, and they had less severe mid-life crises. Erik Gronseth, "Work Sharing," in Rhona Rapoport and Robert Rapoport, eds., *Working Couples* (New York: Harper & Row, 1978), p. 117.

9. *Catalyst Career and Family Bulletin*, vol. 1, no. 2, May 1981, p. 8.

10. Thomas Murphy, speech to Menninger Foundation Convocation, Chicago, Ill., 23 September 1980. Text provided by General Motors.

11. See "Recommended Corporate Policies for Working Mothers/ Parents," Chicago, Ill., Women Employed Institute, 1980.

12. Halcyone Bohen and Ana Maria Viceros-Long, *Balancing Jobs and Family Life* (Philadelphia: Temple University Press, 1981), pp. 127, 135.

13. Margaret Randall, *Women in Cuba* (New York: Smyrna, 1981), pp. 39, 41.

14. Jerry Rankhurst and Michael Sacks, eds., *Contemporary Soviet Society* (New York: Praeger, 1980), p. 234.

15. U.S. Commission on Civil Rights, Child Care and Equal Opportunity for Women, Clearinghouse Publication No. 67, June 1981, pp. 10, 14.

16. Karen Campbell, "The Latchkey Kids," *California Living Magazine, San Francisco Chronicle*, 6 September 1981, p. 12.

17. Sheila Kamerman, *Parenting in an Unresponsive Society* (New York: Free Press, 1980). Kamerman, "The Labor of Women," *Signs*, vol. 4, no. 41, Summer 1979, pp. 632–651.

18. "Women in the World," Ford Foundation Position Paper, 1980, p. 13.

19. *Catalyst Career and Family Bulletin*, vol. 1, no. 3, Fall 1981, p. 1.

20. Chris Mosey, "Even in Sweden Some Women Are More Equal Than Others," *Christian Science Monitor*, 26 December 1980, p. 7. Linda Haas, "Domestic Role Sharing in Sweden," *Journal of Marriage and Family*, vol. 43, no. 4, November 1981, p. 957. Brigitta Wistrand, *Swedish Women on the Move* (Stockholm: The Swedish Institute, 1981), p. 21. Letty Cottin Pogrebin, "A Feminist in Sweden," *Ms.*, vol. 10, no. 10, April 1982, p. 69.

Selected Bibliography for Dual-Earner Couples

Books and Publications

George Bach and Ronald Deutsch. *Pairing.* New York: Avon, 1970. Describes how to achieve intimacy through honest disclosure, fighting fair, and so on.

Catalyst Career and Family Bulletin. 14 East 60th St., New York, NY 10022. Provides current information about advances in corporate personnel policy helpful to working parents. A quarterly publication.

Herb Goldberg. *The Hazards of Being Male.* New York: Nash, 1976. A classic description of the ill effects of the male role on men, although Goldberg seems to blame women for the passivity and dependence of their stereotyped role.

Francene and Douglas Hall. *The Two Career Couple.* Reading, Mass.: Addison-Wesley, 1979. Discusses how to communicate effectively, deal with stress, organize housework, and so on.

Kay Kuzma. *Prime-Time Parenting.* New York: Rawson, Wade, 1980. Gives practical time-saving suggestions for child care.

Letty Cottin Pogrebin. *Growing Up Free: Raising Your Child in the 80's.* New York: McGraw-Hill, 1980. How to share parenting and raise children in a sexist society.

David Rice. *Dual-Career Marriage.* New York: Free Press, 1979. A therapist's view of the particular emotional conflicts faced by dual-career couples.

Graeme Russell. "Shared-Caregiving Families: An Australian Study," in Michael Lamb, ed., *Nontraditional Families.* Hillsdale, N.J.: Lawrence Erlbaum, 1982.

Marjorie and Morton Shaevitz. *Making It Together as a Two-Career Couple.* Boston: Houghton Mifflin, 1980. Similar to the Halls' book, this book deals with how to manage family work and child care, cope with "overload," and what to look for in an employer. Contains useful bibliography.

Elaine Fantle Shimberg and Dori Beach. *Two for the Money: A Woman's Guide to a Double-Career Marriage*. Englewood Cliffs, N.J.: Prentice-Hall, 1981. Raises pertinent issues with breezy suggestions about how to cope.

Jean Stapleton and Richard Bright. *Equal Marriage*. Nashville, Tenn.: Abingdon, 1976. Provides a theoretical model for equality.

Susan Washburn. *Partners: How to Have a Loving Relationship After Women's Liberation*. New York: Atheneum, 1981. Based on interviews with 16 couples who are struggling with dual-career issues.

Randy Meyers Wolfson and Virginia DeLuca. *Couples with Children*. New York: Dembner, 1981. Discusses the impact of an infant on the parents' lives.

Barriers and Bridges: Male/Female Relationships; Swedish Support Systems for Egalitarian Families; Parenting; and Women and Family. 45–50 minute tapes. To obtain, write Gayle Kimball, California State University at Chico, Chico, CA 95929, 1980. Other video tapes in the series: *Women and Careers, Women and Health*, and *Feminist Visions of the Future*.

Couples Who Are Sharing Responsibilities. Martha Stuart Communications, 66 Bank Street, New York, N.Y., 1974. Couples discuss changing traditional roles. 29 minutes.

The Two-Profession Marriage. Buffalo, N.Y.: WNED-TV, 1974. Interview with a couple.

Appendices

Appendix 1. Profiles of Couples Interviewed

	% of Total (N = 150)	Number of Couples
Location		
Northeast	21.3	32
South	17.3	26
Midwest	30.0	45
West	28.0	42
Canada	3.3	5
Ethnic Background		
White	98.3	147.5
Black	1.0	1.5
Asian	0.7	1.0
Length of Marriage (in years)		
1–5	36.1	44
6–10	25.4	31
11–15	21.3	26
16–20	7.4	9
21–25	4.1	5
26–30	4.1	5
31–35	0.8	1
36–40	0	0
41–45	0.8	1
Type of Relationship		
First marriage	71.4	95
Second marriage	15.0	20
(for both spouses)	6.3	9
Second marriage	0.8	1
(for one spouse)	4.5	6

	% of Total (N = 150)	Number of Couples
Third marriage for one spouse, second for other		
Living together, not married	4.5	6
Lesbian couple	1.5	2
Number of Children*		
1	36.0	53
2	40.1	59
3	14.3	21
4	6.8	10
5	1.5	2
6	0.7	1
7	0.7	1

* 21 couples have children from a previous marriage.

	Women		Men	
	% of Total	Number	% of Total	Number
Age				
20–24	3.1	4	0.8	1
25–29	11.6	15	10.4	13
30–34	34.1	44	28.0	35
35–39	28.7	37	30.4	38
40–44	11.6	15	12.0	15
45–49	6.2	8	5.6	7
50–54	2.4	3	6.4	8
55–59	2.4	3	6.4	8
60–64				
65–69				
Education (Highest Degree Earned)				
High school	7.4	10	8.5	11
B.A.	44.9	61	35.4	46

	Women		Men	
	% of Total	Number	% of Total	Number
M.A.	20.6	28	17.7	23
Law (J.D.)	6.6	9	13.8	18
Ph.D. (some in progress)	16.9	23	17.7	23
M.D. (and other medical)	3.7	5	6.9	9
Type of Occupation				
Professional (requires graduate degree)	52.6	71	44.3	58
White collar (requires B.A.)	29.6	40	44.3	58
Doesn't require B.A.	11.9	16	7.6	10
Student	5.9	8	3.8	5

Occupation	Women	Men	Total
Business administration, personnel, etc.	20	15	35
Professor	18	15	33
Science, engineering, computer, CPA	6	21	27
Mental health	16	8	24
Attorney	10	11	21
Medicine	10	9	19
Business owner or co-owner	5	14	19
Teacher	12	6	18
Student	8	5	13
Journalism, writing	7	4	11
Pastor, Christian education	3	7	10
Clerical	7	2	9
Unskilled	5	2	7
Sales	2	4	6
Skilled craft	1	4	5

Occupation	Women	Men	Total
Anthropologist, sociologist (not teaching)	2	2	4
Entertainer	1	1	2
Homemaker	1	1	2
Artist	1	0	1

Interviewed Couples' Location by State

West		Northeast	
Arizona	2	Connecticut	1
California	22	Delaware	1
Colorado	8	Maine	1
Hawaii	1	Maryland	6
Idaho	1	New Hampshire	2
Montana	1	New Jersey	4
Oregon	1	New York	12
Washington	6	Pennsylvania	4
Midwest		**South**	
Illinois	5	Florida	1
Indiana	8	Georgia	5
Iowa	2	Louisiana	4
Kansas	2	Missouri	2
Michigan	7	North Carolina	3
Minnesota	3	South Carolina	1
Nebraska	3	Texas	6
Ohio	5	Virginia	2
Wisconsin	10	West Virginia	2
Canada			
Ontario	3		
Saskatchewan	1		
Quebec	2		

Appendix 2. A Comparison of Egalitarian and Traditional Couples' Biographies and Attitudes

To find out if there were differences in the biographies and social attitudes of egalitarian and traditional couples, I asked both groups to fill out a questionnaire that asked about influences such as working mothers and the couples' current political orientation. (I measured egalitarian and traditional couples' personality types using Sandra Bem's Sex-Role Inventory; results of that survey are contained in Appendix 3.)

The couples were subdivided into four groups according to the way in which they put their ideology about family work into practice (see Appendix 3 for a more complete description of the composition of each group). The four groups are labeled as follows:

E/E: Egalitarian in ideology and in practice of family work

T/T: Traditional in ideology and in practice of family work

E/T: Egalitarian in ideology and traditional in practice of family work

T/E: Traditional in ideology and egalitarian in practice of family work

The following results are based on responses from 71 E/E couples, 38 T/T couples, 18 E/T couples, and 37 T/E couples. (Mike King did the computer work.)

Age: E/T individuals were younger (in their early thirties) than individuals in the other groups (in their late thirties):

	Mean Age			
	E/E	T/T	E/T	T/E
Women	35.8	36.9	32.4	35.6
Men	38.0	38.8	33.3	37.7

Birth Order: More egalitarian individuals were later-born and more traditional people were first-born, but the differences were not statistically significant.

	E/E (N = 142)		T/T (N = 76)		E/T (N = 36)		T/E (N = 74)	
	No.	%	No.	%	No.	%	No.	%
First	69	49	39	53	15	42	37	51
Later	72	51	35	47	21	58	35	49

Among the women, E/E were more likely than those in other groups to be first born. Among the men, those in T/T and T/E were more often first borns than E men.

First Borns by Gender

	E/E No. %	T/T No. %	E/T No. %	T/E No. %
Female	41 59%	18 49%	8 44%	17 47%
Male	28 39%	21 57%	7 39%	20 56%

Mother Employed: More egalitarian people had mothers engaged in paid work than did traditional people (not statistically significant). Males and females in each group tended to be similar in the percentage who had working mothers.

	E/E ($N = 142$) No. %	T/T ($N = 76$) No. %	E/T ($N = 36$) No. %	T/E ($N = 74$) No. %
Yes	75 53	30 39	19 53	28 38
No	67 47	46 60	17 47	45 62

Religious Background: The differences between groups were not statistically significant, although E/E has more Jewish background than other groups and T/E more Catholic background.

	E/E		T/T	
	Men ($N = 71$) No. %	Women ($N = 71$) No. %	Men ($N = 38$) No. %	Women ($N = 38$) No. %
Protestant	40 57	44 62	29 76	31 81
Catholic	11 16	15 21	3 89	3 89
Jewish	15 21	10 14	3 8	2 5
Other	4 6	2 3	3 8	2 5

	E/T		T/E	
	Men ($N = 18$) No. %	Women ($N = 18$) No. %	Men ($N = 37$) No. %	Women ($N = 37$) No. %
Protestant	14 78	12 67	25 68	23 62
Catholic	2 11	4 22	9 24	11 30
Jewish	2 11	2 11	1 3	1 3
Other	0 0	0 0	2 5	2 5

Occupation: Men's patterns are similar in all groups; the majority of men in each group held professional jobs. The women's occupations may be the most important factor influencing role-sharing. Egalitarian women are more likely to be professionals and traditional women to be homemakers.

	E/E		T/T	
	% Women (N = 71)	% Men (N = 71)	% Women (N = 38)	% Men (N = 38)
Skilled	2.9	7.4	5.4	21.6
White Collar	33.3	27.0	8.1	24.5
Professional	62.3	64.7	24.0	51.4
Housewife	1.4		62.2	

	E/T		T/E	
	% Women (N = 18)	% Men (N = 18)	% Women (N = 37)	% Men (N = 37)
Skilled	11.1	16.7	10.8	11.1
White Collar	33.3	38.9	13.5	35.3
Professional	50.0	44.4	32.4	55.6
Housewife	5.6		43.2	

Results were tested statistically. F is the ratio of the variance accounted for by the groupings.

Hours spent on housework: Women spend significantly more time on housework than men in all categories except E/E. The T/T group stands out from the others in the disparity between men's and women's hours.

Average Hours Spent on Housework

	E/E	T/T	E/T	T/E	
Women	10.6	27.5	16.5	17.3	F = 33.50
Men	9.7	3.1	7.2	6.7	F = 12.27

Hours spent on child care: Women spend more time on child care in all categories except E/E. Men in all categories spend more than twice as much time on child care as on housework.

Average Hours Spent on Child Care

	E/E	T/T	E/T	T/E	
Women	21.9	32.1	33.7	28.9	F = 6.45
Men	19.1	7.0	14.8	16.6	F = 7.59

Number of children: Couples with traditional ideology have more children than do couples with egalitarian ideology.

Average Number of Children				Average Age of Youngest Child	
E/E	T/T	E/T	T/E	E/E	E/T
1.9	2.2	1.5	2.3	7.4	4.4

$$F = 6.17$$

Political orientation: Egalitarian individuals are more liberal politically than traditional individuals. Spouses had the same political orientation, with the exception of the E/T group, in which the women were more liberal than their husbands. (Scale: 1 = conservative; 2 = moderate; 3 = liberal; 4 = radical.)

	E/E	T/T	E/T	T/E	
Women	2.9	1.7	3.2	2.0	F = 54.9
Men	2.9	1.8	2.8	1.9	F = 9.50

Attitude toward traditional definitions of masculinity and femininity: Egalitarian individuals are more disapproving of traditional definitions than are traditional individuals. (Scale: 1 = approve; 2 = neutral; 3 = disapprove.)

	E/E	T/T	E/T	T/E	
Women	2.8	1.7	2.9	2.0	F = 36.98
Men	2.6	1.5	2.5	1.8	F = 24.59

Attitude toward feminism: Egalitarian couples are more approving of feminism than traditional couples. (Scale: 1 = approve; 2 = neutral; 3 = disapprove.)

	E/E	T/T	E/T	T/E	
Women	1.1	2.0	1.4	1.8	F = 20.18
Men	1.2	2.0	1.3	1.9	F = 18.40

Questionnaire # 1

1. Sex M_____F_____

2. Birthdate   Month_____Day_____Year_____

3. Address: _____

   _____

4. Grew up in what region?   North_____East _____

                                 South_____West_____

5. Your siblings by order and sex: born_____M_____F _____

born_____M_____F _____

born_____M_____F _____

6. Occupation of: Your Mother_____

Your Father _____

7. Your profession:_____

7b. Number of years doing paid work_____

8. Gender and ages of your children: M_____F _____Age____

M_____F _____Age____

M_____F _____Age____

9. Your political orientation: Conservative_____

Moderate _____

Liberal_____

Radical_____

10. Your religious background: Protestant_____

Roman Catholic_____

Jewish _____

Other_____

11. Amount of time you spend weekly on:

Housework_____(hours)

Child care_____(hours)

12. Would you describe your attitude toward traditional femininity and masculinity as: approving_____

disapproving_____

neutral_____

13. Is your attitude toward feminism: approving————————

                                                    disapproving————————

                                                    neutral————————

14. Educational level: High School——————————————

                              B.A. Degree——————————————

                              M.A. Degree——————————————

                              Ph.D——————————————

15. Years married:——————————

Appendix 3. A Comparison of Egalitarian and Traditional Couples' Bem SRI Scores

Do egalitarian couples have different personality types from traditional couples? Are there personality differences between those egalitarian couples who put their ideology into practice and those who have a more traditional division of family work? Do traditional couples who share family work have different personalities from purely traditional couples? To find the answers to these questions, I administered Sandra Bem's Sex-Role Inventory to 89 egalitarian and 75 traditional couples throughout the United States and Canada between 1979 and 1982.

I defined egalitarian couples as sharing decision making, money-making, housework, and child care. I located the couples through National Organization for Women chapters throughout the United States, through notices placed in feminist, black, and men's liberation publications, and through referrals by other egalitarian couples. Most of the traditional couples in this survey were selected by the egalitarian couples, who were asked to give a questionnaire to a traditional couple in their area. I defined traditional couples as ones who regard the man as head of the household, his job as primary, and the woman mainly responsible for family work. Other traditional couples in my survey were members of a fundamentalist church in Chico, California, who have at least some college education (6 couples); faculty members and their spouses at California State University, Chico (10 couples); and college-educated couples recommended by my colleagues in various California cities (8 couples). (I chose college-educated couples to approximate the educational backgrounds of the egalitarian couples.) These 24 traditional couples were included only if both did not disapprove of traditional sex roles or did not approve of feminism, as indicated in their questionnaire responses.

The couples were subdivided into four groups based on the number of hours they spent each week on housework and child care. Among the egalitarian couples, 71 reported that the number of hours spent on family work by the man and by the woman did not differ by more than 10 hours. This group is referred to as E/E (egalitarian in ideology and practice). For 18 egalitarian couples, the woman's report of family work exceeded that of the man's by at least 10 hours per week in both housework and child care. This is the E/T group (egalitarian in theory but not in practice).

In 38 traditional couples the women did much more family work than the men. This is referred to as the T/T group (traditional in both ideology and practice). The other 37 traditional husbands and wives spent within 10 hours of the time spent by their spouses on family work. They are the T/E group (traditional in theory but egalitarian in practice).

A total of 164 couples, 328 individuals, took the Bem Sex-Role Inventory personality scale. The test lists 20 masculine traits (such as "self-reliant" and "defends own beliefs") and 20 feminine traits (such as "yielding" and "cheerful"), as well as 20 neutral traits ("helpful" and "moody") that are not scored but are included to keep the design from being obvious. The test taker rates how accurately the various characteristics describe herself or himself on a scale of 1 to 7 (1 meaning never or almost never true and 7 meaning almost always or always true). The highest possible score is 140. The couples' mean score on femininity is 96 (or 4.8), on masculinity 101 (or 5.0). Individuals who score over the mean on both masculinity and femininity are considered androgynous; those under the mean on both are considered undifferentiated. A score over 101 on masculinity and under 96 on femininity is labeled masculine, and a score over 96 on femininity and under 101 on masculinity is labeled feminine.

Sandra Bem and other psychologists believe that androgynous individuals are the most flexible and creative people, and that sex-typed individuals are more anxious and rigid.[1] They rate the undifferentiated category as the least strong personality type, with lowest self-esteem. Traits labeled masculine seem to be desirable for achievement and self-confidence for both men and women.[2]

The specific results for each of the four groups are shown in the following table.

In the E/E group, more men were androgynous than any other trait, and more women were in the masculine category than in any other. A study found that androgynous men—but not women—are more autonomous and unconventional than other personality types.[3] Perhaps a woman must have more masculine traits in order to overcome passive female role socialization.

In the T/T group, predictably, most women are in the feminine category and most men in the masculine one. Few are androgynous.

A look at the E/T group reveals that the largest category for men

Bem SRI Scores

		Androgynous	Masculine	Feminine	Undifferentiated
E/E (71) Egalitarian in practice	Female	25% (18)	35% (25)	22% (16)	17% (12)
	Male	31% (22)	27% (19)	18% (13)	24% (17)
T/T (39) Traditional in practice	Female	13% (5)	5% (2)	63% (24)	18% (7)
	Male	13% (5)	47% (18)	16% (6)	24% (9)
E/T (18) Not Egalitarian in practice	Female	39% (7)	39% (7)	11% (2)	11% (2)
	Male	11% (2)	33% (6)	11% (2)	44% (8)
T/E (38) Not Traditional in practice	Female	14% (5)	14% (5)	51% (19)	22% (8)
	Male	22% (8)	30% (11)	24% (9)	24% (9)

is undifferentiated, followed by masculine. The men's low scores on femininity may keep them from engaging in family work. A study found undifferentiated fathers to be less nurturing than fathers with higher femininity scores who spend more time with their children.[4] The women, however, are similar to the E/E group in that they are most frequently in the androgynous and masculine categories.

The T/E group has fewer men in the masculine category than the T/T group, and more androgynous- and feminine-scoring men. The majority of women are in the feminine category so the personality type of the husband seems to make a major difference in actual role sharing as it did in the E/E and E/T groups. We have seen that most women in egalitarian relationships score in the masculine and androgynous categories, while traditional women are more often in the feminine category. In comparison, a study of 369 middle-class Los Angeles women, age twenty to fifty-nine, found their personalities similar to the traditional group: 47% were categorized as feminine, 24% androgynous, 19% undifferentiated, and 10% masculine.[5] The Los Angeles masculine-group women had a "feminist pattern." They and the androgynous women were likely to be college educated, employed, and have high self-esteem. The androgynous women were less liberal than masculine women regarding women's roles and religion. Androgynous and feminine women were most satisfied with their marriages. The feminine women were more conservative and traditional, more introverted, with lower self-esteem and less education than those in the masculine and androgynous categories. There were few differences between the feminine and the undifferentiated women, except that the latter were more liberal about women's roles and disliked housework more. The undifferentiated women had less self-esteem and seemed the least well adjusted of all categories. The Los Angeles study seems to confirm that professional achievement by women is tied to the development of "masculine" traits. Perhaps, then, these personality characteristics should not be labeled masculine but instrumental, and traditional feminine characteristics labeled nurturant or expressive.

In contrast to E/E men's scores (androgynous and masculine), a study of college students (mean age, 22.4) found that 18% of the 128 men scored androgynous and 40% scored masculine (30% undifferentiated), more similar to the pattern of the T/T group.[6] (The college women in the same study scored 44% in the feminine category, 20% androgynous and only 15% masculine.) An Australian study comparing traditional families with 50 shared-parenting families found similar Bem SRI scores[7]:

	Shared		Traditional	
	Mothers	Fathers	Mothers	Fathers
Androgynous	44%	41%	23%	31%
Feminine	25%	16%	49%	12%
Masculine	16%	21%	9%	37%
Undifferentiated	15%	22%	18%	19%

The traditional couples in my study seem to be fairly typical of the general population, and the egalitarian ones were unusual in both their Bem scores and in their lifestyles.

The pairing patterns of the couples by personality traits is charted in Table 1. One characteristic of the E/E group is that the only pairing pattern to emerge is an untraditional pairing: Feminine-category wives and masculine-category husbands make up only 4% of the group. Feminine women most often couple with androgynous and undifferentiated men, rather than with masculine-category men, while feminine-scoring men pair most often with masculine-scoring women. The largest combination is masculine-scoring women and undifferentiated men (11% of the group). Another 10% of the couples are a combination of androgynous women and masculine-scoring men; 10% are a pairing of masculine-category women and androgynous men. Undifferentiated and feminine-category men most often pair with masculine-category women. Undifferentiated women pair most often with masculine-category men. Androgynous women and men are most likely to pair with the masculine or androgynous categories.

In contrast, 34% of the T/T group clusters in the traditional pairing of feminine women and masculine men. Very few are cross-sex typed or androgynous, so untraditional pairings are unlikely. As in the E/E group, the two masculine women were coupled with androgynous or masculine men. Unlike the E/E group, the undifferentiated and feminine-category men do not pick masculine-scoring women.

As in the E/E group, the only distinct pattern that emerges in the E/T group is a nontraditional one that does not pair sex-typed individuals. Again, the undifferentiated men are most likely to pair with androgynous and masculine women.

In the T/E group, there are three most frequent combinations (16% each): feminine women and androgynous men, sex-typed

Table 1. Pairing of Personality Types
E/E Group
(N = 71)

Man's Personality Trait	Woman's Personality Trait				Total Men
	Androgynous	Masculine	Feminine	Undifferentiated	
Androgynous	7 (10%)	7 (10%)	5 (7%)	3 (4%)	22 (31%)
Masculine	7 (10%)	4 (6%)	3 (4%)	5 (7%)	19 (27%)
Feminine	1 (1%)	6 (2%)	3 (4%)	3 (4%)	13 (18%)
Undifferentiated	3 (4%)	8 (11%)	5 (7%)	1 (1%)	17 (24%)
Total Women	18 (25%)	25 (35%)	16 (22%)	12 (17%)	71

T/T Group
(N = 38)

Man's Personality Trait	Woman's Personality Trait				Total Men
	Androgynous	Masculine	Feminine	Undifferentiated	
Androgynous	0 (0%)	1 (3%)	4 (10%)	0 (0%)	5 (13%)
Masculine	2 (5%)	0 (0%)	13 (34%)	3 (8%)	18 (47%)
Feminine	1 (3%)	0 (0%)	3 (8%)	2 (5%)	6 (16%)
Undifferentiated	2 (5%)	1 (3%)	4 (10%)	2 (5%)	9 (24%)
Total Women	5 (13%)	2 (5%)	24 (63%)	7 (18%)	38

E/T Group
(N = 18)

Woman's Personality Trait

Man's Personality Trait	Androgynous	Masculine	Feminine	Undifferentiated	Total Men
Androgynous	1 (6%)	1 (6%)	0 (0%)	0 (0%)	2 (11%)
Masculine	2 (11%)	2 (11%)	1 (6%)	1 (6%)	6 (33%)
Feminine	1 (6%)	1 (6%)	0 (0%)	0 (0%)	2 (11%)
Undifferentiated	3 (17%)	3 (17%)	1 (6%)	1 (6%)	8 (44%)
Total Women	7 (39%)	7 (39%)	2 (11%)	2 (11%)	18

T/E Group
(N = 37)

Woman's Personality Trait

Man's Personality Trait	Androgynous	Masculine	Feminine	Undifferentiated	Total Men
Androgynous	2 (5%)	0 (0%)	6 (16%)	0 (0%)	8 (22%)
Masculine	1 (3%)	2 (5%)	5 (14%)	3 (3%)	11 (30%)
Feminine	1 (3%)	1 (3%)	5 (14%)	2 (5%)	9 (24%)
Undifferentiated	1 (3%)	2 (5%)	3 (3%)	3 (3%)	9 (24%)
Total Women	5 (14%)	5 (14%)	19 (51%)	8 (22%)	37

244 · Appendix 3

pairs, and feminine/feminine pairs. This is in contrast to the T/T group in which 34% are sex-typed pairs. Like the T/T group, however, undifferentiated men select feminine and undifferentiated women.

Clearly, sex-typed pairing is most often found in traditional marriages. The Bem SRI results seem to indicate that masculine and feminine traits are strongly associated with division of family work between spouses. It could also be argued that performing nontraditional tasks causes one's personality to change in response to the requirements of the task. Perhaps as men spend more time with their children they become more nurturant and as women have careers they become more instrumental. This conjecture could be investigated by long-term studies of newlyweds who plan to be role-sharers. It is more probable that certain personalities gravitate to unconventional or traditional styles of marriage. It seems that it is necessary for women to incorporate masculine traits in order to role-share and that it is more difficult for men with low femininity scores to role-share. Androgynous men are likely to be in egalitarian marriages. The thesis that personality traits correlate with division of family work seems to be validated by our comparison of traditional and egalitarian couples.

Notes

1. Sandra Bem, "Androgyny vs. the Tight Little Lives of Fluffy Women and Chesty Men," *Psychology Today*, vol. 15, no. 4, September 1973, p. 60. Bem's findings of flexible sex-role behavior in androgynous individuals was replicated and described by Linda Olds in *Fully Human*. (Englewood Cliffs, N.J.: Prentice-Hall, 1981.) (Olds traces the biographical development of androgynous individuals and finds patterns similar to the couples I interviewed.) The current owners of the Bem Sex-Role Inventory would not grant permission to print it. Readers can find a copy in *Health Behaviors* by R. Reed-Flora and T. Lang (St. Paul, Minn.: 1982), p. 163.
2. Diana Baumrind, "Are Androgynous Individuals More Effective Persons and Parents?," *Child Development*, vol. 53, no. 1, February 1982, pp. 48, 58, 68.
3. Baumrind, pp. 58, 61.
4. Graeme Russell, "The Father Role and Its Relation to Masculinity, Femininity, and Androgyny," *Child Development*, vol. 49, no. 4, December 1978, p. 1179.

5. Donna Hoffman and Linda Fidell, "Characteristics of Androgynous, Undifferentiated, Masculine and Feminine Middle-Class Women," *Journal of Sex Roles*, vol. 5, no. 6, 1979, pp. 777–779.

6. Judith Fischer and Leonard Narcus, "Sex Roles and Intimacy in Same Sex and Other Sex Relationships," *Psychology of Women*, vol. 5, no. 3, Spring 1981, p. 444.

7. Graeme Russell, "Shared-Caregiving Families: An Australian Study," in Michael Lamb, ed., *Nontraditional Families* (Hillsdale, N.J.: Lawrence Erlbaum, 1982), p. 152.

Appendix 4. Studies of Division of Family Work Between Spouses

1. Joseph Pleck maintains that in the 1970s and 1980s men's family work is increasing while women's is decreasing. A 1977 study of two-child households found an increase of 30 percent in men's time and a 5 percent decrease in women's time, unlike the 1960s when wives' levels of housework remained high in comparison to their husbands'. However, Pleck's own description of 1977 data concludes there is "no question that women hold primary responsibility for family work" (see 2, below, p. 487). Even the most recent studies, including my own, show that wives do more family work. (Joseph Pleck, "Changing Patterns of Work and Family Roles," Wellesley, Mass.: Wellesley College Center for Research on Women, Working Paper No. 81, 1981, pp. 2, 5.)

2. A national survey of 1,575 adults (not married to one another) in 1977 found that working men did about 14.5 hours a week of housework and 20 hours of child care; men with working wives did 1.8 hours a week more housework and 2.7 hours a week more child care than husbands married to homemakers. This was the first finding of men increasing their housework in response to wives' employment. Working women did 31½ hours of housework and 33⅔ hours of child care. (Joseph Pleck, "Men's Roles in the Family," *Family Coordinator*, vol. 28, no. 4, October 1979, p. 487.)

3. A study of 1,212 Philadelphia couples found that none were absolutely equal. Even if a wife is working and well educated and her husband is not successful in his work, the man has higher status and the woman does more family work. (Julia Ericksen, "The Division of Family Roles," *Journal of Marriage and Family*, vol. 41, no. 2, May 1979, p. 311.)

4. A study of 681 professors in 15 states found that married women and unmarried men experienced more stress and less job satisfaction and had less time for professional reading. (Cheryl Fields, "Faculty Stress Is Found to Be Highest among Married Women, Single Men," *Chronicle of Higher Education*, vol. 21, no. 3, 8 September 1980, pp. 1, 6.)

5. A study of 200 working women found them overworked and tired; child care was their main problem; it was left mostly to the women. (Jean Curtis, *Working Mothers* [New York: Doubleday, 1976].)

6. A survey of 3,880 married individuals showed that the ideal of "companionship on an equal basis is replacing male and female roles" but that family work is still divided along traditional lines. (Anthony Pietropinto and Jacqueline Simenauer, *Husbands and Wives* [New York: Berkeley Books, 1981], pp. xxxiii, xxv.)

7. A 1977 study of married female physicians in Detroit showed that three fourths did all the cooking and one third did the cleaning and laundry with no outside help. (Caroline Bird, *The Two-Paycheck Marriage* [New York: Rawson, Wade, 1979], p. 87.)

8. A 1975 University of Michigan study of 1,519 individuals' diaries (kept for six weeks) found that working wives averaged 25 hours a week of housework and husbands did 10 hours. Employed women did 3 fewer hours of housework and housewives did 5 fewer hours than in a 1965 survey. This was not due to greater help from men; men's contribution declined about 5 percent between the 1965 and 1975 surveys. Women did the routine tasks and men did more interesting ones, such as playing with children. Some men tried to help and were rebuffed. (John Robinson, "Household Technology and Household Work," in Sarah Fenstermaker Berk, ed., *Women and Household Labor* [Beverly Hills, Calif.: Sage, 1980], pp. 56–61.)

9. A study of 748 households in urban areas in the late 1970s indicated only a small increase in the amount of work done by husbands when their wives returned to work. (Sarah Fenstermaker Berk, "Husbands at Home," in Karen Feinstein, ed., *Working Women and Families* [Beverly Hills, Calif.: Sage, 1979], p. 143.)

10. A Northwestern University study of 309 middle-class two-earner couples in an Illinois suburb found that women did 80 percent of the housework. (*Los Angeles Times*, 28 November 1976, part V, p. 8. Study about women by Joann Vanek, Queens College.)

11. A Cornell University study in 1980 of 1,400 people found that in no family did the husband spend more than 3 hours a day on family work and in no instance did the woman spend less than 4 hours a day. In a typical family with one child age 6 to 11, the working wife spent 42 hours a week and the husband 7. Husbands of homemakers did more work—9½ hours. Their wives spent 49 hours a week. (Study by William Gauger and Kathryn Walker, cited in Louise Cook, "Women Earn the Bulk of Unpaid Wages," *Los Angeles Times*, 12 February 1981, Part V, p. 8.)

12. A study of 205 couples in suburban New York found that women were mainly responsible for work inside the house and men for the outside. Less than 15 percent of the husbands had sole responsibility for portions of housework. The husbands of professional women did more cooking (10 percent cooked almost all the meals and 10 percent shared cooking). Thirty-six percent of the men played a significant role in child care. (Sheila B. Kamerman, *Parenting in an Unresponsive Society* [New York: Free Press, 1980], pp. 48, 66, 69.)

13. A study of 196 couples, all psychologists, found the women had the major responsibility for family work, except for cleaning work done by paid help. This was true even for the younger couples. (Jeff and Rebecca Bryson, "Salary and Job Performance Differences in Dual-Career Couples," in Fran Pepitone-Rockwell, ed., *Dual-Career Couples* [Beverly Hills, Calif.: Sage, 1980], p. 255.)

14. A Stanford University study of 1977 and 1978 M.B.A. graduates found a traditional division of labor, with wives primarily responsible for child care; it also found that wives suffered more from stress than husbands did. (*Los Angeles Times*, 8 March 1981.)

15. Donald St. Johns-Parsons's study of 10 dual-career couples indicated that women did most of the domestic work and made more career accommodations. (St. Johns-Parsons, "Continuous Dual-Career Families," in Jeff Bryson and Rebecca Bryson, eds., *Dual-Career Couples* [New York: Human Sciences Press, 1978], p. 33).

16. Garland's study of 53 professional couples in 1971 found one couple who shared equally. Thirty-eight percent of the husbands did almost no domestic work, and all the women did more work than their husbands. (Kathy Weingarten "The Employment Pattern of Professional Couples and Their Distribution of Involvement in the Family," in Jeff Bryson and Rebecca Bryson, eds., *Dual-Career Couples* [New York: Human Sciences Press, 1978], p. 44.)

17. A study of 120 Nebraska couples who shared child care found that the women still did 77 percent of the cooking, 73 percent of the cleaning, 87 percent of the ironing, and the men did the repairs, lawn mowing, and car work. (John DeFrain, "Androgynous Parents Tell Who They Are and What They Need," *Family Coordinator*, vol. 28, no. 2, April 1979, p. 238.)

18. Of Chicago men who agreed that they should share family work with their working wives, only 7 percent did 50 percent or

more of the housework. Forty-two percent did less than 25 percent of the housework. (Helena Lopata et al., "Spouses' Contributions to Each Other's Roles," in Fran Pepitone-Rockwell, ed., *Dual-Career Couples*, [Beverly Hills, Calif.: Sage, 1980], p. 132.)

19. A 1975 study of 750 wives and 350 husbands (not married to one another) found that two thirds of the men with working wives made almost no contribution to after-dinner tasks or to morning tasks on weekdays. (Richard and Sarah Berk, in Sarah Fenstermaker Berk, ed., *Women and Household Labor* [Beverly Hills, Calif.: Sage, 1980], p. 279.)

20. A study conducted in 1979 by an advertising agency of men age 18 to 50 in 20 cities found that the men felt it was all right for a woman to work but that she should also do the housework and child care. The number-one characteristic they looked for in a wife is that she make a good mother. It reiterated a 1969 study of men in their senior year at liberal colleges: Only 7 percent said they would be willing to modify their career and domestic roles to help their future wives' careers. (Paula Kassell, "Any Changes Ahead?," *New Directions for Women*, January–February 1980, p. 1.)

21. A study of randomly selected Seattle couples found that 92 percent reported the wife did almost all the housework. Increases in husbands' income reduced sharing. (Robert Clark, F. Ivan Nye, Vikor Gecas' "Husbands' Work Involvement and Marital Role Performance," *Journal of Marriage and Family*, vol. 40, no. 4, February 1978, p. 15.)

22. Preschool children of dual-career couples were questioned in 1978–79 about their parents' task assignments. Few instances were mentioned of a man's total responsibility for a task or even of sharing a task. (Joan Aldous, ed., "Dual-Earner Families," *Journal of Family Issues*, vol. 2, no. 2, p. 240.)

23. Lynda Holmstrom's study of 20 dual-career couples found the men's careers and time were more valued, domestic work was the women's responsibility, and only a third of the husbands helped regularly with a number of tasks. Holmstrom explains that culturally men are seen as more valuable than women. (Linda Holmstrom, *The Two-Career Family* [Cambridge, Mass:. Schenkman, 1972], pp. 38, 156.)

24. A study of 20 Los Angeles nurses and their families between 1976 and 1978 found that the women did most of the housework except repairs. Only three men shared cooking and shopping. Child care was the most shared task. (Carol Mukho

padhyay, *Sexual Division of Labor in the Family*, unpublished dissertation, University of California, Riverside, June 1980, pp. 105, 112, 191.)

25. A *Ladies' Home Journal* survey of readers found 86 percent of the working wives did all, or almost all, the housework and 70 percent of the child care. (Terry Schultz, "Does Marriage Give Today's Women What They Really Want?," *Ladies' Home Journal*, May 1980, vol. 92, no. 4, p. 152.)

26. A Louis Harris poll of 1,503 adult family members in November and December 1980 for General Mills found that, although 83 percent agreed the parents should play an equal role, 36 percent shared equally in child care, the child care was done mostly by the mother in 59% of the couples and mostly by the father in 29 percent. Working mothers had much less time for themselves than did working fathers. (*The General Mills American Family Report, 1980–81.* [Minneapolis, Minn.: General Mills, 1981], p. 28.)

27. A study of Iowa couples found that more young wives than husbands perceived their role as unequal, although overall couples felt fairly equal. (Robert Schafer and Patricia Keith, "Equity in Marital Roles Across the Family Life Cycle," *Journal of Marriage and Family*, Vol. 43, no. 2, May 1981, p. 366.)

28. A comparison of federal employees using flexible work hours and those using standard hours found that men on flexi-time spent 16 hours a week on housework, 17 if they had a working wife. Women spent 26 hours. Men working standard hours spent 14 hours on housework, 18 if they had working wives. Women on standard hours spent 23 hours on housework. Working mothers spent 7 hours a week more on household chores than did nonmothers. Fifty to 60 percent of the men said family work was equally divided, while less than 40 percent of the women thought so. Fifteen percent of the men wanted their wives to spend more time with their children, but 65 percent of the wives wanted the same. (Halcyone Bohen and Anamaria Viveros-Long, *Balancing Jobs and Family Life* [Philadelphia: Temple University Press, 1981], pp. 132–134, 136–137.)

29. A study in 1967–68 of household work time among 1,400 families found that the wife's average time never dropped below 4 hours a day and the husband's or children's time never was more than 3 hours a day. Husbands' time averaged 1.5 hours a day. They spent more time when babies were involved. Employed wives averaged 2 hours less than homemakers. A sample of 210

families in 1977 was consistent, with some minor changes, such as husbands doing more nonphysical care of preschool children. (William Gager and Kathryn Walker, "The Dollar Value of Household Work," Cornell University Information Bulletin No. 60, 1980.)

30. Other studies showing that wives do more housework than husbands are cited in Jerome Tognoi, "The Flight from Domestic Space: Men's Roles in the Household," *Family Coordinator*, October 1979, vol. 28, no. 4, p. 602.

31. A study of California professional women from 1973 to 1975 found that they all followed a traditional division of housework. (Linda Beckman and Betsey Houser, "The More You Have, the More You Do," *Psychology of Women Quarterly*, vol. 4, no. 2, Winter 1979, p. 171.)

32. A study by Slocum and Nye in 1976 found that 70 percent of the husbands and 55 percent of the wives had egalitarian attitudes toward housekeeping, but nearly all agreed that more housework was done by women. (Sharon Araji, "Husbands' and Wives' Attitude-Behavior Congruence on Family Roles," *Journal of Marriage and Family*, vol. 39, no. 2, May 1977, p. 311.)

33. Using data from 1965–66, John Robinson found that working women spent 28.1 hours on housework (homemakers 53.2) while employed men did 11.3, mainly repairs and shopping. They spent only 2 minutes more on child care on Saturdays (and 6 minutes more on housework) than on weekdays. (John Robinson, *How Americans Use Time* [New York: Praeger, 1977], p. 62.)

34. A recent study of faculty women at Northwestern University found that they spent 24.6 hours a week on housework, while their husbands spent 8.6. The wives spent 35.1 hours on child care and their husbands spent 12. The women spent 48.5 hours a week on their careers, while their husbands spent 57.9. (Sara Yogev, "Do Professional Women Have Egalitarian Marital Relationships?," *Journal of Marriage and Family*, vol. 43, no. 4, November 1981, p. 867.)

35. A 1976 study of 31 couples committed to role-sharing in Madison, Wisconsin, discovered equal division of labor between wives and husbands. The wives averaged 16 hours a week on housework and the husbands 16.2. Mothers spent 12.2 hours on child care while fathers spent 10.4. The couples were mainly professionals under 30. (Linda Haas, "Role-Sharing Couples: A Study of Egalitarian Marriages," *Family Relations*, vol. 29, no. 3, July 1980, p. 289.)

36. My study, from 1979 to 1982, found the mean number of hours spent on housework by 71 egalitarian wives was 10.6 and by husbands 9.7. Women spent 21.9 hours on child care, and men spent 19.7 hours. Among E/T couples, the wives spent 16.5 hours on housework and their husbands 7.2; their hours spent on child care were 33.7 and 14.8, respectively. Among 38 traditional couples (T/T), the women did 27.5 hours of housework and 32.1 hours of child care. The men did 3 and 7 hours, respectively. Among T/E couples, the women spent 17.3 hours and the men 6.7 hours on housework and 28.9 and 16.6 hours, respectively, on child care.

37. A 1979–81 study of 545 Toronto families discovered that employed women, on a weekday, spend 128 minutes on housework and 64 minutes on child care. Their husbands spend 57 minutes and 22 minutes, the same amount as husbands of non-employed wives. (Non-employed women spend 251 minutes and 105 minutes.) (Lynn Smith, "How are Supermoms Doing?," Los Angeles Times, 5 July 1982.)

Appendix 5. Three Interviews

The three complete interviews contained in this appendix represent three types of marriages I found among the interviewees. The first type is the marriage that began traditionally and changed to role-sharing in mid-course. Couples experienced this as a difficult struggle but they were able to persist and feel proud of their growth. Annie and Jack fit this pattern. Married for ten years, they live in Wisconsin where they are co-owners of a small record store. He was thirty-six and she was twenty-nine when I interviewed them. They have two sons.

The second type of couple began their marriage with a desire to role-share. Lisa and Art are an example; they too face difficulty working through the results of male/female role socialization. They are among the unusual couples who married in their teens and stayed together, probably because of their commitment to equality. Married for twelve years, Lisa is thirty and Art is thirty-one. They are both professors in Indiana and have a four-year-old daughter.

The third type is a second marriage entered in reaction to an unfulfilling traditional first marriage. Barbara is a lawyer, age thirty-nine. She has two sons—ages fifteen and thirteen—from her first marriage who live with her. Slack is a consultant, age fifty-nine, with two adult offspring—ages thirty-one and twenty-one—at home. This is his third marriage. They have been married for three years and live in Wisconsin. Having previous marriages seems to lead to real appreciation for the current spouse.

In the interviews, initials are used for the interviewees, and G is the author.

ANNIE AND JACK

G: Let me ask you some basic questions, like how long have you been married?

A: Ten and a half years.

G: And your boys are how old?

A: Six and a half and ten.

G: What do you do?

A: We are partners in a small record store.

G: I see. How long have you been doing that?

A: Well, Jack began it in seventy-two and I joined part-time in seventy-four and full-time in seventy-six.

G: What did you do before that?

A: Before then, I was a full-time homemaker and before that I had a secretarial-type job. I worked in a bank once.

G: How is it working together?

J: We don't.

A: That is not exactly true. We have a schedule set up whereby one or the other of us is at the store. Almost never both of us. The purpose was so we wouldn't have to get outside child care. It also works better because we are both bosses, so we don't work well together, but when we have to we do.

G: How much time do you end up spending at work?

J: Thirty-two hours a week, each.

G: When do you have time together?

A: Both of us have Sundays off and then a couple of evenings a week. Tuesday is a good evening, Friday is a good evening, Saturday is usually a good evening, when we are both home.

G: And then do you make a point of going out or is that the time you spend with the kids, or how do you work time for just the two of you?

A: It is usually spent with the kids. We don't go out often for a number of reasons. Number one, it's hard to find baby sitters; number two, we don't have the money for baby sitters; and number three, our interests are really not geared toward outside things. I mean, we enjoy going out to dinner once in a great while. We don't have money for movies. What we will basically do when we do go out is visit with friends.

G: In terms of the business of both being bosses, the fact that Jack's been in it longer, does that mean that you are more of a boss, Jack? Or really make decisions equally?

A: Do you want to answer that, Jack?

J: Yeah, yeah. We have different areas.

G: Like what?

J: Annie takes care of advertising. She does a lot of the personnel work, raises, etcetera. I take care of the buying of certain areas. Annie takes care of buying in other areas.

A: I do all the accounting.

J: Yeah, there are ten different responsibilities in owning a business like ours and we split it pretty much down the middle.

A: On major decisions we always work together on it.

J: Yeah, there is never a decision that has not been discussed at the dinner table or on the phone or something like that. We are both two different kinds of bosses, and we deal with our boss things on our own. Like I'm a boss when I'm working and Annie is a boss when she is working. There are a lot of decisions that are minor decisions that are dealt with because we have discussed them already, or by the person in the situation.

G: What you are saying makes so much sense and it seems so right and simple, but I think with most people it doesn't work that way at all.

J: You see, a lot of people do not have the situation we have. We are incredibly lucky in our situation, because we have flexibility, tremendous flexibility.

G: Because you are the bosses.

J: Yeah, and because we are in a small-business situation. There are tremendous disadvantages, I mean, we haven't taken a vacation since seventy-four. It is constant, it's constant. It's ten P.M. and Annie is doing the books and tomorrow she works twelve hours. She works ten to ten and that is standard. That is nothing to get sympathy over, that is just the way things work out. There are advantages and disadvantages and one of the main advantages is the flexibility that allows us to do this. It is a pure schedule split.

G: So what do you do about dinner hours as a family?

A: The way that is set up it works out fine. We set this up in 1976 when I started working the split shift with Jack. Whoever is home that day makes the dinner. And then two days a week we work the full twelve-hour shift, so then again, whoever is home with the kids makes the dinner. We also set it up that whoever cooks doesn't have to do the dishes and it has worked out really well that way. Jack had to resurrect his hidden cooking skills when we started this.

J: There were no hidden cooking skills.

G: They were nonexistent?

J: They were totally nonexistent.

G: Then how did you learn?

A: He called me up and said, "How do you do this?"

J: When I was a bachelor, I kept myself on a subsistence level and in those days you could live cheaper. And I would eat out and I was a one-meal-a-day person. Two Whoppers and a

Coke was a dollar fifty-six. I lived on those for a year. No, my cooking skills did not exist. I am a semigood cook. I am not a gourmet cook. I'm not a good utility cook. Annie is a good utility cook. Every once in a while I get a bug and I like to make something fancy, but it usually costs too much and the kids don't appreciate it anyway. You make something fancy and they go, "Eh."

G: What do you do about other household tasks like cleaning and doing the clothes?

J: At home we are two different people also; Annie is a worker and I am a schelp. A schelp is a person who can sit with a book and spend the night there. Right, Annie?

A: Yeah, I've got to be doing something.

J: She is always doing something—it used to drive me nuts—and so she has always got jobs. She is always doing something, and I'm usually the person who washes the kitchen floor or cleans the bathrooms. I do the laundry every week, Monday and Friday, because I happen to be home those days. Whoever is home on Monday and Friday does the laundry. And I do the general housecleaning, right?

A: Right. Every once in a while I will fill in and do something, but . . .

J: And screw it up. I'm kidding.

A: Basically, he does the housework.

G: And then what do you do your days at home, Annie?

J: Give her your schedule for today, this is a classic day.

A: After I got up I made a couple of phone calls. These were family related. I'm a volunteer. I work quite a few hours a week for N.O.W.—National Organization for Women. I finished up some last-minute details on a mailing and got that ready for the mail. Then I went grocery shopping, went over to my son's school. It's the end of school and they had what they call the Olympics.

J: You saw that?

A: I saw part of it. It was kind of boring because there were a million kids and I couldn't even see Jason, but I went there and then I came home and I started working on the books, and then I made supper. So my time at home is half store related and then the other half is either volunteer work or personal things. You know, yard work or something that needs to be done for the kids or once in a while I will sit down and read a book or do something for myself.

G: I bet not very often.

A: No. I'm a workaholic. I try to learn to take time for myself, but there are so many projects I want to do that it is hard for me to sit down, unless I have a really fascinating book. It's hard for me to sit down and take time for myself. I've tried to learn that, but it is very slow coming.

G: Well, my philosophy is that it makes you happy. You kind of get hooked on achieving, don't you? You get one little task done and you think, Oh, what is next to do?

A: Yes.

G: It's kind of like an addiction.

A: Yes, yes. I think two years ago I nearly drove Jack nuts, because I was working at the store and I was taking a really tough accounting course and I was doing my volunteer work and I was busy every second of every single day. I've slowed down a little now.

J: It's a disease.

G: Well, yeah, I think any kind of compulsion is.

A: I've also come to the conclusion that I'm just a very ambitious person. There is a lot I want to accomplish. And I can't accomplish it unless I keep working on it step by step. I'm able to put it aside sometimes.

G: Well it sounds like you balance each other out.

J: Oh, God, we are a yin-yang in a classic. We are, aren't we?

A: Yeah.

G: How else are you yin-yang?

J: I tease a lot and Annie doesn't tease, right? I'm a big joker. I goof around. I enjoy goofing around. How else are we different, Annie? I'm tall and she is short.

A: You have gray hair and I don't.

J: Yeah. I'm old and she is young.

A: Well, not exactly.

G: Are you two in your thirties?

J: I'm thirty-six and she is twenty-nine. The big thirty is coming and she is going to pay.

A: One way that we're different, that isn't in accordance with a lot of our other differences, is that Jack is generally more concerned about the kids than I am. I'm a little more relaxed about them.

J: That is my phobia.

A: Well, it's your phobia, I think it's also that I come from a very large family and most of the things that the kids have had, whether it's growing pains or illnesses, I've already seen in my brothers and sisters. I also have a pretty definite idea of how I want the kids to be raised, etcetera, so I will usually have an answer for a crisis or a question or something, whereas Jack doesn't have such formed ideas and he tends to get real worried and concerned about some things.

J: Hyper is the word. I lost sleep when the kids got colds. Did you ever read *Garp*?

G: No.

J: Oh, what kind of an educated person are you? Read *The World According to Garp* by John Irving. Garp is me. The kid.

G: Well, what is that, since I haven't read it?

J: I'm a fanatic. I prepare myself for crises. I always look at the bad side. I mean, I'm driving down the road and I think, now what happens if the truck in front of me blows up and I run into it? What happens if this, what happens if that? And I prepare myself for everybody's death in my life. My parents, Annie's, I've prepared myself for it. I'm ready for it. I will be sad. I will be hurt, but I will survive. But if one of the kids dies, I will go totally out of my head. I have no way of handling it. I will crawl into a corner and just vegetate until I've come out of it. And this is no exaggeration, this is something that I have thought a lot about and I get a nervous stomach just talking about it. I don't like to think about it.

A: But, Jack, that is not really descriptive of how you are different with the kids than I am.

J: No, but I am saying that I am very, very close to the kids. Annie is close in a different way. She is an incredible mother. I did not become involved in parenting until our oldest was six and our youngest was three, so she did an excellent job those first years.

G: What do you mean you didn't become involved in parenting?

J: I was a nine-to-fiver. I was a classic nine-to-fiver.

A: He worked six days a week.

J: Yeah, I was putting in the sixty hours that we are splitting now.

A: There were a couple of years, particularly when our oldest was small, where he worked twelve hours a day, six days a week, when our business was new.

G: Oh, boy, then you would come home and they'd be asleep.

J: Oh, yeah. I'd talk to them over the telephone. That's no exaggeration. Remember the Cookie Monster, Annie? It would be the way that I would get through to my kids. The past five years or four years that we have been doing this, I think, has just been a revelation. I'm getting to know my kids again. I'm a parent. I am a born and bred parent. I don't think I will be a nine-to-fiver if I have a choice. I'm more of a parent than I am a nine-to-fiver.

G: Can you see that there is an impact on the boys?

J: Annie can answer that.

A: I'm sure there is. Some of it is hard for me to see because in many ways it seems as though it has always been this way, but I think their relationship with Jack is different, it's nontraditional, because they see him as a person. He is not someone who disappears in a suit and comes back and maybe takes you to a ball game and tells you that he is tired and that he doesn't want to talk to you, which is the way that a lot of fathers operate, some out of necessity and some out of ignorance. They see Jack as a father and they can go to him. For instance, if they are hurt, they don't automatically come to me. If they have a problem or something that they want to talk about they don't automatically come to me. It's whoever is at home and available at the time.

J: Or whoever is in the best mood.

A: They are proud of him. For instance, on field trips teachers ask parents to come along and Jack has been able to go along a couple of times and the boys are absolutely thrilled and all the kids in class talk about, "Oh, you have such a neat father." They are so impressed that there is a father along. They feel real good about this.

J: If I die, that is what I would like on my headstone, that he was a neat father. I'm serious, because I can see no more important things to do than to be a neat father. I mean, I would like to have a nice prosperous record store, but I would much rather be a neat father. Basically, I think that I am a romantic and Annie is not. Okay, there is the yin-yang. Right, Annie?

A: Yes.

J: I'm a real sucker for things like that. I don't see it as being wrong and I don't see Annie as being wrong, just two different people. But we love each other.

G: Do you think that is part of what makes you work well, that you have those balancing things?

A: I think that is one of those things that we have to work at.

J: Opposites do not automatically attract. We have discovered that.

A: As people, there are a lot of times that we really have to work at getting along, because we have such differences.

G: Like, it would bother Jack that you are so active and would it bother you that he is just sitting and reading or something?

A: Right. And just the way we do things, we do things differently. I am a very thorough, meticulous person. Jack will slap things together last minute and that is fine with him and it drives me nuts. I can't see how anyone can't prepare and, I mean, I'm a slight perfectionist too, and he is nowhere near that.

J: Slight perfectionist? I'm sorry, you let that slide right by. Slight? She is the world's biggest perfectionist. No, but she is phobic about her perfection.

G: So when you say work at it, what does that mean?

J: For me, the first thing to work at in a real relationship is that you have got to sit down as an individual and decide whether it is worth it. It's like a job, and you have to decide whether you want to change, if you think you are wrong, or if you want to quit. If you decide that you are going to work at it, that means that you have got to look at yourself objectively, and look at what she is saying to you. Look at what you have got around you, and decide whether you want to go through the effort to analyze and find out whether she is right or you are right and sit down and discuss it; because that is what you have got to do to work at it. That's what working means. It's talking about it. Here's another yin-yang thing: She is good at words, and as a romantic I get all emotional and I forget and lose my train of thought. Working at it is pure exactly that, working at it. You have to, it's an effort. Annie, rescue me.

A: Yeah.

J: That is a yin-yang. You are seeing a yin-yang right here. I know what I want to say, but I can't say it and she'll say it for me and I'll agree.

A: All right. One piece of information that I want to give you is background on this particular topic of how we work our relationship. We were not always an egalitarian partnership couple. We began our marriage as a very traditional couple. We were very traditional until 1975 when I read Betty Friedan, and I found out that I was not the only person who was unhappy with nameless problems. I then began to analyze my life and analyze what I wanted to do and then the changes started fast.

J: She is a change maker.

A: I went back to school. I did more and more feminist reading. I found more and more things that I said, "Yeah, I agree with that. That's right, that is what I have been thinking." A typical story of a woman awakening to feminism. From there, I started making slow changes to add things to my life. At this point I had a three-year-old and a baby.

G: How old were you then?

A: I was twenty-four, twenty-five. I started making changes to add other things to my life. I began going back to school on a part-time basis. I also began to get involved in the business. First, just because there was help needed, and then because I got more and more interested, I felt more self-confidence, I started learning things about business through school and I wanted to get involved. I thought, My life is also tied up in this business. This is also my sole source of income. I've lived with this store through Jack telling me the trials and tribulations and successes for so many years that, why should I not be involved in creating my financial destiny instead of sitting back and watching it? I also needed some kind of outer activities. I could no longer put up with being in a house with small children. We didn't always live in the suburbs like we do now, but it was just as isolating in a more city area.

Well, we went through some big changes. There were a lot of late-night discussions. There were a lot of arguments and there were tears and harsh words, but we kept at it. We have slowly worked to the point that we really believe in each other as equal partners and we value each other's opinion. Working at it is really a lot of talking, discussing things, being willing to sit and let a problem work itself out—not expecting an instant answer. Being able to give in when you can see that what you want is really not going to work out for the best and you will do it the way the other person wants, or coming up with compromises. It's a lot of communication. It takes an immense amount of time, but it has to be done, because it is the only way to let each other know where you are and where you are going and to keep in constant touch so that there is not misunderstanding. When we work so closely in business, is well as in personal life, without a lot of communication, misunderstandings easily come up.

G: And then they can just kind of simmer.

J: Gunnysack. Who am I stealing that from?

A: *The Intimate Enemy,* Dr. George Bach.

J: That was an important book.

A: Yes, that was an influential book for us.

J: When we were going through it you have to realize that she was the change maker. She is coming up with all these ideas and I am going, "Oh, that is crazy." And you, as a man, have to decide whether or not you want to stick it out. There is no reference book to go to. There is no reference book that you can go to and say, "It works. See, they did it."

G: That is why I am doing these interviews.

J: There was nothing for me to go to. Two men, with feminist wives who left them, have come to me and said, "What do you do?" And I sit and try to talk to them and tell them books to read but there is nothing about how to make a marriage work. How to make a feminist marriage, an egalitarian marriage, however you want to talk about it, and this is important. What you are doing is very important.

G: I'm glad you think so; I am struggling in a relationship, too.

A: It's particularly important for a relationship like ours. I have friends now, who are feminists, but their husbands are not at all involved. It's as though what they do is kind of their side activity. Our relationship is such that we share everything. There is no way that I could have been a feminist and Jack not fully understand what I was doing. There was no way that it could be a separate part of my life. It was too all-encompassing and I felt that a lot of the things that I was learning and feeling, he needed to know about. I wanted him to know about. If he didn't agree, at least understand what was going on.

J: I think, Annie and I haven't talked about this, and Annie you correct me if I am wrong, but I think that if, hypothetically, if we would have stayed in the nine-to-five relationship and she had not read Betty Friedan, I don't think that we would have still been married, because I was slowly killing myself.

G: You didn't see each other much and you were tired when you saw her.

J: I didn't respect Annie as an individual. I respect her as a person. In pre-1975, I don't think I did as much as I do now.

G: You thought of her as a mother and a wife and not as a person.

J: Exactly. She is raising the kids well. I was a little different, though. I don't know any men like me. I don't enjoy bowling with the guys. I very seldom go out with men. I don't dislike men. I don't have very many friends, which is not negative. The friends I have I feel fairly strongly about, but I am not an average, typical male. I think with that and the fact that she was pointing out some things that I could relate to in my family life. Okay, my parents are married and all that sort of stuff, but theirs was not a happy marriage. There was no wife beating or any of that sort of thing, but it was not happy and I could see it. I did not like my father and I could see myself becoming like my father, and I didn't like that. When she came in with some points, pointing out the fact of being more of a "parent" father, more than a "nine-to-five father," I could relate to that.

A: Everything that we describe to you is a minute portion of the things that have actually happened in the last five years. Some of it is hard to even describe, because we don't often sit down and think about the changes, a lot of them seem now as though they always were.

J: But, Christ, we would go for days talking about little things, I mean literally. I mean there were three o'clock and four o'clock in the morning discussions and that is not exaggerating. And getting up with a three-year-old kid for about a year. It was really work during that time. I got to like her, to like and respect Annie. I respect her ability to make a decision where I didn't before.

G: She hadn't had the chance, it doesn't take much decision, "Do I do the wash now?"

A: Well, also, I think part of that, not to diminish your changes, Jack, but I think part of it is that I began to operate in his

J: sphere, in business. I did make some changes in our business that have made a great difference.

J: A difference. No, continue. It was a cheap joke.

G: (laughs)

J: She likes it, Annie.

A: He was able to see that my knowledge, my understanding of the situation was good and I think my working at the store also brought us closer together because, after a couple of months, I began to see the things that he had talked about, the fun and the hard parts. I began to experience for myself.

G: You had more empathy for him, too.

A: Yes, and conversely, he was home with the children and the housework, he began to see real life, he was really experiencing all the things that I had talked about.

J: Nobody has ever written about the boredom of being a full-time nine-to-five *hausfrau*, with a child at home. The incredible tension, that was the thing that I could not believe. You cannot relax when you have a kid in the house.

G: I think the problem for me is feeling that you can't get enough done, so you feel like you haven't done anything worthwhile during the day. Is that what you mean, though?

J: Yeah, but then there is the boredom, when you have got that quiet time, okay, and the kid is sleeping and you sit down and you realize that you've spent six hours, done not a goddamn thing, and you're exhausted.

J: There were phone calls, literal phone calls that I would make to Annie and say, "I believe you now." Right?

A: Yeah.

J: I mean, it was just incredible, but working at it is constantly working at it and it is an ongoing thing. It has a spark. Eleven years, I mean when we hit ten, I couldn't believe it.

G: The men that have feminist wives that left them, even when you talked to them, what didn't they understand that you understood?

J: No, see, I didn't understand. God knows I didn't understand. The main thing is that it was political and emotional. Okay, the political I could understand, because Annie knew me well enough to be able to put it into areas that I could see in my family. The emotional takes a long time. You have to be politically committed before you become emotionally committed. These guys were a long way from becoming politically committed. I mean, it is a lot easier to be macho crazy than it is to be a feminist male, because you are bombarded hourly with all the television commercials, the *Playboy* and all this sort of stuff. It is a lot easier to say, "Yeah, that is the way it is," than to try to change. These guys were far from doing that, I've come to realize now, after spending a lot of time with them. I don't know if that answers your question.

G: I guess no one wants to give up that privilege. I don't want to do the dishes if someone else is going to do them for me.

J: I think it is more than that, but that is one way of looking at it.

A: I think that is part of it. I think also that—at least one man that I can think of who ended up in this situation where his wife left him was very, very emotionally dependent on her and she began to refuse to give him the kind of motherly support that she had in the past and said, "Look, you have to recognize me as a person and I'm not going to prop you up and I also want you to start doing this, this, and this," he just fell apart. First he said, "No, that is ridiculous, you're crazy," and I think their relationship was not real good as it was, but he refused to take any of it seriously to the point where she thought, "To hell with all this," and she left.

G: Sounds like he just didn't have the tools of emotional expressiveness at all and it was too threatening to try and develop them.

A: Exactly.

J: Both men were classic, Milwaukee macholemos. Bowling, hunting, fishing, a night out with the boys, poker games, and that sort of stuff. One of them had the beginnings but it could possibly be to just placate the wife. The first reaction a male has is, "It's a phase and she will get over it." I had it and I think these men had it. One of them tried to play the game and his wife finally saw through it and left.

G: You say a few pat phrases and . . .

J: Exactly. Equal pay for equal work, they believe in that. That is a big line.

G: I'm still trying to think about what made you have the capacity to stick with it.

A: I think Jack, being the kind of person he is, could do it. He's, I wouldn't call him an intellectual, but he is a thinker. He doesn't have a peer group, so he feels no pressure to be like the guys. He is also . . .

J: Cute, handsome, and has gray hair.

A: I think that he has worked at . . .

J: Being different.

A: No, be quiet, you are making me lose my train of thought. He really worked at finding and living with his emotional side.

G: That is the key.

A: And that was a very, very big ingredient. It was very, very hard for him. It came about as a result of the changes we were going through.

J: This is interesting.

A: Adjectives are very hard to come up with. He is not a typical man, as he said. He does not go out with the boys.

J: Never have.

A: He doesn't go bowling, he doesn't go drinking, he doesn't go womanizing and he never has, even when he was a bachelor. He is a reflective, quiet type of person, who spends a lot of time by himself. He enjoys that. The changes were hard for him, but there was no peer pressure.

G: And also you could appeal to him on the basis of intellect, what he calls political thinking.

A: Exactly.

J: I've always been politically active. Okay, I'm thirty-six. I went through the sixties. Now, for the first seven years of the sixties I was a right-wing conservative. From then on I became a left-wing liberal, in fact, a radical, while I was in Chicago and the whole shooting match. I've always been interested in what is going on. Didn't I suggest or recommend *The Feminine Mystique*?

A: Yes, you gave it to me.

J: I did not expect what happened to happen, of course, but she is very correct, I've always been this way. I've been that way and that is a beautiful way of putting it, Annie.

A: Well, that is one of the things that I like about you. That is one of the things that attracted me to you. I have never appreciated the typical macho man. I have never liked them. From the time I was a kid I thought they were brats.

J: One of the high points of my bachelorhood was a talk I had with the guy who was the best man in our wedding. One night, we talked and drank a bottle of cognac, the two of us.

We talked until four o'clock in the morning and it was the most beautiful talk I've had with anybody. That would give you an idea and that was almost fifteen years ago. That's one of the things I remember about the sixties. One of the strong memories I have is that one talk. That is more important to me than parties. God, we don't go to parties at all. I don't enjoy being around people that I don't know. Annie, I guess, answered your question.

A: Does that answer it?

G: Yes, except in terms of what shapes that kind of sensitivity? It must come from . . .

J: From a weak father and a very strong mother. I have had all of my life negative role models. Whenever anybody wants to hurt me, they can say, "You're being like your father." No, I don't hate my father. I understand where my father comes from. That doesn't mean that I have to like it, but I do not agree at all with the way my father brought me up and I am not going to raise my children like my father. It is interesting, this is a little sidelight—I ran a men's consciousness-raising group. I didn't run it, I was one of the leaders of a men's C.R. group. The first one Milwaukee N.O.W. ran. It was really boring, except one time, and it was cosmic. There were seven of us sitting around this guy's place and it was supposed to be on parents, and we started talking about fathers. We all had the same father and the same mother—strong woman, weak husband. Some hate their fathers even to the point of violence, hating their fathers. They would say, "You're kidding, you're kidding. My father used to do the same thing. Did he ever do this?" And it just raised goose bumps on your arms. We spent two hours talking about the similarities in our upbringing. All of us were the same and we were all feminist males.

A: But, Jack, you know, negative feelings about the way your parents play roles does not necessarily create a feminist man. We would have most of the country as feminist men.

J: This is an insight that has been newly discovered three years ago into my past and it troubles me, because I am a very heritage-oriented person. I'd like to know more about my family and my father. It troubles me a tad. I don't lose sleep over it, but it is something that I would like to correct. It has not been, as a typical cliché goes, the older I get, the smarter my father is. The older I get, the angrier I get at the way that he brought me up.

G: He didn't have any options.

J: Oh, none at all. None at all. I mean he was a non–high school graduate, was on the road and working his buns off. I can see that, but during the time at home he was not a very good father. That is his problem. I am a good father.

A: You know, parenting is something you learn. It is not something you "know." I learned a lot of positive parenting from my mother who, for all the negative things she has, was in many ways a very good parent. I was the oldest of twelve. I spent a lot of time working with her, taking care of younger children, and I observed a lot. I also read, I mean, I am a reader, not fiction, regular, hard-core reality books. And I have read quite a few books on parenting that really showed me, instead of just *not* doing the negative things my parents did, it showed me how to do positive things.

G: Communication skills.

A: Right, treating children like people. Really communicating with them. Positive ways of motivating them and directing them and I think I have shared a lot of that with Jack. He has learned a lot of that from me.

G: Well, then you must see the impact on your kids compared to their peers, in terms of them having more respect for women and being more whole.

J: Oh, yeah. Our oldest is just a beautiful person. I mean, he is the type of person that I would not mind marrying. He is just a beautiful kid. The youngest, hmm, but we are working on that.

G: What does "hmm" mean?

J: He is a typical second child. He is a hell raiser.

A: He really is. He is very independent and he is very stubborn. He is very sensitive yet he spends a lot of time trying not to show that. He is a much harder child to raise. He was an easier baby, but as a child now, he is a lot harder to raise. He, on the one hand, wants to do what his big brother does, but on the other hand, he still, in many ways, he doesn't want to grow up. He doesn't want to pick up his clothes. He doesn't want to dress himself. He doesn't want to eat when everybody else eats. He doesn't want to help around the house.

G: Sounds like he is really trying to establish his own identity.

A: Yes, he is. And his older brother is so good at everything that it is really hard. He finds it hard to accept the fact that he is younger, therefore, he doesn't—we don't expect him to do as well.

G: That is hard, to follow in someone's footsteps like that. What do you think about the men's liberation movement, Jack?

J: There is a men's movement, all right, and I look at it as hand-holding. They are basically hand-holders and watch me cry. They have got to become politically involved before I start becoming excited about the men's movement.

G: You mean like working for child care?

J: Yeah. "I'm a stock broker nine to five, I'm making my fifty thousand, but I can cry." These guys are not doing anything involved in women's problems. They are more involved in themselves. It is like EST and all the other cult things that grow up. They are bellybutton gazers. Nice to have men walking around in the ERA marches and abortion rights and marches and stuff like that, but I really, deep down inside I don't think that they are all that committed. We need more people like Warren Farrell, I think. People who actually live it, and don't write best-selling books about it. He was an important person in my trying to understand.

G: You read *The Liberated Man?*

J: Yeah, *The Liberated Man,* and then we saw him. I was never so scared in my life, but we went to see him.

G: You went to his workshop?

A: Yeah, he did a workshop a couple of years ago and we went to see him.

J: University of Wisconsin. I was scared to death. I thought he was going to pick me for the men's beauty contest.

G: He didn't?

J: No, thank God. We left before it was time for it. Remember, Annie?

A: Yeah.

J: That was, I think, one of the first political things I went to.

G: And that kind of reinforced the direction you were heading in?

J: Yeah, oh, God. And all the men there. I mean, there were men there.

G: So you felt like you weren't the only one out there.

J: Right.

A: Another big thing for you, Jack—and at least I think so, you can correct me if I am wrong. I was involved in N.O.W. for quite a few months and after I joined the chapter I got involved in working with the chapter newsletter, which I have been working on ever since 1975. I have been editor for a couple of years now, but the woman who was editor then, that I work with, is a wonderful, dear, neat, super woman. I can't say enough about her. We started doing the collating of the newsletter here at our home because here, in our basement, we have all our mail-order equipment. We sell records through the mail and have equipment, and I said, "Well, let's use the collator." It was a lot faster than everybody walking around the table picking up one page at a time. So we did that for two or three months, and one evening Jack came down and helped us and he found out that "Hey, these women are just regular-type women. They are really nice," and they were really nice to him. That evening, after everyone left, he handed me a filled-out application for a N.O.W. membership, then I knew that things were going to be okay, because he could see these were just regular women.

G: Romantic love is what I want to talk about next. We really get barraged with that, that love should mean bells ringing and weak knees.

A: It does for about three months and then you wonder what happened.

G: That is what the studies show. Ninety days, so I wondered how you cope with that.

A: A couple of things were influential in my dealing with that question. Number one was feminism, because for the first few years I was a full-time mother, homemaker. I convinced myself that what I was doing was really interesting and really valuable. After that, I began to realize that what I was doing was very valuable, but it was not interesting. I like children, but I would never work with them for a living. Though I like my children and I love them, I'll be glad when they grow up. I began to realize that the role that I was in, I was not happy with and then I started reading and I started getting names for all the things that I was thinking. One of the influential books that I read was Intimate Enemy, where he talked about the expectations that we get from parents, church, movies, TV, the media in general, and I began to say, "Yeah, that is right. That is all baloney. That is not real life."

Through reading and talking to people, I began to form ideas about what is real life and think about what really is love to me. What do I want out of a relationship? That is where I got the ideas that I have now. I cannot watch old movies on TV. I don't watch most of the new ones either, but I cannot watch them, because they are so fake and I think, how many years was I fed those lies about how I was going to feel and how it was going to be? Hey, it isn't that way for anybody, I don't care if you are rich or poor. I don't care what your jobs are, what your family situation is, it isn't that way, it's not real. So I slowly began to build real models. There are still times when I have trouble with it.

G: I know. We all do. You always expect the prince or princess to come.

A: I get really disgusted with myself sometimes, because I find myself expecting the types of things that are from movies. They are old ideas that I picked up when I was a kid about what is love and what's involved in a marriage. The biggest one is that the other person is going to automatically know what you want and do it for you. I still sometimes want Jack to know what I want and say what I want him to say at that moment. It's sometimes really hard, but I think I am getting a lot better at learning to express my needs and my wants and knowing that there are going to be times when we just don't get along.

I have found that there is a two-, three-month cycle where things will be going fine and then, for a week or two, everything he does and says annoys me to the point I think I cannot stand to be around him. Then it usually builds to a peak and something triggers it and we sit down and we talk and we always end up discovering or expressing something new that we haven't told each other before and I feel closer to him and everything is cool again. It's never on an even keel. It's always up and down. It's the realities of life.

G: That was well said.

A: It's not what you get in movies.

G: Jack, do you want to say your two cents' worth about the romantic love business?

J: I am frustrated over the lack of it, but I can understand it.

A: What is romantic?

J: Oh, the romantic is all the stuff that she doesn't like. I mean all the movie stuff and all the touching and the hugging and the kissing and all that sort of thing. I'm a big sucker for that. I mean, the man and a woman in the film *Elvira Madigan*, and all the great movies in the late sixties. I was deeply touched, but I can understand. I really can. I don't lose sleep over it. Let me put it that way.

G: That *Elvira Madigan* film is a good point, because in romantic love, it always involved some kind of anxiety or loss or separation.

J: Or throwing up while you are eating, what were those, mushrooms? At some point there was a beautiful scene where they are running through, with Mozart's piano concerto. I really have to agree with Annie. That doesn't mean that I like it, but I agree with what she is saying, okay?

G: What I want to know is if you think it's possible? Do you think there can be that "romance," whatever that is?

J: Not in a political relationship.

G: What do you mean by a political relationship?

J: Everything she says. You can't look at *Elvira Madigan* without getting pissed at where are they getting the money for all this? You have to look at it with your reality glasses on.

A: I think another problem with the romantic love idea, at least of the impression I have gotten of it, is that I don't see the people really communicating in the "romantic" movies. People just kind of come together. There is very little day-to-day nitty-gritty stuff, or if there is, it is treated in such a way that you think, "Wow, they really handle those things well." Nothing in life is like that. You know, emotionally, I grew up prepared only for romantic love and I had to learn to discard slowly the false ideas and start dealing with the realities. Romantic love, to me, is something for rich people. We have never been rich and we probably never will be.

G: You mean vacations in Europe?

A: Yes. You take these vacations. You go to these nice restaurants, have these nice clothes. You also have these rich, no-cares friends. It isn't real life.

J: Maybe for some people, but it is not for us.

A: Yeah, it's not for us. I think the kind of sharing of responsibilities, sharing of successes and failures, is much more meaningful than the kind of put-on. To me, the romantic love idea is you're presenting yourself to a person as just part of yourself.

Particularly the women in this situation are portrayed as docile, quiet, sexual things. They don't have minds, they don't have intellects, they never argue forcefully for a point, they don't have strong opinions. It is not real.

J: It would be nice if we could make it, but there is no way to be that way, to have a romantic relationship. Now, that does not mean that Annie and I are not romantically inclined. Do you follow? I'm not trying to make it sound like we are two individuals living under the same roof. You know, we kiss a lot. But it is not me walking up behind her and giving her a peck, a kiss, and then it turning into symphony orchestras going up in the background and all this stuff. It's just two human beings who like each other.

A: How can I say this?

J: Very carefully.

A: Yeah, and don't throw anything at me, Jack.

J: I'm close enough that I can.

A: We haven't touched on this topic and maybe this isn't part of your study, but since feminism, etcetera, our sex life is a whole lot better than it ever was in our past life in our typical roles.

J: Oh, really?

G: Do you know more about female anatomy?

A: Jack knows more about female and I know more about male anatomy. We communicate better. I think we have stronger feelings for each other, because we share so much now that we didn't share when we were playing the male-female role.

J: Oh. God. Our sex life went to hell when I was working the long hours.

A: Running a small business is a very stressful, all-consuming position, and Jack tried to do that all by himself for quite a few years. I spent a lot of my time trying to get him to communicate and relax and he spent a lot of his time not telling me the problems that he was running into, because it would only upset me. And it did. When he would share things that I knew nothing about, that I wasn't involved in, I didn't have any kind of business experience, so I didn't know what to do with it. It was just one more problem to heap on me. Since we have shared it, the problems are not so large, because there are two of us working at it and we both know what is going on. We both come up with ideas. There is nothing that has to be kept inside anymore, that one person is brewing on, not wanting to tell the other person.

J: It's a lot easier sharing. And I agree with Annie about the sex. The sex pre- and post-1975 is like grade school and married life. It's a lot more fun. I really don't think that traditional marriage has a place if either one or the other of the people has any kinds of brains at all, unless, being a wife to a doctor where, when you get bored, you can go out and spend your money, go out shopping and all that sort of stuff. That, I think, could be a possible way of surviving a traditional marriage. But a traditional marriage in a middle-class situation is work, constant work. And if the husband is very inward it's not very much fun for either person.

G: I think probably what most traditional middle-class women do is get their needs met through their children. I mean, not really, but that is where they turn.

J: And the poor kids end up being neurotic by the time she does it.

A: I see a lot of changes in that, though. I don't have a hell of a lot of contact with other women, other than my N.O.W. friends and the people that I run into at work, but I do see a lot of changes, for two reasons. Number one, the women's movement has made a hell of a lot more changes than we sometimes give ourselves credit for. I think women working outside of the home has made a big difference, because they are not isolated anymore and there are a lot of problems that people no longer feel uncomfortable talking about. I was standing next to another mother on my oldest son's soccer team today. We were waiting for the kids. They were getting their team pictures today and she started talking about how she finally got a sitter for her son this summer. Talking about how difficult it is to find child care. Four years ago, it was still, "Oh, my God, you have child care? You are not home with your child?" And now, all of a sudden, I see it being accepted. In this neighborhood, you know, middle, lower-middle class, most women work. It's exceptional to find mothers who don't work.

G. This is a corny question, but if you had advice to give to some young couple just starting out being married and parents, in a nutshell, what kind of advice would you give them?

J: I'm quick. Don't have kids until you know that you want to stay with that person, because kids will totally destroy your marriage if you don't have the foundation. The other side of the coin is, if you have your kids right away, you don't have a foundation so that you can be flexible. When you have kids, your life is totally turned inside out. You totally lose your independence, you totally lose your own self. Your self is the kids. If you want to make love and the kid wants to eat, guess what happens? And that is very hard for a person to accept. You can either have your kids right away or wait ten years. I wouldn't get married, unless I could find somebody like Annie.

A: Ahh.

J: Here comes the intellectual response. You just got the emotional response.

A: Give me a break. What I think of as a young woman—the patterns are still too similar to what I grew up with and you grew up with—but I think a real big point for me is that she be a person. That she know who she is and that she have accomplishments, self-confidence. When she goes into a marriage, she is not giving up her person, she is sharing her person. Of course, that she go into a relationship where she has a partnership with this man. That she, that they respect each other. They like, they respect, and they know each other.

That is another big point for me. Forget this romantic business. Really find out who that person is. Don't go in there with preconceived ideas of what you want and place them on that person, only later to realize that that isn't that person. Make sure you know that person. That is not to say that the marriage will then work out, but it really gives it a better chance than what I went into marriage with and many, many, many people today are still going into it with.

G: I think that is useful. Can you think of any areas that we haven't covered or questions that should be raised in terms of making a relationship work?

A: One thing that Jack and I really look for, we would really like to know other couples like ourselves. There are so many times that we feel like pioneers. We come across a problem and there is nowhere to turn. There is not even anything written down, much less do we know anyone else who has gone through it before. You can't read about, hear about, talk to that person and they say, "Well, I ran into that and this is what I did." We really feel like pioneers often times and it is very, very frustrating, for me anyway. I just get to the point where I am at a loss because everywhere I turn, I see people who are not doing what we are doing. They are doing the traditional thing, or they are not married, period. They are single.

LISA AND ART

G: How old were you when you were married?

L: I was eighteen and he was nineteen.

G: You were babies and you made it.

L: I know. I teach family courses and am always telling them, Wait until you are twenty-five, at least, to get married. They say, "What a hypocrite you are."

G: Would you start with child care and tell how you have done that between the two of you and when you are at work?

A: We have arranged our teaching schedules so that we work on alternate days. Lisa works on Mondays and Wednesdays and I work on Tuesdays and Thursdays. Basically the person that stays home is responsible for the child that day. And then we are more or less even on Friday, Saturday, and Sunday.

G: How do you do housework?

L: That is sort of based on the child-care arrangement. To some extent, whoever is home is responsible for making sure the place is cleaned up and cooks. We don't both always eat together because sometimes we are out with evening classes and so on, but that person is still responsible for cooking that night. In terms of other things we have a special system worked out whereby he is responsible for certain things and I'm responsible for certain things and each person does what they are supposed to do and we don't ever talk about it.

G: How have you divided it up?

A: I do vacuuming and Lisa does washing floors.

L: I clean the three bathrooms. He does all the laundry and it just appears clean in my drawers.

A: She did it for me for the first year or so, after we moved to this house (we went to the laundromat together the first years after we got married) and then I began to complain and took over.

L: He really does the laundry better than I do. I don't get the wrinkles out of the permanent press. Everyone does their own ironing except I tend to do the kid's. You know how ironing is.

A: Wrinkles don't tend to bother me as much as Lisa. That's the reason for that.

G: What about yard work?

A: Lisa does more yard work than I do.

L: That has been rotated too. I decided to mow the lawn more often when we moved to a smaller place.

A: She has been doing flower gardens more than I am into. I just believe in mowing. She takes more initiative there to start what needs to be done and then I'll come out and help with the labor. I don't think about it.

L: Sometimes you do. You make it sound like I make the decision and you do the work.

A: Lisa basically handles the bills but I balance the checkbook at the end of the month.

L: I don't like to do that.

A: I tend to be lazy and the bills will sit on my desk for a couple of weeks.

L: I have always paid the bills. He's not good at that.

G: What about social stuff like birthdays, Christmas cards?

L: Everybody's family is their own responsibility.

A: I take care of mine and she does hers. In practice that means I have more responsibility because I have more relatives.

G: How do you manage to be dual-career parents in terms of research? Because it's hard to do that when your daughter is there, right?

A: It wasn't hard until she came.

L: Unfortunately, she came the year we both started to become professors. We got our dissertation topics in 1977 in August and she was six months old, and then we started working on them immediately.

A: We alternate getting Friday. Each week one of us gets an extra day and then we try to put her in preschool so the other person doesn't have to be there. She now goes to preschool on Monday through Friday for two and a half hours. I do more stuff at night after everybody has gone to sleep, because I need less sleep.

L: It's just hard. Whoever is up against a deadline gets a break on the weekend. It's not just getting the task done but it's having patience when it comes to the child. I think you have to believe in your life. In some ways it's easier now than if we would have been in graduate school and both had the the same deadlines all the time. Now our deadlines don't usually coincide unless we are grading midterms and finals.

G: Do you find that she bonds with both of you and you have a kind of closeness in the relationship that most fathers don't have?

A: Yes, I would say so. Another father on the block I'm aware of seems never to be home. I think he sees his kids a couple hours a week and often when he's home he doesn't talk to them.

G: All the studies show that the time per day fathers spend with their kids is incredibly small.

L: I want to say something about that. When I came back from a conference (I had been gone for four days) I noticed that when I came home she was a little more cuddly to daddy. She had grown to depend on him solely for those couple of days. She wasn't shutting me out at all, but there was a little more of that that hadn't been there before. When we are both taking care of her all the time she relates to both of us to an equal degree. It seems to me that it's clear the more time you spend, the more impact you have.

G: What are the influences that led you to do this kind of role-sharing? What about the family that you grew up in?

A: When I was young in Sweden my parents both worked in a metal factory. They had different shifts. My father worked while my mother took care of the kids and then vice versa. I had seen my dad do cooking and child care and things like that. Later, when we came to the United States, my mother became a full-time housewife but by that time my ideas had been formed. Then, when I met Lisa I told her right off that I thought a relationship should be an equal one where I didn't want to support a lady housewife and I expected her to work and share the responsibility. It really seemed like a strange idea to her but it was very natural to me.

G: Did that kind of thinking get strengthened by any kind of political ideology or your college experience?

A: This was before we had gone to college. At the time I was also questioning things in terms of discrimination against blacks and felt very strongly about it. I basically had developed an anarchist philosophy all across the board and I wouldn't give up my belief in sexual equality.

G: What about your siblings? How many are there?

A: I have three. I'm the oldest one. I have one sister close to me who is twenty-nine and a brother twelve years younger and a sister who is eighteen years younger.

G: Did the kids do all kinds of tasks at home or were there boys' tasks and girls' tasks?

A: I was encouraged to do things for fun, like sewing. When I showed an interest in needlework my mother didn't discourage me and saw nothing wrong with it, in terms of hobby things. In housework we really didn't do that many chores around the house but I noticed that my sister was expected to do more than I was at home.

G: Lisa, what about your family?

L: My family was very traditional. My mother had been the kind of person that had worked before she had me and had always really enjoyed her work. She decided to stay home and have babies in the fifties and always acted like that was what she wanted to do. But you got this feeling that there was something more to life than that. I was discouraged from climbing trees and not encouraged to go to college. I could think about being a secretary. You couldn't be much more traditional.

G: Did you think your mother felt resentment about not continuing work?

L: I don't know. I sort of wonder sometimes. My relationship with her is ambivalent on that point. I really think that she didn't enjoy my upbringing as much as she likes to pretend that she did. Now that I have a child of my own, in terms of my responses to that, I feel like she reacts in a strange way sometimes and makes me think it wasn't all she wanted it to be with me. I wonder whether or not I didn't pick that up. I was really interested in school and nobody encouraged me to go on to college. I just decided. I started working and doing different things when I was fourteen and then when I was sixteen I got a regular job as a clerk-typist in a downtown office and looked out the grimy window one day and said, I'm not doing this the rest of my life. I decided that I was going to go to college no matter what, even though my parents didn't support it, financially or otherwise.

Once I was in school I became more achievement oriented

and then I had these weird ideas about male-female relationships. When I was a sophomore in college I wrote a paper
about women's status in employment, so it wasn't much longer
after I got into college that I became aware that I was interested in women's studies. I belonged to a N.O.W. chapter and
consciousness-raising groups. That began when I was eighteen
or nineteen. It was reinforcing the kind of things I would
like. When I was seventeen or eighteen it was the Vietnam
war era. I see it just as a questioning of tradition. To do
something for traditional reasons is just not the reason to do
anything. Sex roles are just one of those kinds of things. And
I still feel strongly that way, that tradition is just no reason
to do anything. I'll probably die thinking that.

G: That is what is so frightening, that people in their twenties
that didn't experience any kind of radical movement don't
question any of this.

L: I know. When I think of my latest studies in married women
and work, the youngest women are the most traditional of all.

A: The sister that came closely after me also experienced that
period in Sweden and she is rather untraditional in her attitude to career and being a housewife. In terms of picking a
male friend and her husband, she looked for a nontraditional
man, not the macho type, but one who would allow a woman
to create a nontraditional lifestyle. I think we are alike in that.
The other siblings who come a little later tend to be more
traditional. My brother is not more conservative in political
attitudes but in the way he treats his girl friend: He has
double standards in terms of freedom to date around and this
kind of thing. My little sister is the most traditional of all and
is really into makeup.

G: Lisa, are you the only child?

L: No, I have a brother younger than me.

G: How did the tasks get arranged between the two of you?

L: It was traditional. My mother did the dishes. I dried the dishes
because that was more feminine and he dried the pots and
pans because that was more masculine. However, my brother
refused absolutely to do any of these things. It was a constant
fight. That was the expectation but not the constant and actual thing. He was expected to do the more traditional things
like the garbage and my father would watch ball games and

races and do things with him. I really wanted to be more involved with them but my mother expected me to be with her.

G: So you grew up feeling like you were being cheated in some
ways?

L: It was very clear. I can remember sometimes when my brother
would be taken to the races and my parents would give me
money instead. They would say, "Your brother is going to do
this so here is five dollars as a compensation," and I would
say I really wanted to go to the races and they would say,
"Here is your five dollars." If he got new baseball equipment
I would get his hand-me-downs, and I was older. They wouldn't
go to my games but they went to his baseball games.

G: That must have turned you into a feminist.

L: That is typical, though. I was a typical tomboy and sort of got
over it by the time I was fourteen or fifteen and probably
would have bought the tradition and stuff if I hadn't been the
clerk-typist and didn't meet Art. That changed things. I guess
a lot of women go through that and turn out very traditional.

A: I think we were ahead of our time and had already decided on
this and happened to be living in New York City and were
pleasantly surprised to see other people were thinking the same
things.

L: But my classes see me being egalitarian as some type of thing
you don't find in real life.

G: They are right in a way. It's not common.

L: I know that we are unusual. But I know if I had married anybody but Art I would have eventually come around. I was
college-bound before I met Art. I would have gone to college
and stayed with women's studies and whoever I married would
have been in big trouble. I would have awakened one day and
said, "Why am I doing the housework?" With Art it was even
worse in a way. When I was in graduate school and felt like
quitting he said, "Look, you quit and I quit. You have as much
responsibility to earn money as I do and you can't stay home."
Even though my mother was economically dependent, I didn't
grow up thinking that I wanted a college education because I
wanted to earn money. I wanted a college education because
I was interested in books. I wasn't money oriented. Now I am
very conscious about wanting to support the family.

G: Do you have pressure from your family, Lisa, that you are deviant?

L: They just kind of ignore it. Art gets a lot of positive strokes because he's a "good father."

A: They have a lot of respect for me and I can intimidate my mother-in-law without trying. She is very worried about hurting my feelings, so she wouldn't say or do anything to bother me.

L: She perceives him as being very smart and very knowledgeable. I don't know why, but sometimes she'll say, "Art, you have a Ph.D., now answer this question for me . . ." She drives me crazy. They essentially ignore me. Every once in a while they'll get to something like, "Is it right that Art does this?" The basic approach that my parents take is to ignore it. I get no support—just the reverse—and it bothers me. I go out of town on a trip and they say, "How can you leave that baby?" And when I say, "I had a great time and didn't think about her for four days" (I tell her just to shock her) my mother says, "Oh, you terrible person, you don't mean that." "Yes, Mom, I do," but she doesn't buy it. I see his mother as somebody who gives me silent but emotional support. I don't think she understands how egalitarian we are but once in a while. It's clear that she respects me being a person with a Ph.D., a professional and still choosing to be married and have a child. That makes me feel good. Art's father pretty much ignores it, although he is aware that I know some things about computers and stuff; he thinks it's neat because he repairs them for a living. But that's the professional aspect, not the family aspect.

A: My mother also speaks up for us. I have a great-uncle in town that is very traditional indeed. When we first got married he questioned some things about our lifestyle. My mother was very quick to speak up on how we were both working and what a good job we are doing.

G: That really helps and makes a difference. In the literature, people talk about dual-career couples having competitive feelings about each other's professional achievement, especially being in the same field. Do you feel that?

A: Lisa thinks it's there. She is doing better at this point than I am.

L: He thinks that but I don't agree with that. He has always been worried more with respect to getting into college and getting into graduate school and applications accepted and getting a job—more than I ever have. I sort of feel that I'm lucky to get as far as I have, though at every point he has been worried about the achievement aspects.

G: That is the male socialization, don't you think?

L: If you were to ever tell him that, he wouldn't believe it.

G: Don't you believe it, Art?

A: Well, I don't know. It's a possibility. I don't think that we should assume that everything a person feels is translated into sex roles. If a woman has achievement orientation it's seen as untraditional, and if a man has it, it's traditional socialization, when maybe they both resulted from something else. I wouldn't jump to that conclusion. It may be untraditional in other ways.

G: It's impossible to escape that achievement-performance thing for a man.

A: I think it's a lack of appreciation, more than achievement. I have been very successful in the past, straight A's and did very well in graduate school. I have always done very well in what I've been doing. This is the first time really that the success hasn't come as quickly. That bothers me.

L: That's sort of like an external thing. I don't have any feelings that I'm better than he is because I knew for a long time there when he was clearly smarter and I had the feeling that I was inferior and always had that feeling.

A: That was a sore point in our relationship. I got very irritated at the sense of inferiority. I got tired of having to convince her that she was going to do all right.

G: People talk about relationships needing work and that seems to mean work at communication. How do you deal with conflict?

A: We have very different philosophies about that. My feeling is that if you love someone, you don't need to spend a lot of time talking about it and trying to build the relationship. To me, it's mystical and is just there—the common understanding to fall in love and that's it. You don't have to work at it. There is a commitment that you make and that's it.

L: You still think that?

A: Yes. From Lisa's point of view it is something that is continually tested by new circumstances and you need to rethink the relationship.

L: You need to keep working at it and don't take anything for granted. You have to communicate about your goals and your feelings on a regular basis or else you wake up one morning and there won't be anything left. We really do disagree on that.

G: It sounds like what you are saying, Art, is that there is some kind of bond that exists on some level—almost a metaphysical plane—but that wouldn't negate the fact that you have to work on day-to-day interaction.

A: Life can be much more pleasant when you are talking to the person, but it's not a necessity to me for the relationship like it is for Lisa.

L: It seems like if we go for a whole week and we just tap each other and see each other in the hall that's not going to make him feel different about me, but sooner or later we will catch up with each other. He feels the same way about me whether I'm in this country or the next country. And I don't feel that way. People need to talk and give each other a lot of emotional support.

A: I think it's insecurity. After we dated one summer we ended up going to different schools and Lisa felt that the relationship was over because we were going to be physically separated for a long period of time. I didn't see the problem because I thought we had made a commitment for a long period of time.

L: One reason I think it's insecurity is that since I've had my daughter it has pointed out to me the inadequacies in my relationships with other people that I should have been intimate with. It has always been rather insecure. Basically I know her love for me is unconditional. I have a lot of leeway. There has never been anyone in my life that I felt that way for. I even feel insecure about her sometimes and wonder if, when my daughter is a teenager, will she still love me? I think my parent's relationship with me was utilitarian. They took care of me within their budgetary means, but the other things were lacking. I didn't get the emotional support or intimacy from my parents and I still don't. I think, therefore, that I don't get it anywhere and I want a constant reminder that it is there.

G: It seems to me the only way it would work to exert no effort is if you were both perfect persons. That's why things have to be dealt with. No? What if one of you wants to get a job at Berkeley and the other one doesn't?

L: There would be a problem with that one and that's the kind of thing we handle real well. That's not the problem. We don't handle it well when I come in and say I don't feel you have been hugging and kissing me enough lately. Or I'm coming in and saying something about my work that I feel insecure about. Then the sparks fly.

G: How would you handle the Berkeley thing?

A: We never disagree when we have a problem like that. We talked it through when Lisa had a job offer and I had a chance to do research somewhere else. We found what the points were and got the idea of having her ask if she could postpone her appointment and then we could do both. We have been able to work out something that pleases both of us.

L: But then, we are lucky too. When we were both going to graduate school he got a National Science grant from Berkeley and they wouldn't even let me in. It was one of those years when they did discrimination. So instead we went somewhere where we both got the same package. It was never an issue. We have been lucky but also have compromised on some stuff. Art compromised for me. He could have gotten a degree at Berkeley, but he didn't.

G: What about the little irritants of living with somebody day to day?

L: We both are certainly irritated by a certain number of things, but not the same things. Usually you just tell the other person that it bothers you. And they usually say, "Yeah, I'll try to watch it," and if they don't, you remind them again.

A: I'm very mindful of the fact that everybody does some things that drive me up the wall. Conflict there doesn't bother me so much. I realize there are things she does and there are things I do, too, that irritate her so I try to keep that in mind.

L: He is more tolerant than me. I'm more likely to say something.

A: I come from a family where one of the great pastimes is to argue politics constantly and there are no hard feelings left. It can get very intense between my dad and me about the war in Vietnam or other things and when Lisa is around she thinks we are going to go to fisticuffs any minute and thinks it's upsetting, but actually my dad and I are having a great time and there are no hard feelings. I think she comes from a different background where things did not end pleasantly and she was not treated as an equal in the discussion. That, I think, carries over to some extent in our relationship.

L: He doesn't like it when I bring up something that bothers me. We have a real problem with that. I try to use a lot of "I" messages and sometimes try to let things go, which is what he does, but that doesn't work with me because I'm not as easygoing, so that by the time I'm ready to bring it up I just explode. Even if I don't explode there usually is some emotion there that turns him off. It's like not playing fair or something. So we usually get into a round-robin of him denying that he does it or saying, "Why are you so petty all at once?" or some other thing that might even be true but doesn't change my feelings about it. It turns into a real problem because sometimes I just want somebody to see my feelings.

G: The active listening business.

A: I have come to the realization that I'm sort of like Mr. Spock. I try to be very rational with a problem and get to the point and she doesn't see how rational my suggested solution is and I get frustrated. I guess I don't realize that she is looking for emotional support. She is just looking for someone to say, "I understand."

L: I need someone to do that.

A: I don't want to see the feelings. I just want to see the problem and get to work right away . . . find the solution and go to something else. We have a lot of misunderstandings about that.

G: Are you making any progress?

A: No, not much.

L: We understand what goes on, anyway.

A: There is a spot in each of our personalities, like Mr. Spock can't be Dr. McCoy. We try to get along with it the best we can.

L: I think we are coming to some understanding better and Art will step outside his rational role and hug me or do something else to support that, but it's often not enough, so every two or three weeks there is probably going to be a clear-the-air fight. Probably not that often, but sooner or later. The accumulation of what I feel are unmet needs of emotional support comes up and something will touch it off and we'll get into an argument. We'll end up saying, "I'm this way" and "You are this way," and there is no right or wrong with this and we are just going to have to learn to live with it. I've learned to develop a lot of friendships that have all kinds of emotional support and that makes a lot of difference. That helps when it comes to work things, but it doesn't really help when I'm concerned with matters here.

G: What do you do for fun?

L: She asks this in the middle of the fall semester.

A: The coming of our daughter has changed the things we used to do together like go to the library or go on a hike, things we aren't able to do anymore. Like I go off skiing or canoeing by myself now because we can't find a baby sitter who will take care of her while we both go out. I don't know if more shared activities are seen in the future or not.

L: Until she can ski.

A: Then I'll wind up taking her along and Lisa will stay home. Then I'll have the person to do things with. Lisa never really liked those things, she just did them for company. I have to find someone else to do those things with. Because there is just one kid, we all go do things together a lot. We like to go camping in the summer, all three of us, just like when there were two of us. Periodically we try to schedule things together and have her stay for the weekend at my mother's, because my mother keeps her overnight and gives me a couple of days peace. It's not very often that we go to a concert together.

G: A lot of us were raised with romantic myths about love. Did you have to deal with unreal expectations about marriage and love and parenthood, or did you escape it?

A: I think I did to some extent by not being exposed to that much. I saw TV just once when I was a kid in Sweden and then over there it was a big event. I remember in terms of school years, looking for someone to have a crush on and be romantic and it always had to be a woman with intellect, one I could talk to. I wasn't attracted to dumb blondes. Maybe I haven't escaped the thing of something permanent when they get together, like on the movie screen. The message was that they were going to stay together, and I do have that notion.

L: I think that when I was really young I had a romantic thing about getting married because being married for a woman is like a big deal—it's how you become a woman. The people around me, like the girls I shared the dorm with and the girls around me, really saw me as different. There was a little romantic complex there, that thinking that I was becoming an adult. We wanted life to be very simple and that's why we got married rather than run across the country back and forth to visit one another. So I just saw it as making a more permanent setting since we had been going together for quite a while. In terms of parenting, I didn't have our daughter until I was twenty-six. I would have thought most of my ideas about parenting would have been very romantic if it were earlier. I do think I was prepared. She was a very hard baby to take care of. I don't hear myself saying some of the things I hear my my students saying about parenting. I didn't have that romantic complex about how this baby was going to change my life and make it whole and wonderful.

G: But it does change your life.

L: My students are talking about staying home after they have a baby. The main goal of their life is to have babies. It's obvious that they are under an illusion.

G: If you were asked to give advice to a young couple starting a family and wanting to be egalitarian, what kind of advice would you give them?

L: Have you ever read the Stapleton and Bright book called *Equal Marriage*?

G: Yes.

L: I often recommend that book to the people in my class or to couples. It has a lot of things about the way you conceptualize your relationship and so on. In terms of specifics, when I talk to women I feel as though an egalitarian relationship requires change on the woman's part. The woman has to be ready and prepared to give up complete responsibility for the home and child. If she is in between being Mother and Susie Homemaker, if she is not prepared to support herself, then she is not ready for an egalitarian relationship. It's not going to be egalitarian until women change their minds about what their role is.

A: If a couple already have a notion of that type relationship and have a commitment, then I'm not sure they need any advice to find ways to bring it about. We have had to change our ways. You have to adjust and are not going to find a way that is going to be satisfactory to everyone. When we first started out we wanted to split every activity fifty-fifty and did it that way for a couple of years and that became a source of tension. If she was asking for something that I didn't feel was that important, I would postpone it because I didn't feel it was that important. So now we have tried to even that workload by having her do things she feels aren't that bad and I'll do things I feel aren't that bad, and it doesn't necessarily follow male-female lines either. She does yard work, which is a traditional male activity, and I do the laundry and other things, but we have specialized because of personal preference. It is basically satisfactory at this point, though at first we thought we would divide everything fifty-fifty for all the time.

L: During the time that we shared it fifty-fifty, both of us learned some things about the other one and that they might be better. I'm the one who is responsible for the yard but during the time that we were doing it fifty-fifty I hadn't been responsible for the yard, so I learned about it then and the lawn mower and things like that. The same about ironing and mending. There were things that I was better at and because we were doing it fifty-fifty the other one learned how to do it. Now the arrangement is not so sex-based. I don't think we would have come that far. We only lived a year on our own before we got married. And there wasn't time for either one of us to become great cooks or be anything special, so we we learned how to take care of the household together.

I know lots of people say they share the general responsibility for their children, but the man doesn't take responsibility for some of the things. I really feel like child care is something that we shared equally and never had to think about. We don't spend money on housework help. I'd rather spend money on something else. There are people I know who have housekeepers and say they are egalitarian, but the housekeeper is doing all the things the husband won't do. The wife is responsible for the housekeeper and gives the housekeeper instructions, so that means to me that she is in charge of the home. It's still woman doing domestic work, and until that is shared in this society and at the family level, then we haven't progressed any.

A: I think the difference in standards should be emphasized. They should really think through what each of them expects. There will have to be compromise there and neither one will have exactly the type of household that they would like. The dif-

ferent personalities involved have to communicate. The problem we had in the beginning and is better now is that we
would essentially try to be carbon-copy personalities and we
would both try to approach things in the same way. If I didn't
approach things at first the way she did, then we ended up
being unhappy and feeling something was wrong, instead of
realizing that we were both different personalities in many
ways. We sometimes have other directions.

L: You have to be ready to compromise and by the time we had
our daughter I realized that we have different standards. He
allows her to do things that I consider are dangerous and I
would never let her do. I realize that I have to compromise
and the woman can't have it her way. If she is going to share
the care with her husband, then she has to be willing to accept that it's not going to be the way she might want—like
she might find if she were married to a traditional man. In
our personal growth we aren't carbon copies of one another
and in any relationship people have to grow together. What
makes it a strong relationship is that each person feels that
they have and are doing what they want in most areas of their
life. In egalitarian relationships you could feel like you have
twice as many responsibilities, more than in traditional marriage, because you are sharing all the roles. I don't feel that
way personally. I feel like when I go away for three days I
don't have to worry about it and I could support the family
if necessary. We feel less burdened overall with two incomes.
If I felt that Art couldn't take care of the kid sometimes I
would just be in a panic.

A: Is there a chapter on sex?

G: No, I'm always too shy to ask.

L: He must not be if he's asking you to make it up.

G: What do you say about it, Art?

A: One thing that occurred to me—I'm trying to be relevant—
we have different sexual appetites. They are somewhat different. Lisa tends to be a little more inhibited and shy. She is a
very active sexual partner, but I still feel like in the past, anyway, I have had to take the initiative more often. Though not
a major difficulty, it did call for some discussion in terms of
what were the sexual problems, and then again we have come
around to seeing that basic personality difference. You could
have inhibited males and uninhibited females in another cir-

cumstance. For a long time, I was thinking of ways to re-socialize her and get her to open up on this and she was thinking of ways to cool me down and get me away from this traditional male response. I don't know whether it comes from sex-role socialization or not. There is less of a difference now, in the past year.

L: I'm getting closer to my sexual peak and he is going away from his.

A: She keeps saying that, but I don't think it's true.

L: In a paper about conflict over marital intimacy that I recently read, the man complains that there is not enough sex and the woman complains there isn't enough emotional support.

A: We got into the argument about what one has to come first. She was saying she can't really expect to have sex unless the emotional connection is there. And I say you can't expect to have a full emotional relationship until you have physical communion. We had that basic difference from our very first date. It's not a new issue. Males first find a woman attractive and sex is one of the first things you do with them. If you like her, you stay with her and then love grows out of that.

L: I think it has become less of a problem. As you become older you get less socialized and break away from your socialization; my theory for why women peak in their thirties is that they are finally getting away from that. I find it easier to have sex in the five minutes before the kid wakes up than I ever used to. I think part of the reason is that even if he hasn't given me twenty-five hugs in the last two hours or said the right thing when I said the chairman was driving me crazy, I sort of realized that whether he shows that or not, I know how he feels and that is the way he is. We compromise and that is the whole point of marriage.

A: In terms of the personality traits, I think one of the things that's becoming apparent is not only that our behavior is egalitarian and we share housework and so on, but when it comes down to arguing about how we should be or what is desirable and undesirable, I find that I tend to decide along sexual lines. I think that male traits are more desirable than dependence and irrationality. That's really the way things work.

L: But you don't think that for every male trait down the line. He doesn't like macho men.

292 · APPENDIX 5

A: I don't like wimps either.

L: He has a real problem with gay liberation because of that. In the past we have done papers together on sexual things like that and he basically is not interested in reading more about that, the personality aspects. The power part, no problem. The emotional part, he has a problem. He thinks I have a problem because I should be more like men.

A: That may be a cultural thing rather than a sexual thing. My Estonian family is like that. They are stoic and try to be rational.

L: It drives me crazy. They all drive me crazy sometimes.

G: Are you going to have another baby?

A: I would like one more.

L: And I told him if he wanted to stay home all year and take care of it, I'd have one in a second.

A: That's a very unfair demand. We should both share.

L: It's been real hard. I always thought I'd have two children and thought they would be a couple of years apart. The first one was crazy. She cried all the time and it was just awful. And living with that is so strong in my memory and if we had another incident like that I'd have a nervous breakdown. We never had a baby sitter, you know, we were always with the kid until nursery school. We had a baby sitter to go out but not for work. I just can't do that again. It was really problematic. That is why I've changed my position on how we take care of kids. If he would discuss having a twenty-hour-a-week baby sitter I might have a kid real quick. But he'll say, "No," and I think, "Oh, my God." So we sort of postponed it until later on.

A: We are in agreement that it's not a good time if there is a lot of stress. If one of us or the other had to change jobs, we don't want to have that on top of the other.

G: You have time. There is no hurry.

A: When we first got together we decided we were going to wait ten years until we were thirty to have our babies. Then we got tired of waiting.

L: I do love babies. I wouldn't wish our daughter away for anything in the world. After we are both tenured maybe things will be different. As time goes on I think about going back to diapers and going back to breast-feeding every two hours, and I just get tired thinking of it. I guess I'm selfish. As my daughter has gotten older and you will see this, Gayle, as your son gets older, that you get more and more freedom. She can have her own playmates and more and more free time. It's great to have time to yourself again. I worry about starting all over again. I also know that I really like kids and really think babies are neat. My relationship with her surpassed all expectations I had for that relationship. And I'm thinking, What am I missing out on by not having another one? I think it could go either way. I tend to be real practical and plan out how much time I have to do things and whether or not I can have the time. Art is always the one who wings it. I have a very tight schedule and how am I going to fit a second kid into my day?

A: I say we'll do it somehow but I don't want to think about it.

L: He'll say if you want it bad enough you can do it. That's a different philosophy of life than I have anyway. If I have a paper coming up, I can tell Art exactly how I'm going to get it done week by week, and Art will come home and say, "Oh, I'll get it done somehow." It's a different style.

G: It will be interesting to see what will happen.

A: I don't think we are having another one.

L: Because I have doubts—he'll assume it was all over. Gayle can probably tell by the way I present my arguments that I'm looking for more of a rational kind of thing. I've told him so many times that if I really felt that he would be sympathetic to my concerns it would probably be enough to compel me into a decision about it. But I feel like he is basically unsympathetic to my concerns. He just says, "Would you have one? I think we should have one. It's your body, it's up to you." He's very rational. That makes me stubborn. I can't say he's not going to take care of the second one; he has taken care of the first one. But what if the second one is too much work, even if I'm only doing half the work? I really do feel like it's up to me because I know what he wants. I know that and feel like if I don't have another baby he'll be gypped because he can't have one himself. I'll feel bad either way probably.

G: It seems like a third option is hiring help.

L: I think he won't consider it. I think the third option is adopting somebody older, frankly.

A: I want to make it clear, though, that there is no hidden agenda here about me wanting a boy. It really doesn't matter to me what the second one is. I feel like if you just have one then you are putting all your eggs in one basket. If anything should happen, that is a tremendous loss. I think the second time will be easier because you learn from your mistakes from the first one. It just seems like each individual should replace himself or herself with one other individual. I don't see anything wrong with that. I think it would be easier now if we had a second one. Because with Valerie around, she wants attention and thinks she's an adult like us and has adult privileges and she keeps telling us that we're not the boss and she wants to act with us on an equal basis. That is fine in principle but in practice we are busy and need to get things done. She is chattering and driving us crazy. It would be nice to have another little one around.

G: Then they would both be going, "Hey, Mom, hey, Dad."

A: When another child comes over from the neighborhood, there is no problem and they go off upstairs and play.

L: My brother was a year younger than me and we fought like cats and dogs. Even Art and his sister fought. I didn't see my brother as a playmate at all. We never played together, we only fought. We didn't save my mother any time at all. I don't think all the literature about how only children are spoiled or weird is true; in fact, they have some real advantages in life. I know that the intellectual stuff that propels people into having another kid is that sometimes they worry about the kid being spoiled. Those things don't affect me in the slightest. But I probably have an advantage because I've replaced myself with a girl already.

A: Lisa and Valerie are more sexist in that area than I. Lisa really wanted the first one to be a girl, and Valerie is four years old and kept discriminating against me at the table and other places because I wasn't a girl.

L: That wasn't just it. Also she thought that because she knew little about reproduction that Daddy didn't have anything to do with it.

A: They have some same sex bonds. I may have more of the male role to me than I care to admit, but I am open.

BARBARA AND SLACK

G: How long were you married in your previous marriages?

B: My first marriage was thirteen years. I got married right after graduation from college and had two children in the first four years. I got a divorce the first time after seven years and reconciled after going through the whole court proceeding. I stuck it out another six years, then divorced the second time. I'm a lawyer and I have been practicing for three and a half years. I had a B.A. degree and two years of graduate work before I had my kids. I decided when my youngest was ready to go to school that I wanted to go back to school and went to law school.

G: I'm interested in how you run your household. I imagine with your youngest being thirteen that you have a lot of driving and taxiing kids around. What are your tasks with the kids and how do you divide those up?

B: Okay, the youngest two are from my previous marriage and they are pretty self-sufficient but we do live in an area without public transportation, and in the winter bicycles are pretty cold to ride around. They each ride school buses so we don't have a school transportation problem. With their social life, we do have transportation duties. Very often the two of us ride together, when taking the kids somewhere, mostly for the company of each other . . . or I will take them or once in a while Slack will take them. We pretty well share it and most often we go together. School conferences—we participate equally in those. The kids' father sees them quite often. In fact, we have joint legal custody and tomorrow we're going up to school for a conference and the three of us will be there.

G: What about the things like cooking and shopping?

B: We do both things together too. Weekends are generally relaxed for us. We don't have a very heavy social life. Generally, we do the grocery shopping together on Saturdays. We do the planning before we go and cut the coupons out of the paper and make a list and do the grocery shopping together. I don't think I can remember a time that either one of us has done it separately since we've been married. But we both enjoy it and we really enjoy being together. We're separated all day long most days and really enjoy spending the weekends together. When we get home from work we generally have fairly simple meals. Something you can cook with hamburger in a half-hour or pop a pizza in the oven or a fish that cooks in a hurry. We share it. We both just start working when we get home and do different parts of the job.

S: Barbara is of course far more expert at cooking with all of the experience she's had. My first marriage was very conventional with a "housewife" for twenty-six years. My second marriage was even worse from that standpoint. My second wife didn't want me to help with the shopping and thought that her whole mission in life was cooking. So it wasn't until this happy time around that I have been permitted to participate, and I think Barbara would agree that she answers most of the questions on how things are to be done but I have also gotten competent enough to do it by myself.

G: What about cleaning the house? Washing clothes and all that stuff?

S: You didn't finish up the story about Saturday...

G: Oh, sorry.

B: Well, Saturday evenings we generally do the laundry, or in the afternoon if we have evening plans, but we share that also. We collect the dirty clothing from various places; all of the the kids throw their own stuff down the clothes chute and we do the laundry for the four of us—the two of us and the two younger kids. The older kids all do their own laundry. The kids change the linen on their beds whenever they feel they need changing and take care of the bathroom linen, putting it in the laundry. We sort the clothing together and we take turns or go down together and switch the loads around and generally spend Saturday evening in front of the TV in the summertime, or in front of the fire in the wintertime, slowly folding clothes up and putting them away. We sometimes do a double-crostic puzzle while we're doing that or enjoy a TV program. But we do that together.

G: Sounds kind of relaxing...therapeutic almost...to fold clothes.

S: It is.

G: What about yard work and car repair, that traditional man stuff?

B: I think Slack takes more of the initiative there. He remembers far more often than I do to check the oil in the car. I've been under the car and am gradually learning some of the things to do.

G: That's terrific.

S: We solved the yard work problem by growing a natural wild-flower yard. So we don't cut grass.

G: Sometimes people have brought up that the administrative tasks of remembering appointments, making lists, falls on women without anybody thinking about it; have you avoided that kind of trap?

S: I think so, don't you, Barb? We each of us have some separate work-related commitments we keep track of individually, but our joint enterprises like the American Field Service, Americans Abroad Program, I think that's a very joint obligation to remember where we're supposed to be and what to do.

B: Yes. And we together developed a system with our bills. Generally Sunday nights we go through the mail. We each have a mail box. We go through the two of them and pull out all the bills and take them upstairs and then arrange them by date for when they are due. We have a rack that we put bills in and put them by dates and generally pay them for one week. I guess we most often go up together and one of us may have a project from work and the other writes out bills or we may do it together.

S: We maintain one joint checking account which is used for all of the usual obligations of all kinds. Each of us has a little separate checking account of $100 or so which we would use for buying gifts but I can't think of very many things that we consider separate obligations.

B: I think it's gotten to be fewer and fewer things, but I carry the joint book around in my purse. I work in the building where we do our banking. It's very convenient for me. I also like having it but I don't think Slack objects and I think he uses his own separate account more because he's got that checkbook to carry around when something comes up. If he wants to write a check then he's got it.

G: Right. So it doesn't add up to a lot. Where did the model come from for that kind of role-sharing, was the women's movement an influence, or the kind of families that you grew up in?

B: I would say a lot of it came from each of us separately becoming very disenchanted with a prior marriage, with sex-determined roles. At least for me, I was unhappy in the prior relationship and it seemed after so many years to not be possible to rearrange it without a lot of underlying tension and hostility.

G: You did a fairly traditional splitting of tasks in that marriage?

B: Yes, and I resented it. I think I was resentful about the things
    I had responsibility for. I often felt that I had three children
    instead of two and that I had too much of a responsibility,
    and yet I really like being responsible and being active. When
    I have a partner I think that it makes all the difference. I just
    enjoy doing it. I do as much or more of it now, but I don't
    resent having all the responsibility.

S: My father died when I was eleven years old, and my mother
    worked throughout the rest of my early time so I think I was
    probably fairly independent. I wasn't subjected to a view of
    a mother in the home doing all the work from sunup to sun-
    down, that kind of thing. But I think I have always con-
    sidered myself a feminist in the present sense of the word.
    I don't know whether this is relevant, but one of the first
    things I asked Barbara when I first met her was whether she
    considered herself a liberated woman or believed in women's
    lib.

B: I used to say that Slack was more of a women's libber than I
    was and I really believed that for a while because he so
    strongly advocated equality and really doing away with the
    sexual stereotypes. I think I've grown a lot and gotten at
    least comfortable with thinking of myself as being active and
    an equal partner.

G: Slack, where did that come from? That's terrific. I want to
    know what made you that way.

S: I wish I could identify it all for you. I just remember all the
    way back when I was much, much younger I used to say
    things such as if there was a choice whether my female or male
    children went to college, I thought it was much more im-
    portant that the females went. My rationale at the time,
    which is not so radical today, was that women had more to do
    with the success of society than men did because all the man
    did was get up and eat what was given to him and go to work
    and do what his boss told him to do and come home and eat
    again and read the paper. I do think I have a very sincere
    contempt for the participation that most men devote to what
    I consider the most important part of society, and that's sort
    of always been with me. I think my first wife would have been
    a feminist if she had survived. My second one was a prime
    example of what I characterize now as the Phyllis Schlafly
    school of social affairs.

G: Why do you think you married her?

S: Gee, it was about nine months after my first wife died, and I was ... I think it's a little cavalier to say I was lonesome. I had a sudden intense infatuation and that lasted for probably a year or a year and a half. We generated all kinds of problems because of an immense diversity in intellectual interests.

B: She brought four children into the marriage and I think Slack had two or three at home most of the time.

S: Yes, and the kids were very different in the degree of responsibility with which they faced life.

B: The expectations of the kids were different. The educational expectations of the kids were a lot different.

S: I consider myself extremely fortunate to have encountered another flaming school romance.

B: We met at law school.

G: I see. Was your mother a strong woman, Slack? She must have been to keep the family together.

S: Yeah, I think she was. She was a strong, independent woman. She did not remarry after her husband died when she was thirty-eight. Yeah, I think she made her own way and in a very subconscious way provided a real image of an individual who could survive on her own effort.

G: That sounds like an important influence in terms of shaping what you think a woman really is.

S: Well, I've never really been a big, strong, masculine protect-the-woman type. I'm glad of that. Barb, do you remember the book?

G: *The Male Machine* by Marc Feigen-Fasteau?

B: Was there an idea of androgyny in it? It seems to me there was. That was one of the influential books shaping my thinking about our marriage. We used to talk a lot about androgyny or use the term anyway for no-sex-differentiated roles.

G: So that book helped. Can you think of any other things that shaped your attitudes?

S: I think I read *The Feminine Mystique* somewhere along the line to make sure that I was in agreement, and generally speaking I was, and such books as *The Women's Room* and *The Bleeding Heart*.

G: What about your kids? Do you see that they are more independent or the girls are more achievement oriented or that they are more strong individuals because they have you two as role models?

B: They didn't have us as role models. Leigh [Slack's daughter] was twenty when we got married and not around very much. She lives separately out in her cabin. In fact, Leigh has been, I would say, our one big problem. I wouldn't characterize the relationship as a problem right now, but for me at least it was a big problem between Slack and me.

G: Was she resentful of you?

B: I don't know. I think I was jealous and resentful of her and the way she was operating. It all came to a crux over money and spending habits and over borrowing from us, and it was at a time when money was tighter for us than it is now.

G: With so many bodies, physical persons, around, how do you two find time to be together? You said that you have some time just driving. When else do you find time to talk or to have fun?

S: In the evenings, usually the younger kids are upstairs doing homework or Paul [one of Slack's children] is out seeking his friends for a short period of time and we don't have a lot of people around under those circumstances. Saturday afternoons we always take a nap.

B: We have our time alone together. Usually my boys visit their father over the weekend. Since he has remarried they spend more time at home on weekends and we see more of them and I guess we have less privacy. Normally, we would be alone most of Saturday.

S: On that score we have a very simple solution to the privacy problem. I have stolen a few Do Not Disturb signs from motels and if we hang them on the doors that is all that is needed.

G: That's simple.

S: And the kids are old enough of course to respect our desire to be alone. I don't think we encounter much of a problem.

B: We ride down to work together and ride home together and generally talk to each other on the phone. We used to have lunch together more times than not when Slack's office was closer to mine, but he has moved about five or ten miles away so we are lucky if we have lunch together once a week now. We generally talk on the phone some time during the day and then have one half-hour down in the morning and about one half-hour back in the evening to talk.

S: And all the time we are fixing dinner.

B: Doing all the chores together is a real nice thing because we have lots of opportunity to talk.

G: That is a positive way to look at it. I think that's inspiring.

S: We are just very lucky. The honeymoon isn't likely to end the way it's been going, and the mad desire that people in love have to spend every waking minute with each other, which usually lasts until after the wedding, seems to be prevailing.

B: We really just enjoy each other's company and enjoy similar activities. I would say I was more athletic, spent more of my time in active activities before we got married, but I have adjusted and I really don't mind not being as active. We swim together one night a week when we can when the pool is open. We have been swimming about a quarter mile in laps. I guess this is the second winter we have done that. I play on a softball team at work in the summer one night a week and Slack comes out for the games and enjoys being a spectator and talking with the people I work with and spouses. Let's see, we take walks together, we ride bicycles together. We don't lead a very athletic life. It's pretty sedentary but we enjoy doing those things together.

G: That sounds pretty active to me.

S: We diet strenuously. (Laughter.)

G: Are you serious about that honeymoon comment? It sounds kind of unbelievable.

B: We are very serious about that.

G: How do you account for that?

S: Maturity. (Laughter.)

B: I don't know. I so often look at Slack and think what a wonderful person he is. He is so genuinely generous and such a warm person and really goes out of his way for everybody in his family and his friends. I think that generosity of spirit generates love. I have a lot of respect for things he stands up for. On certain political issues he is more willing to speak his piece than I am and I admire that a lot. I have always thought of Slack as a very stable kind of person. He's an eternal optimist. He has an inner bubbliness and strength and I get such a lift out of that.

I used to be depressed a lot of the time and I suffered from migraine headaches, and I think part of the difference I feel in myself is my career—the intense interest I have in prac-

ticing law and the real enjoyment I get out of being productive. But I think the personal relationship we have is probably just as much an important part of the change in feeling
good about myself as a person, and I think I've relaxed a little bit. I would consider myself a perfectionist. I think I felt
a lot of stress, more stress before I married Slack than I do
now, and I think some of his personality rubs off on me. I'm
very grateful for all those things; I think I'm constantly reminded of what a wonderful influence he is on me.

S: We're both just bright kids who finally found each other,
that's all.

G: What do you do about the homework you have from your law
practice, Barbara, does that get in the way? People I know that
are attorneys have their nose in their yellow legal pads all the
time and it's a real strain on their marriage.

B: I think I brought work home more in the first two years than
I do now, and I used to go in Saturday mornings more often
than I do now. It's very rare that I go in Saturday mornings
now. After work, in the evenings, I get calls from clients at
home once in a while. I have a specialty in family law at this
point and once in a while people in an emergency call me at
home. I wouldn't say I spend a lot of hours working at home. I
really like coming home at night and not having to bring my
work home and having my weekends. Fortunately I'm in a
practice where there is a commitment to families and to having time for things other than work. We get me down to
work usually between eight and eight-thirty in the morning
and I leave work between five-thirty and five-forty-five most
nights. So I put in a long enough day when I'm there and I
figure when I go home I deserve the time to be doing something different and my mind needs to relax.

Slack is fortunate, I think, in not having to bring work
home very much. He travels from time to time, not very frequently anymore. He rarely has to bring work home with him.
When I have a brief to write and I just can't get the concen-
trated time I need at the office, I will do it at home. I haven't
done that for a number of months. But I will work late into
the night if I have to, here at home, or spend the weekend
working, and Slack is very supportive and will take over and
do whatever household chores there are to do and will field
phone calls so that I am not disturbed. He will be solicitous

and get coffee and help me take breaks . . . totally supportive, I'd say, never jealous and never resentful that I have the work to do. I would say that if the shoe were on the other foot I would not be as patient and understanding as he is.

S: It's a thoroughly two-way street because when I go out of town it's usually for three or four days at a time and there's no question but that Barb is left here holding the fort and minding the ship and being totally responsible for everything while I'm living in a Holiday Inn someplace in Memphis or New York or Idaho. She's still way ahead of me in having to have done more on her own than I ever had to do.

G: When you say maturity, Slack, you mentioned that word, do you think you have gotten more patient and whatever over the years? Or have you always been this good?

S: I've always been fairly phlegmatic and not quick to fly off the handle. I was never appreciated before, that much I'm certain. I feel loved and understood and appreciated more now. Beside, generally I'm too lazy to get excited about things that I can't do anything about.

G: People talk about the need for communication skills in a relationship. Do you ever have those times when you get irritated with each other, resentful about the toothpaste in the basin or whatever? If so, how do you deal with those little frictions?

B: It's hard to remember when things are going well. (Laughter.) I'm trying to remember back to the last irritation. I think I'm more likely to say something when I get irritated. I don't know if Slack gets irritated as often as I do. I can't remember the last time.

S: We don't really have very many.

B: Oh, I can think of one. Our bedroom is on the first floor separated by a hall from the family room and the kitchen. I'm more concerned with personal privacy, I think, and when we're both in the bedroom dressing it's an irritation to me when Slack goes out and leaves the door open and the kids are out there. I would rather not have anybody have the opportunity to look in. Chances are remote, but it is an irritation to me. I guess I pout a little bit and I complain about it and Slack's pretty good about not doing things that are irritating when he realizes that they are. I guess I was accustomed to a different way of a spouse reacting, and that's to be resentful of being criticized and then to sort of subtly on purpose not comply with the wishes of the other spouse just because you didn't want to be bossed around or told what to do. There isn't any of that. Slack is very unusual, I think.

G: I do too.

S: I think a lot of that could be explained partly by the difference in our ages. Although that's maybe superficial. I think I just feel so lucky that Barb and I ran into each other and if I ever had a mental image of an ideal person that I could be married to . . . I found her.

G: This is beautiful, really.

S: Well, it's sort of a pleasure to be able to tell someone else . . . how terribly lucky I think I am.

B: It really is peaceful and loving. We've had our differences.

G: I'm glad to hear that.

B: We've had our arguments, but it's been such a long time. We were going to a counselor for a while really at my insistence. I don't know if we just outgrew the problems or going to the counselor really helped. We had some dandy arguments afterwards on the way home from the counseling session so I really don't know what was going on there.

G: Over Leigh?

B: Well, I guess that was the primary motivation for it, yeah.

S: And I wasn't very much help because all I would say in the face of the irritation was "relax and in a couple of years it will be gone."

B: Yeah, he kept saying, pretty soon she'll move away, she doesn't stay very long. And Slack really loves his kids and I think enjoys and appreciates them when they're living home and he doesn't want them to move away. So when he would say that, I guess I would realize how important they are to him and yet the problem wouldn't go away from me. It's not a great big mystery what was happening. I think Leigh was what I would characterize as not very responsible about money and she borrowed money to go on trips and really lived to the full extent of whatever money she had and what she could borrow. As a consequence I think others got left in the lurch. A couple of times her automobile turned out to be a lemon. She had a number of major breakdowns and had to be bailed out and we lent her money for those times and, mainly for me, it was the thought that she wasn't asked to be responsible or to repay. She wasn't told, you're expected to do this or to do that, just sort of an unspoken understanding that she would become responsible.

S: What is called by most people excessive permissiveness is a characteristic of my relationship with the kids. Barb and I would get into a big philosophic argument about should children be permitted to stay at home beyond their age of adulthood, and we were probably reacting to immediate circumstances. We used to argue about whether kids ought to go away when they're eighteen years old and come back for Thanksgiving.

B: The other thing I think was going on was that I felt that Slack ought to take more responsibility for my kids when they need a lecture on discipline or setting a limit of some sort. I have done it because it's natural but also because I think I should and I think at least for Slack's younger two kids there were times that I felt Slack should talk about being responsible, maybe not set down rules but at least do more talking about being responsible. He really isn't comfortable in the role of talking about responsibility or setting limits. I think he has a philosophical bias against it. He's an advocate of Summerhill and very permissive non-limit-setting. That I think is a problem for us. If we had children to raise together, I think we may have had more problems. But the way it works out now, we sort of have two different styles of dealing with my kids or with his kids, and I think that's appropriate.

G: What kind of skills did you learn from the counselor? Did that help resolve anything?

B: I don't know. I think we had the opportunity to sit and talk about things and focus on them. I was anxious when we were between sessions because we would not talk about it at home and when I would bring it up and try to talk about it and force the issue, it did result in some arguments. Slack's philosophy was that if we ignore it, it will go away, she will grow up, she will become responsible or she will move away.

I think he wanted me to just be patient. Going to the counselor forced the issue in the sense that when we were there and sitting down, we were there for a purpose and that was to talk about the situation. We did make some progress. We took some steps. I think maybe the resolution of it is accidental. The fact is that Leigh did get more responsible, but we had a couple of discussions and maybe some of that helped. Those were involving Leigh in the family. They were sort of hostile and sort of angry discussions, at least on my part, but at least some of the words were said and maybe that helped.

One thing we did between the two of us, and I think the counselor helped us to arrive at this, was to say that whenever Slack thought she should have money to tide her over to help her out, I would take an equivalent amount of money and what I did with it would be discretionary. We did that to the tune of maybe two thousand dollars' worth of bills and I have that money in a separate account. So far, it's just sitting there drawing interest, but it made me feel better and I think it made us realize that we could make independent decisions. Slack could be generous to Leigh if he wanted to and it wasn't my business. He had the right to decide about the money, aside from the question of what a parent's role with the child is, and I had my bone, so to speak, to keep me happy. That was the way of resolving the problem at that time. I think that was helpful.

S: I heartily agree with everything Barb just said about circumstances concerning Leigh—very accurate. We managed to get past my poor performance as an authoritarian parent, a guiding parent is a better term. I don't think I do any kind of a job in that area at all, as Barb says. Guiding your children simply by unrelated example I don't consider to be the best way, but it's my unfortunate disability. Barb has done a good job of accommodating ... which I think is quite different from what her background would lead her to expect from a parent. So we have pretty well resolved it. Furthermore, I quit drinking three years ago and that helped.

B: That was the problem before we got married. I thought Slack drank too much.

S: I did, too. But I found something better to do. It changed my life in many ways.

G: So you really have been growing. It seems you need some kind of conflicts or it's just marshmallows. I'm not clear about your first marriage, Barbara. You said it was very traditional. Did you feel constrained under that kind of framework?

B: Yes. I felt as if I just fell into it. I had a child and became a housewife and was really not very happy. I liked the kids. I liked being a mother but I really didn't like the role of cleaning up after everybody and organizing the whole life except for the important job that was outside the home that my husband did. I really did not like that way of operating. I had another child because we had planned to have more than one. I wasn't any happier with the way things were going. I did not want to be the kind of wife who was handmaiden and secondary to her husband and aided his career, and I really resented when my husband came home late for a meal and I had it ready and it was sitting and getting cold. I really resented the whole housewife role.

My mother is a meticulous housekeeper. She is a very traditional housewife. My father's income was never very ample and yet my mother had a philosophy of not working outside the home; she believed that a mother should be home taking care of her home and that when the kids left she was still a housewife, a meticulous housewife, and that's still her role. That's still the kind of marriage they have. I don't think I was ever very happy with that. I didn't like housework as a kid at home and got out of it as much as possible by using schoolwork as an excuse. I excelled academically. That was always my thing.

Law is the perfect field for me. I love it. I love the logic and the reasoning and matching wits with people and the social service aspect of being sympathetic to clients and helping them solve problems and helping with the planning. I just love the whole bit, and I don't know how I existed in the housewife role and stayed in it for so long. I remember having migraine headaches every winter and just not liking life very much. I used to feel there was a void at the very center of it.

My husband was a computer programmer and had his own personality problems; he was not very happy with himself. He was a good father. I think that's his best virtue—that he always liked the kids and liked spending time with them. He was very helpful when I was in law school. I think my first husband really has problems with women. I think he's anti-woman from some of the incidents that he related and that his mother related.

I really like his mother. She was always sort of the victim of verbal abuse in their family for taking over too much and making too many of the decisions, being too active in volunteer work, and she has been criticized by her family. I think my first husband had this tension and hostility to women who were active and made decisions and sort of preempted the male or wanted to participate equally. I don't think we would ever have worked things out even if Slack hadn't come along.

I was just waiting. After the first divorce, I reconciled mainly because I was destitute economically, didn't have a skill, didn't have a job, had these two little kids to raise by myself, and it was too much. I also felt sorry for John being deprived of the company of his kids. When I went back to that marriage, it was with a lot of resignation and a lot of regret that I was giving up on life and with a lot of sadness. I was biding my time and I kept saying to myself, I won't divorce John again, I won't put him through that, but when the kids get out of high school, I'm leaving. So it was really a compromise, done for the sake of the kids and I couldn't hack it. It wasn't worth it. Once in a while the hostility would surface, and both times that I decided to get the divorce John finally exploded with anger and hostility and hit me, and that made me very angry and made me both times decide, this is it. I don't care what pain he's got to go through, I won't be abused and so there was a lot of buried anger and hostility in both of us.

I think too if I had started out with a career and insisted on it that things probably would have been different. I don't know that I would have been any happier in that relationship, but I think it just was all wrong. I expected too much of him, things that he couldn't give in the way of being decisive and planning and taking some of the initiative; I think I put too much responsibility on him and was not willing to do enough of it myself. I think he put too much responsibility on me for the traditional housewife things women are supposed to do . . . a bad set of expectations mutually.

G: Yes, but it's very hard to escape those when you are programmed . . .

B: It's very difficult to change one's role when a relationship like that has lasted for years.

G: If you had advice to give to some couple that were just starting out, what kind of advice would you give them?

S: My advice as the male member of this couple would be to realize that the other partner is discriminated against and the victim of thousands of years of slavery. She is an individual person who needs some respect in all the little things that tend to separate the male stereotyped role from the female.

B: I'm afraid I end up sounding negative, but I guess I would say to the male member of the couple don't be so afraid of your image. Risk a little bit and try it; maybe you will like sharing the roles without such rigid differentiation between the sexes and what men should do and what women should do. And I think pretty much the same advice for women. Although I think I agree with Slack that there is more that has to be done from the *male* point of view, to not look at women in a certain role and for men not to look at themselves in these straitjacketed roles. But I think women too should risk a little bit. Do the unconventional things and do your share of the traditional male jobs. Take an interest in the car and the mechanical things around the house and the decision making and the planning of the money, and do it with a feeling that you are a full and an equal partner and that it is fun being active. Making decisions and sharing in that role is a fun thing to do and a lot more rewarding than being taken care of or being watched out for and being done for. I guess, break out of the traditional roles that society would have you fit into.

G: Can you think of anything we have left out in terms of what makes an egalitarian relationship work?

B: We didn't talk about sex.

G: I just don't know what to say to people, how is your sex life?

B: Finally, our counselor brought it up: "You haven't mentioned it, what about your sex life?"

G: Well, what about it, Barbara?

B: Our sex life is great. I feel very free. I feel a lot freer. A comment that my ex-husband made to me some time after we split was, "You really didn't like sex, did you?" I thought that was so funny! One of the differences between Slack and me, especially in the beginning, is that I wanted to have sex every night and that was too often for Slack. I simmered down a little bit. We have sex three or four times a week on the average and Saturday afternoons is the best time. One of the things that was a real revelation for Slack was making love in the light, not always in the dark, and doing it in the daytime. When we were courting (when we were on the sly, we were both still married) we had this little apartment and Slack was even unemployed; it was such a risky thing for us to do. It was $95 a month. A really cute place but really a hole, a one-room apartment with a fold-out bed. We would sneak away from our jobs and make up meetings that we had in the early evenings.

S: It's the kind of thing you had to pay cash for . . .

B: . . . put a phony name on the money order. It was the most romantic thing. We love our Saturday afternoons together.

S: On that subject, I used to characterize my sex life as something I didn't know anyone did when they were sober. I really would have to say that I had had practically no sexual activity for other than a brief flurry at the time of my second marriage that lasted a couple of months. I didn't know that I was capable of being interested to the degree that I am and I still don't suppose I would be with anybody else.

B: Well, I hope he doesn't get the urge and go out and find out . . . I have heard about that, but then I like to keep him busy. I like to be on the top and I think we both enjoy that and that's very fortunate. Anatomically we fit together better that way and I am a little bit lighter than he is and that works out together just fine.

S: The important things are in not making an absolute ritual of it and, as Barb says, the daylight and daytime . . .

B: Yes, we are more relaxed . . . at night we are tired. We have worked full days and sometimes we get to bed late because we have family responsibilities and discussions and sometimes work is so demanding.

S: All the experts say it is an important part of life but so few people really take any time for it. It's just something that gets to be an obligation once a week or once a month, after midnight, and that's really not satisfactory.

Appendix 6. Survey for Role-Sharing Parents

* Please, each spouse fill out a separate survey.

* Your name will not be identified in the book that will describe shared parenting, unless you would like acknowledgment.

* If you know of other couples who share parenting equally, I would appreciate your duplicating a copy for them or letting me know their address.

* Please return to Gayle Kimball, EWS-420, California State University at Chico, Chico, CA 95929

1. Your name, address, phone number, occupation (will be kept confidential).
2. Age and gender of children. Please give a thumbnail description of your child or children's personality(ies). In what ways are they like or unlike you at their ages?
3. On a typical week day, how do you organize child care when you are at home? On a weekend day?
4. Describe your philosophy of child rearing and your goals for your children's development. What factors led you to this philosophy?
5. a) Do you find yourself treating sons and daughters differently? If so, how? And why or why not?
   b) How do you counter the prevailing messages about sex roles provided by T.V., schools, children's friends?
6. What duties, responsibilities, and share in family decision making do your children assume? How do you motivate them to do housework?
7. Please add any other remarks about shared parenting and non-sexist child rearing, including benefits and difficulties.
                                                                Many thanks.

Gayle Kimball, coordinator of Women's
Studies at California State University
at Chico, has written and produced
books, articles, and videotapes on women
and the family. Currently she is doing
research on shared parenting.